ADAPTIVE ACTION

ADAPTIVE ACTION

LEVERAGING UNCERTAINTY
IN YOUR ORGANIZATION

GLENDA H. EOYANG and ROYCE J. HOLLADAY

STANFORD BUSINESS BOOKS
An Imprint of Stanford University Press, Stanford, California

Stanford University Press
Stanford, California

Special discounts for bulk quantities of Stanford Business Books are available to corporations, professional associations, and other organizations. For details and discount information, contact the special sales department of Stanford University Press. Tel: (650) 736-1782, Fax: (650) 736-1784

Printed in the United States of America on acid-free, archival-quality paper

Library of Congress Cataloging-in-Publication Data

Eoyang, Glenda H., author.
  Adaptive action : leveraging uncertainty in your organization / Glenda H. Eoyang and Royce J. Holladay.
     pages cm
  Includes bibliographical references and index.
  ISBN 978-0-8047-8196-1 (cloth : alk. paper) — ISBN 978-0-8047-8711-6 (pbk. : alk. paper)
  1. Management. 2. Adaptability (Psychology) 3. Uncertainty. I. Holladay, Royce J., author.
II. Title.
  HD31.E659 2013
  658.4001′9—dc23

                                                                    2012046533

ISBN 978-0-8047-8540-2 (electronic)

Typeset by Classic Typography in 10/14 Minion Pro

CONTENTS

ACKNOWLEDGMENTS

Appreciation may be one of those infinite games. It certainly feels like it as we reflect on who influenced our work and how. Every cycle of our separate and shared Adaptive Action has been informed by those we depend on, the ones who depend on us, and the many communities that shaped us all. Though a complete thank-you is impossible, we will touch on the bits of coherence and clear sparks of energy that enlightened our journey.

Many people helped this particular manifestation of our work come to life. Margo Beth Fleming, our editor at Stanford University Press, not only inspired this book, she waited for it and shepherded it from beginning to end. Special thanks go to those who shared their Adaptive Action stories with us: Denise Easton, Brenda Fake, Vickie Gray, Wendy Gudalewicz, Mary Nations, Kristine Quade, Paul Reeves, Janice Ryan, Larry Solow, Mallary Tytel, and Ilir Zherka. All of them planted the HSD seed in their own gardens, and each one reaps a different harvest. The field of human systems dynamics is fed by them all. Beatrice Favereau lent us her eyes, hands, and heart as she created the wonderful illustrations that give life to our Adaptive Action models and methods. Peer reviewers—formal and informal—helped us find and file down the rough edges of how we think and write about Adaptive Action. Our thanks go to every one of these colleagues for their insights, good humor, and high expectations.

Through the years, we have been fortunate to engage with a wide variety of teachers, students, and clients. Most of the time, we couldn't tell the difference among them, as we shared puzzles and possibilities with all. Thanks to all of you for building adaptive capacity for all of us. Our work has been particularly informed by a wonderful community of HSD Associates who are committed scholar-practitioners. They are a diverse lot, but every one of them has contributed to the emerging theory and practice we share in the following pages. Thanks go to them for sharing the journey with us and with each other.

Our thanks to families will be relatively short, as we share so many of them. Ruth Holladay, our mother, would be beaming while she checked for typos in the manuscript. Toni, Tori, and Rai will be sharing the adventures to come. Leslie and JoTisa speak and listen with the same ears and hearts, because those sisters share more than just genes with us. To them and all of theirs, many thanks for inspiring and sustaining us.

Adaptive Action and the other models and methods of human systems dynamics evolved from generations of work in many fields. Traditions of inquiry from mathematics to mothering have provided both the questions and the emerging answers that are captured on these pages. Even when we are not conscious of drawing on the intelligence of those who went before, we know that our insights depend on theirs. We also know that their learning and ours are part of the infinite game of Adaptive Action that shapes our experience of uncertainty in organizations.

Finally, we each thank the other as a thought partner and friend. Our similarities and our differences contribute equally to the patterns of our collaboration.

Glenda Eoyang
Royce Holladay
Circle Pines, Minnesota
May 2012

ADAPTIVE ACTION

PART I

WHAT CAUSES UNCERTAINTY? WHAT CAN YOU DO ABOUT IT?

No one denies that uncertainty is on the rise, but there is little agreement about how to understand where the uncertainty comes from and even less clarity about what can be done to make sense of it. We begin our exploration of making sense of uncertainty in organizations by outlining our assumptions about today's complex contexts, explaining what we understand about the dynamics that drive uncertainty, and proposing a practical and simple approach to taking intentional action, even when you can neither predict nor control the future.

1

WHY SO UNCERTAIN?

It is the bottom of the ninth; the game clock ticks to zero; the goalie has a weak knee; the star forward has five fouls; and the soprano just missed her cue. It is your move; you have the puck. What do you do? What game are you playing and how can you win? This may sound like the punch line of a nightmare, but for many of us it feels more like Tuesday at the office. We often find ourselves in unfamiliar territory, working toward shifting goals, with colleagues who seem to be from another universe. Today, it is sometimes hard to tell who works for whom. Relationships are shaped by inconsistent and often confusing cultural, social, emotional, and business practices. We are never quite sure what to expect or how (and by whom) our success would be judged. It is increasingly difficult to make sense of complex and uncertain patterns in organizations. There are questions about goals, rules, equipment, and skills that separate winners from losers. Relationships that might have held over the long haul are challenged by changing expectations and loyalties. Careers do not follow predictable, predetermined patterns. Economic indicators are confusing even to the experts. All of us have trouble making sense of the game we are playing and figuring out what we have to do to win.

The Infinite Game

What rules prove to be constant in your day-to-day experience at work and at home? If you are anything like our clients or like us, you live and work in an environment where new rules are written and old ones are broken every day. James Carse[1] saw the emerging complexity of the world back in the 1980s. He wrote a lovely little book called *Finite and Infinite Games* to distinguish predictable, closed-system games from the ones that were open and unpredictable. Traditionally, finite games have shaped our experience and our success.

In a finite game, it is easy to make sense. Everyone agrees on the goal; the rules are known; and the field of play has clear boundaries. Baseball, football, and bridge are examples of finite games. At one time in the not-so-distant past, we expected careers, marriages, parenthood, education, and citizenship to be finite games. When everyone agrees on the rules, and the consequences of our actions are undeniable, responsible people plan for what they want, take steps to achieve it, and enjoy the fruits of their labor. We know what it takes to make sense in a finite game.

Most of us realize that we are playing a very different game. We are playing an infinite game in which the boundaries are unclear or nonexistent, the scorecard is hidden, and the goal is not to win but to keep the game in play. There are still rules, but the rules can change without notice. There are still plans and playbooks, but many games are going on at the same time, and the winning plans can seem contradictory. There are still partners and opponents, but it is hard to know who is who, and besides that, the "who is who" changes unexpectedly.

Every day, the newspaper is full of examples of unexpected and sometimes unknowable developments. The mortgage market tanks, an Interstate bridge across the Mississippi River collapses, youth in London turn into lawless mobs, earthquakes hit Washington, D.C., and a tsunami devastates Japan.

In such complex and unpredictable environments, important factors that shape the future are unknowable. Social, economic, climactic, and political changes erupt without warning. We can plan, but we expect our plans to go awry. We can work toward our goals, but we understand that our work may be in vain. We experience unintended consequences that too often punish what should be rewarded and reward what should be punished. We need new ways to make sense in complex organizations. As individuals and organizations, we need the capacity to adapt to the unexpected. We need adaptive action.

Every day, forces we do not control reshape the landscapes of life in the twenty-first century. Not only are the rules of the game of life changing, but the game itself is being transformed. Not only are we playing a different game, but we are called on to play many games at the same time. Not only are we playing many games, no one knows who will get prizes in the end, and for what. It's your move. Life is uncertain. What do you do?

Economic foundations sit on quicksand of derived values and float on bubbles of speculation. Would it be possible to see, understand, and respond to economic turmoil in ways that reduced risk and increase value for us and our organizations?

Cultural and national loyalties shift too quickly or lock in too tightly for civil stability to be sustained. Might we see early signals of dissatisfaction so we could understand and influence the public discourse toward peaceful and productive dialogue?

Technology moves from imagination to reality to obsolescence at breathtaking speed. Can we consumers, producers, suppliers, and service providers develop the capacity to keep up with the pace of technical change?

Massive, ubiquitous, and direct communications contribute to both intractable stability and incomprehensible disruption. Can we read the landscape and establish media and messages that support the patterns we choose to reinforce?

Local climactic conditions change more quickly and more unpredictably than farmers, multinational corporations, or emergency services can manage to respond to. Can we collect data from around the world, consider it rationally and openly, and take collective action for the good of people and the planet?

These are the kinds of questions that shape our ability to thrive—perhaps even to survive—in the uncertain world of the future. As individuals, we face similar challenges in personal development, home, and health. As community members, such challenges appear in threats of violence and opportunities for collaborative action. At work, our abilities to manage planning, marketing, human resources, and supply chains all depend on the ability to see, understand, and influence emerging change in complex environments.

We don't think these problems are beyond human intervention. We believe that humans can make sense of patterns in a fast-changing environment and build the adaptive capacity they need to thrive in such volatile uncertainty.

We are living and working in a world—indeed in multiple worlds—that are changing before our very eyes. This massive disruption is no secret. Every scholarly and practical discipline has tried to describe how these fundamental changes affect decision making and action. In our work, we engage with people from many sectors: educators, public health professionals, politicians, bureaucrats, military strategists, leaders, health care professionals, technology gurus, industry giants, mechanical engineers, entrepreneurs, product developers, middle managers, academic researchers, funders, and grantees.

The particular challenges faced by each of these people are unique. They work with different resources, conceptual and practical tools, places and times, and shares of the power picture. Still, they have one thing in common: they and their organizations all get stuck trying to deal with uncertainty. They struggle to understand and adapt to the ever-changing rules of the game.

Our research and practice, our personal and professional lives point to Adaptive Action as a path through these uncharted territories.

Our Infinite Journey

We are sisters, Royce Jan Holladay and Glenda Kay Holladay Eoyang, so our shared journey and our infinite game started decades ago. Our parents were in the school business in the Texas Panhandle. Daddy coached high school football, Mama directed plays, and both taught whatever was needed in rural classrooms in the High Plains. That environment introduced us to infinite games early in our lives. The flat horizon and sparse vegetation introduced us to unbounded spaces on the ground and in the sky, so we became accustomed to seeing and thinking about the unbounded and far-reaching nature of the "big picture."

As a successful football coach, our father was in high demand and moved his family every year or two from one school to another that was larger, or more committed to the game, or more prosperous, or any combination of the three. We became pretty good at learning the rules of a new community, and playing in ways that always continued the game.

Sitting in the back of the high school auditorium watching play practices, we learned the words and characters of the classics before many of the players did. The theater, and its ability to transcend reality, was part of our daily life. Our parents read, so we read. Our parents talked and wondered, so we did too. Our family tradition in the United Methodist Church instilled in us a love of singing, a taste for reasoned argument, and a commitment to the common good. Before we knew anything else, we lived an infinite game.

In late adolescence our paths parted for a time. Royce moved toward the study of education, teaching, and school administration. Glenda studied history and philosophy of science and practiced technical training and entrepreneurship. Royce's path took her to North Carolina, Washington State, and New York City. Glenda's led to New Mexico, Oklahoma, and Minnesota. Holidays always brought us together with family to celebrate and reminisce, but in

practical and entertaining cases will help you see how Adaptive Action shapes effective decision making and action.

Chapter 8, "Capacity Building," focuses on using HSD models and methods to build knowledge and skills in treating Alzheimer's patients (Janice Ryan), in innovative instructional design (Larry Solow and Denise Easton), and in surviving Lean and Six Sigma implementations (Larry Solow and Brenda Fake).

Chapter 9, "Leading Change," applies Adaptive Action to leadership issues, including sustainable school reform (Wendy Gudalewicz), complex change (Kristine Quade), and integrating work and life during transitions (Mallary Tytel).

Chapter 10, "Working as a Social Act," focuses on Adaptive Action connecting work to social change with the power of self-organizing teams (Paul Reeves and Vickie Gray), transcending cultural bias through generative engagement (Mary Nations and Royce Holladay), and Adaptive Action in public policy advocacy (Ilir Zherka).

Part III, "*Now What* Will You Do?" reflects the lessons Adaptive Action offers and points the direction for how it can shape organizational work in the years to come.

Chapter 11, "Gaps Revisited," reintegrates the theory and practice of Adaptive Action in the context of major challenges that face human systems at all levels, including organizations.

Chapter 12, "Lessons for *What?*"; Chapter 13, "Lessons for *So What?*"; and Chapter 14, "Lessons for *Now What?*" draw on lessons we have learned across time and those we continue to learn today about the individual steps of Adaptive Action, as illustrated in and informed by the experiences and reflections shared by Associates in their stories.

Finally, Chapter 15, "Adaptive Innovation," offers a number of ways Adaptive Action has informed our practice in response to sticky issues in leadership and organizational practices. It offers specific insights for how our approach can help you deal with some specific challenges and opportunities found in particular organizational functions. It poses an invitation to you to join us in exploring the possibilities and opportunities of using Adaptive Action in your own work.

Throughout the book, we hope you find ideas that resonate with your own experience in coping with complexity and uncertainty. We also hope you find concepts that shock and disturb you. We hope you will question your own ways of working against what we have learned and continue to explore. We hope you find the models and methods as powerful as they are simple and that the paradigm shifts are as simple as they are powerful. In short, we hope that you see rich and enlightening patterns in Adaptive Action theory and practice, and that it helps you make sense of your experience in the past, present, and future. And we hope that through the newfound sense you find ways to take courageous and creative action to engage with the systems that are becoming more complex and adaptive every day. In short, we hope it helps you play the infinite game in a way that sustains and enriches the play.

2

WHAT CAN YOU DO?

It is easy to become paralyzed by uncertainty. The challenges of our changing and infinite games can lead us to spend time and energy admiring a problem rather than addressing it. It is easy to find creative ways to describe the difficulties and bask in the hopelessness of complex change. In our work and in this book, we choose a different path—maybe because of our hometown roots, maybe because we are leaders in our organizations and communities, or maybe because we simply get bored finding new ways to talk about why we are stuck. Whatever the reason, our work is to make sense of what is happening and take action in the moment. We play with meaning-making approaches that can inform reasonable options for action. We take intentional action to influence patterns in the world around us.

In this chapter, we share the fundamental observations and worldviews that inform human systems dynamics and Adaptive Action. On the one hand, these ideas will be commonsense and match your own successful practice in human systems in relationships, organizations, and communities. On the other hand, these ideas will challenge many of your long-held assumptions about how the world works and why things change as they do. We cannot predict which of the ideas will be familiar and which will be surprising to you, but we encourage you to keep track for yourself. How often do you nod in agreement or smile in recognition? How often do you bristle or shake your head in confusion? What can you learn from the ways in which our writing reinforces or challenges your current modes of seeing, thinking, and acting?

We begin with a definition of complex adaptive systems (CAS), which forms the foundation for how we explore Adaptive Action. Next, we consider some of the implications of CAS for the nature of change and individual and institutional options for taking effective action. Finally, we explore opportunities for Adaptive Action in greater depth and set the stage for a deep dive into each of the steps of the Adaptive Action cycle.

Complex Adaptive Systems

We may think of ourselves as twenty-first-century thinkers, but our usual view of the natural world is quite ancient. It is built deep into our perceptions and practices. It shapes what we see as possible and how we plan and execute actions. It sets the stage for playing a finite game.

This ancient perspective that so strongly influences contemporary thought and action is called "atomism," and it goes something like this. Solid substances are solid. They have edges and boundaries that are reasonable, clear, stable, and permanent. Fluid substances are fluid. They have boundaries that take the shape of whatever holds them. Except, of course, on the surface, where the container is called "surface tension," and it is a self-made container. Gaseous substances are gaseous. They take the shape of their containers on all sides, without generating any "edges" of their own. We can take a sample of any of these substances and divide it up, take the part and divide it, and divide that part, and so on until we come to the basic, indivisible particle. We call that an atom.

Modern science has advanced this perspective somewhat by allowing the atom to be cut into electrons, protons, and neutrons. More recently, even these "atoms" are being broken into observable and nameable parts. Still, the expectation persists that physical reality is an aggregation of uncuttables. Many scientific thinkers (some are professional scientists and others are not) use this view of the world to observe, understand, and act. They believe that if they can divide the world into small enough bits, they can understand and manipulate it.

On the other extreme, there is a "nonscientific" worldview that rejects this atomistic perspective. It, too, is ancient. From this perspective, there exists a fundamental wholeness from which everything that is comes to be. Concrete and abstract realities merge and emerge as this all-absorbing whole is divided or defined by word or action. Many spiritual traditions, mystics, and some philosophers recognize and work within the constraints of this worldview.

Both of these worldviews generate many problems for those of us who try to see, understand, and act in the complexities and uncertainties of twenty-first-century reality. To begin with, we are forced to select one perspective or the other. Depending on our cultures, interests, temperaments, educations, social networks, personal histories, and a wide array of other determining factors, we live in one or the other of these two realities. For many people the choice is unconscious, but others consider both options and make the choice with intention. Having chosen one as dominant, we find it necessary to denigrate the other. We have many ways to label these two worldviews: rational-irrational, material-spiritual, reductionist-synthetic, analytical-holistic. Each labeling brings with it an assortment of biases and assumptions. That is problem number two.

Problem number three is that neither worldview explains everything. Sometimes cutting something apart destroys its essence. Sometimes a unified whole hides important distinctions. The nature of light has become a classical example of the insufficiency of these separate worldviews. In some ways, light behaves like a stream of particles—uncuttables. In other ways, it must be understood as a continuous wave—an indivisible whole. It is both. It is neither. Its essence depends on when and how we view it, which brings us to problem number four.

Having reached this particle-wave impasse in the early twentieth century, scholars in many disciplines rejected both worldviews. They were able to do this because they denied the existence of an external reality altogether. If reality exists only in our minds, then we can choose at any moment to think of it in whatever way fits our fancy. This was a fine solution, until it became obvious that such a worldview made many important human activities difficult. If each of us could pick, and it didn't matter what we picked, then social connection, ethical action, shared meaning, and judgment of quality and value all became problematic. This postmodern view of the world abolished absolute good and bad, but it also erased better and worse. Ultimately, if the fundamental worldview didn't matter, nothing mattered.

Of course, this description of scientific and philosophical thought through the ages is somewhat abbreviated. Many scholars and wise practitioners have found productive ways to navigate the shoals between atomism and holism. Some twentieth-century philosophers found ways to hold both without annihilating reality. Fundamentally, however, on a day-to-day basis these flawed sets of assumptions limit what we can see, understand, and do in response to the complexities of life in the twenty-first century.

One gift of complexity science, as we understand it, is a path out of this dilemma that maintains meaning while flexing to embrace both reductionism and holism. This path is captured in a description of reality in terms of complex adaptive systems (CAS).

A CAS is a cluster of individual parts that interact with each other, and over time systemwide patterns appear. Parts. Interactions. Patterns. A simplified

CAS appears in Figure 2.1. Following the arrow on the right, you can see the shift from the individual parts into a coherent pattern, but you can also see that the process does not stop there. After the pattern forms, it influences the parts so they are encouraged to fall into the pattern even more completely in future cycles.

It is easy to see from this diagram how CAS resolves the part-whole dilemma. It builds a worldview in which reality is both continuous pattern and agent-based parts at the same time. On one hand, you can divide up the system components into smaller and smaller groups, and each group can generate holistic patterns of its own. *As an industry grows, it consists of successful companies that depend on productive divisions that rely on innovative teams made up of creative individuals.* On the other hand, the characteristic patterns of the parts work together synergistically to create the larger, coherent pattern of the whole. *The successful patterns of innovation and productivity of individuals, teams, and organizations contribute to the sustainable success of the industry, as a whole.*

An individual is still required to choose, at any place and time, whether to focus on the part-like nature or the whole-like nature of reality. The difference is that focusing on the one does not deny or denigrate the presence of the other. If you see the one, and I see the other, we can share our ideas through inquiry and see a reality that is greater than the sum of our respective parts.

A CAS worldview solves problems of the past, but it presents a few challenges of its own. The agents in a CAS are constantly changing, as are the

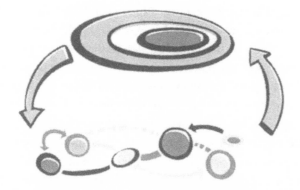

FIGURE 2.1. Complex Adaptive System.

Semiautonomous agents interact such that they create systemwide patterns.
Those patterns subsequently influence later interactions of the agents.

relationships between and among them. That means that a stable, permanent reality is impossible; uncertainty becomes the rule. Because one CAS may share members with other systems and extend beyond immediate view, there is no natural edge to a CAS. It is impossible to say that something is permanently inside or outside of the bounds. For example one individual agent may be a member of a team, and be influenced by patterns outside of the team inside the organization, by the patterns in his or her own family and community, even by political forces on a national or global level. The patterns inside the team are not solely dependent on the actions and interactions inside that team particular team, but neither are they controlled by a single, intentional, external force.

The fact that complex adaptive systems are many and massively entangled means our finite minds and institutions may be quickly overwhelmed by the apparent infinity of the unbounded systems. Because every part can influence the changes of the whole, and every change in the whole may affect every part, it is impossible to predict the future state of either the parts or the wholes. It is even impossible to distinguish part from whole because every one is, in fact, the other.

Though using the CAS as a worldview does us the favor of resolving the atomistic and fundamental wholeness worldview challenges of the past, our work is not done. We have to reframe our ways of observing, understanding, and acting if we are to see clearly, assess wisely, and move with integrity through the uncertainty of a worldview founded on complex adaptive systems.

CAS and Human Systems

This simple diagram of a CAS, with all of its complex implications, is how the world looks through the HSD lens. We find this view gives a reasonable explanation of human systems at any level, from intrapersonal emotions to international trade. We also find it accounts for relatively stable and predictable situations such as government bureaucracies and parental love, as well as for highly volatile situations such as innovation, riots, and mob violence. Differences of level or relative stability simply change the conditions and relationships among the parts of the system and between the parts and the wholes; they do not change the system in any fundamental way.

You see examples of CAS in many facets of human interaction. In a team, members work together and create a product, while the product line influences plans for the future. In a family, parents and children love each other and create a happy home, while the happy home shapes how people feel and behave. In a neighborhood, families chat over the fence and plan block parties, while block parties encourage over-the-fence chats. In an industry, companies compete and create new markets, while new markets fuel healthy competition. In a dictatorship, students Tweet each other and a riot explodes in the city center, while the event sparks Tweets around the world. When an individual reads a book, new ideas clash with old ones and a new "aha" leads to new insight, while the emerging insight frames a new question that reaches out for new books. Clashing insights lead to action, and action leads to new evidence, which leads to new insights, and so the cycle goes. In all of these cases and many others, parts interact to generate emergent patterns while patterns influence parts and their interactions. The result is a self-generating, self-organizing reality of human systems dynamics.

So, what is the role of the individual or institutional actor in such a self-organizing reality? The role is to pay attention to patterns as they emerge; to consider what patterns mean in the context of other patterns in the past, present, and future; to take intentional action to influence new patterns; and then to pay attention to the patterns that emerge in response to action, starting the cycle over again. We have a name for this cycle of seeing what is happening, making meaning of what you see, taking action based on that meaning, and looking again at what is happening. We call it Adaptive Action. It is the only way to engage wisely with complex adaptive systems to see, understand, and influence change as it emerges, and it is the focus of this book. But before we go there, we need to talk about the implications and applications of CAS particularly for patterns in human systems.

Why Is Change So Difficult?

We could go on and on describing the difficulties of productive change in the complex organizations and communities of today. But our bias for action turns us quickly to the possibilities for the future that emerge from the present mess. We want to do something in response to what we see. The trick is to describe a problematic situation in a way that supports wise action. We know that how we talk about our difficulties will ultimately frame the data we collect as well as what we imagine as our options for action. The name of the game ultimately shapes the plan and the play, so we need to understand the nature of this emergent game.

Throughout the book, we will introduce various applications and implications of CAS in human situations, but three particularly inform the foundations for Adaptive Action by helping us describe and explain the uncertainty and possibility we experience in complex change: interdependent pairs, kinds of change, and conditions for self-organizing. We will explore the theory and practice of these three applications and implications next.

Interdependent Pairs

In our experience, every unstable, surprising, or unpredictable situation sits on a framework of interdependent pairs. Each pair represents a single dichotomy that is essential to the survival of individuals in a group or the group as a whole. Strategic decisions rest on such dangerous dichotomies: Centralize or decentralize services; plan for long-term or short-term actions; collaborate or work independently; optimize the whole or optimize the part; work locally or globally; build face-to-face or virtual communications. Others may be more important in your environment, but if you are successful today and want to remain successful in the future, you will be able to recognize and manage such irresolvable dichotomies.

In his groundbreaking work *Handbook of Polarity Management: Identifying and Managing Unsolvable Problems*, Barry Johnson[1] talks about these pairs as polarities. He outlines a vision of polarity dynamics and an approach to polarity management that helps uncover the power of dynamic, interdependent pairs.

Consciously living in the midst of an interdependent pair is hard enough, but to make things even more challenging, the pairs are not independent from each other. A movement along one pair to resolve one challenge can lead to radical transformation along another pair. An example from product development will clarify the simplicity and the complexity of a set of interdependent pairs. To be most productive, a product development effort will focus on dynamic relationships between quality and speed, quality and cost, and cost and speed. This is one of the simplest and most obvious sets of interdependent pairs we have observed. It is easy to see how these pairs and their complex interdependencies could disrupt any simple plan for success. One decision might slide the product along the continuum between quality and speed. Even considered independently, that decision may be very difficult to make, but the interdependency with other pairs makes it even more challenging. The move toward quality will generally decrease the speed of production, distorting the shape of the quality-speed continuum. This shift has ripple effects on the cost-speed continuum; slowing speed increases cost. The decision space is unstable because any single, simple decision reshapes the landscape for all subsequent decisions.

That is the underlying challenge of interdependent pairs and one of the sources of uncertainty and instability in our complex adaptive world. It is possible to find an optimal solution that makes the best fit along the most important pairs, but the problem is that no simple algorithm will lead to that optimal solution. Well-informed trial and error is the only viable strategy. Being well informed means understanding the pairs that are essential to success, understanding how they relate to each other, and having the knowledge and skills required to make wise moves. Excellent leaders and gifted technicians have mastered the ability to navigate their complex interdependent pairs. Because their mastery is often intuitive, however, it is limited. Being well informed is not enough, unless your insights are put into practice. That is where the trial and error comes in and why Adaptive Action is such a powerful tool in uncertain times.

Ignoring, misunderstanding, or mismanaging interdependent pairs is one of the easiest ways to get stuck in a complex human system, and the symptoms can take many forms. Members of a team may have disagreements that seem intractable or so basic as to threaten the team's identity. Over time, a group may alternate from autonomy to independence, giving the appearance of a pendulum and inciting cynicism among staff. One team may focus on optimizing cost and speed, while another optimizes quality and cost. Any of these conflicts can lead to silos, rework, conflict, or blaming. A manager may value reliability while staff values creativity, leading to internal conflict, bad customer service, confused supervisors, or tough union negotiations. Whenever there is an apparently intractable problem, there is a good chance that some dysfunctional interdependent pair is driving an unstable dynamic. Once you find the pair and agree on a way to manage it, the intractable problem resolves itself into a series of decisions, which may be difficult, but at least they are not impossible.

Every situation has its own unique set of most important interdependent pairs. We often begin management interventions by asking teams to define their own. Besides revealing foundations for future decision making, the conversations uncover a wide range of misperceptions and disagreements. Over the years, we have commonly encountered three essential interdependent pairs as we talk with clients and explore the nature of their challenges and how they are stuck. These show up with a variety of names, but the dynamics are undeniable.

Bounded and Unbounded   Any thing or any idea about any thing is bounded, unbounded, or somewhere in the middle. Technically this is known as the relative openness of the system. Try it out yourself. Think of any human system; consider a family, for example. At one time a family was bounded by a shared name, shared gene pool, common living space, cultural practices, and the hour when they serve a family dinner. Over the past decade, in most parts of the world, we have come to recognize families as they move toward the unbounded end of the continuum. Multiple names, step relationships, mobility, cultural diversity, personal technology, and easy transportation are only some of the things that are moving families between the extremes of bounded or not. Whatever specific example you choose to consider, you have probably seen it drifting from bounded to unbounded in the recent past. Business examples of this shift are everywhere: Cross-functional or cross-organizational collaborations, virtual teams, telecommuting, ad hoc projects, matrix management, out-of-the-box thinking, and outsourcing. Bounded-unbounded is one of our critical interdependent pairs because identity, rules for success, and ways of thinking and talking are all radically different, depending on where a system falls along this key continuum. It is also critical because a wide range of circumstances today constantly shift the balance between the two. To adapt successfully, you must know about the boundaries of the system and work effectively within or across them.

This is the dichotomy we met earlier in finite and infinite games, when there was or was not a defined field of play. Complex systems are, by definition, relatively open systems where overlapping or unclear boundaries contribute to their complex dynamics.

Few Factors and Many Factors   This pair has to do with seeing what is relevant and what is not. When few factors are important, it is easier to anticipate and influence what happens over time. But if a situation depends on many factors, it may surprise you when you least expect it. Technically, this pair is known as low dimensionality (few factors) and high dimensionality (many factors).

Try it yourself. Pick a particularly sticky situation, and list the most critical factors. Are there few, or are there many? Consider professional development as an example. At one time, by far the most meaningful determinants of a career path were what you studied and where. As long as you focused on these two choices—going to a good college and studying the "right" things—your professional future was secure. Today, how many variables influence a professional career? There must be thousands: locale, social network, economic landscape, technical changes in the field, organizational mergers and acquisitions, languages spoken, technical abilities, life cycles of industries or technologies. . . . In fact, recent studies show that in today's marketplace choice of school and choice of major have minimal influence over lifetime earning capacity. The number of relevant factors is one of our interdependent pairs because the complexity of decision making increases exponentially as a system moves toward the high-dimension end of this continuum. If an organization focuses only on profits and falls prey to unethical behavior, you can see that it moves too close to the "few factors" end of this continuum. On the other hand, when an organization fails because it tries to be all things to all people, you can see that it wandered too close to the other end.

This pair shows up in finite and infinite games when there are one or many goal(s) or measure(s) of success. Complex systems are also, by definition, high-dimension systems because a large number of variables are working at the same time to influence the behavior of parts and wholes.

One-Way and Two-Way Causality   This pair has to do with the relationships among things and how those relationships change over time. One-way, sometimes called linear, causality means that one side has all the power to cause change in another, but the other has no influence on the one. Two-way, or nonlinear causality, means that one causes change in the other and the other causes change in the one. Over time, there is a mutual dependency that emerges where a change in either one affects both. Consider an example from your own experience, or think of an office conflict. Jane makes a decision that irritates Joe. Joe makes a snide remark. Jane hears it and makes another decision, this time with the intention of irritating Joe. Pretty soon, the two-way causality leads to open conflict and broken relationships. How have you seen one- or two-way causality play out in your own situations?

One reason this is a key pair in our evolving world today is that nonlinear causality tends to magnify situations over time until they explode. Sometimes the explosion is for good (optimal performance in a group) and sometimes for ill (unethical behavior). As the complexity of our systems increases, we become more and more aware of the amplifying effects of causes that work both ways.

Nonlinear causality shows up as an infinite game when we choose to change the rules rather than letting either side win the game. The goal is to keep playing, so being influenced is just as important as influencing someone else. Again, complex systems, by definition, experience nonlinear causality and the exponential explosion of change over time.

Many who have studied systems dynamics talk about and use the concepts of nonlinear causality and causal loops. They describe vicious and virtuous cycles that amplify and damp movement and activity in a cycle over time. In HSD we add to this description to help us explain this phenomenon in complex adaptive systems.[2]

So, these three interdependent pairs help us understand why it used to be so easy and is now so difficult to focus on what's important, to understand what is happening, and to take effective action. Today our world is much less bounded, dependent on many more factors, and more driven by two-way causality than it has ever been before. No wonder we think we're in the middle of a nightmare. No wonder we feel stuck and don't know how to move ourselves or our organizations forward. No wonder our world is so uncertain. No wonder our organizations seem so unmanageable.

There is no need to despair. Even if the strategies of the past fail more often than they succeed, there is hope. Human systems dynamics draws concepts and models from chaos science and complexity theory to help you build capacity to adapt and resolve issues that arise in unbounded, multifactor, and mutually causal situations. Human systems dynamics helps you leverage the uncertainty in your organization.

Rethinking Change

In both human and physical systems, we understand change from models and metaphors that work well in bounded, low-dimension, linear space. One of the critical revolutions we face in the future is to rethink what it means to experience and support change as it unfolds in an infinite game. In this emerging and complex world, we and our institutions experience change in many ways, and each way requires its own data collection, analysis, and response methods.

Change at the bounded, low-dimension, linear ends of our critical interdependent pairs is called *static change*. This is change when an object is moved from one place to another—simple. Before the move, everything is stable and still. After the move, everything is, again, stable and still. In between, nothing interesting happens because we are only interested in the "before" and the "after." The object being changed may be moved to another place, but the thing itself stays essentially unchanged. Sometimes we think of change in human systems as if it were static change. From this perspective, we expect easy transitions from pre-strategic plan to post-strategic plan; bad employee to good employee; expectation to outcome; unproductive team to productive team; toxic culture to generative culture. Of course, change seldom really happens this way, but sometimes it is helpful to think of it in this simple, direct way. The more bounded, low-dimension, and linear the situation (or the more we can convince ourselves of these conditions), the more likely it is that a static description of a change will be good enough. On the other hand, if we have static expectations and the change surprises us, then we need another, more complex, way to think and talk about change.

As the boundaries open, the factors multiply, and the causality gets more messy, change shifts to become more *dynamic*. Sir Isaac Newton, with his calculus and definition of forces and momentum, gave us ways to think and talk about dynamic change. In dynamic change, the motion is along a smooth course to end up at a predictable point. If you know enough at the beginning, you should be able to plan a smooth path to a predetermined end, and then manage a change process to meet your expectations from beginning to end. Of course, change seldom really happens this way, but sometimes it is helpful to think of it as if it does. Project management, capacity development, outcome evaluation (at its best), strategic planning, and most software development methods assume that change takes a smooth and predictable course. When reality steps in, and the path or endpoint is no longer predictable, dynamic change breaks down. It is easy to assume that the planner was not competent, the process was not well managed, or some irrelevant force disturbed the process. All these things may be true, but the challenge may be somewhat greater. The problem may be that in open, high-dimension, and nonlinear systems no amount of planning or management is good enough.

When system conditions are unbounded, when the number of relevant variables is high, and when causation is not simply one direction, the nature of change changes. New understanding of the underlying dynamics of change has labeled this dynamical change.[3]

An earthquake is an excellent example of dynamical change. It looks as if the system is still, and it certainly is still at one level of observation. At the level of the complex adaptive system underneath the ground, though, change is happening as rocks and soil shift and tensions among them accumulate. At some point, the tension overcomes the system stability, it breaks loose, and change at the lower level becomes visible at the higher level. No one can predict when or where the earthquake will happen, but if you know where the fault lines are, you can have some idea about where a transformative change will occur at an undetermined point in the future.

Malcolm Gladwell[4] talks about one instant in this kind of change—the very center of the breakthrough—and calls it a "tipping point." In an organizational setting, it is important to know that tipping points can happen, but it is also important to think about the changes that are visible only underneath the surface, so you can consider your options for Adaptive Action before the dynamical dam breaks. It is also important to recognize a dynamical change has occurred, so you can take action to influence patterns of stability and resilience after the system has tipped.

Many changes in business and social settings follow the dynamical path, among them a shift to violent conflict, an individual a-ha of learning, the journey from addiction to recovery, an innovative insight, the first unethical act. In each of these cases, some underlying tensions accumulate over time and release in an unexpected and dramatic way. The accumulation of the tension ahead of time and the system response following the change offer options for action, while the observable change itself may be impossible to influence.

If it is your job to lead, support, or stimulate change in human systems, you can identify the critical interdependent pairs and consider where your system sits on the continua between the interdependent pairs. Does it lie predominantly on the stable end of the spectrum for most pairs? Or is it precariously balanced in the middle? Is the system wide open and ready for dynamical change, or is it held in a stable place and prepared for a static change? You can figure out the most likely category of the change to come, and you can interact with the system to see and influence the dynamics of the change as they emerge. We talk even more specifically about the kinds of change and their direct application in Adaptive Action in the next chapter.

Still, in an open, high-dimension, nonlinear complex adaptive system, whatever you do, the future remains unknowable. Open to external influences, many factors and nonlinear causality, complex systems are by nature unpredictable. The best you can hope to do is to build adaptive capacity to coevolve with the system as it changes over time.

Conditions for Self-Organizing

The interdependent pairs influence the stability of change, and the three kinds of change help you know how to interact with a changing system. But it is helpful to have a more granular and nuanced way to see, understand, and influence change in complex human systems. For this, we need to consider the conditions that influence the speed, path, and results of emergent dynamics.

When new patterns emerge from interactions in complex adaptive systems, we say they self-organize. That's because emergent patterns are shaped by connections within, rather than forces from outside of, the system. You see self-organizing patterns in human systems every day, from a meeting that "goes south" to a dinner party that delights, to a public bus full of people singing seasonal songs. At every level of human action, self-organizing patterns shape and are shaped by meaning and behavior.

Even though it happens all the time and in every place, self-organizing never happens in the same way twice. This is the profound effect of open, high-dimension, and nonlinear systems: they never let the same thing happen exactly the same way twice. Sometimes the self-organizing process is fast and clear, and the outcome is easy to see and understand. Other times, though, the parts may wander around and try various patterns. They settle into a coherent pattern only after a long and confusing process. And sometimes the system wanders and wanders and never settles into a pattern that is coherent or persistent.

You have certainly been in meetings that matched each of these evolutionary patterns. Follow the agenda; get to work; finish the successful meeting. Begin with voiced confusion about why the meeting was called and what it is about; talk, talk, talk; and finally, in the closing minutes, describe a clear and compelling purpose for ongoing work. Meet, meet, meet with changing players, changing interests, confusion about needs and resources, and abandon the effort when patience and good will are completely exhausted. Each demonstrates one common path of self-organizing processes.

It is important to note here that none of these scenarios is static change. Because we are interested in the path of change, just the simple, static before-and-after picture isn't good enough. On the contrary, any of these paths may seem dynamic or dynamical, depending on the speed of the process and the point of view of the observer.

Seeing these various paths—smooth, bumpy; straight, winding—is one thing. Knowing what to do to nudge them in productive directions is something else. In the late 1990s, a circle of us began to ask about the conditions for self-organizing. What factors helped a system self-organize clearly, well, and toward ends we valued? What happened when these factors were missing or insufficient? What can we know about conditions for self-organizing that can make us supportive partners in a process we do not predict or control? Like many powerful answers in complex systems, this one is profoundly simple. In her research on physical, conceptual, and mathematical systems, Glenda found three conditions for self-organizing. Not surprisingly, we found that the same conditions were relevant when we considered self-organizing patterns in social systems. The three are surprisingly simple, deeply profound, and as commonsense as dirt. They are represented by the CDE Model, which identifies the three conditions that influence self-organizing processes: container (C), difference (D), and exchanges (E). Figure 2.2 depicts these simple components and their complex interdependencies.

Any complex adaptive system will form patterns when conditions are right. (You can also say that the CAS will form whatever pattern is right for the conditions because patterns determine conditions and conditions determine patterns. That idea is on the more complex end of simplicity and will come up again in later chapters, so let's leave it alone for now.) Any complex adaptive system will form patterns when conditions are right.

Something has to hold the parts of the system together close enough and long enough that they will interact to create a new pattern. We call this holding-together condition "container" and represent it as C. It doesn't really matter what does the holding together. It might be a shared idea, a charismatic

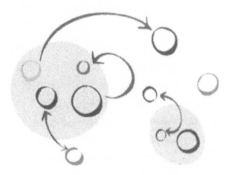

FIGURE 2.2. Eoyang CDE.
Containers (C), differences (D), and exchanges (E) influence the speed,
path, and outcomes of self-organization in the system.

leader, a closed room, a national boundary, a mountain range, a time period, a shared language, an institutional boundary, or any other physical, emotional, social, political, or conceptual feature of the system. The smaller, tighter, clearer the container is, the faster and more coherent the self-organizing process will be. This is pretty obvious. If a small team has a clear membership list and an unambiguous goal, it will get its work done quickly. If it isn't clear who's on the team, and the goal is unclear, and people don't know when or where to meet, the work may never get done at all. You see this effect of container conditions whether you focus on individuals, pairs, teams, communities, neighborhoods, companies, or nations. At every level, the container is one of the critical conditions for self-organizing processes. The container influences the path, speed, and results of the process, and if you can influence the container, you influence the process. If you influence the process, you influence the emergent pattern.

In a complex adaptive system, the parts of the system have to be different in significant ways, or no pattern will emerge. This condition we call "difference" and represent with a D. Differences can be of any kind, as long as they are significant to the players. At a bar, late on Saturday night, gender or level of inebriation might be a significant difference for those who want to get home without undue complications. In commercializing her intellectual property, a scientist finds that business acumen and connection to markets (irrelevant differences in the laboratory where the idea was hatched) become differences that really count. In a classroom, differences in experience and expertise should be relevant, and differences in age and cultural background should usually be ignored. Under what circumstances might age and background be significant differences in a classroom? What if the class is massage training for parents of newborns? What if the class is about cultural history or racial bias?

Difference is also critical at other levels of human systems organization. Competitors in an industry, vendors, partnerships, mergers and acquisitions, customer relations are all situations where differences within and between containers draw the line between success and failure.

In all these cases, and every other social system you ever experienced, differences that make a difference determine the speed and path and outcome of self-organizing processes. If there are too many differences, the system can't settle down. If there are not enough differences, change can't get started. Just the optimal number of significant differences will support a robust self-organizing process. In 2011 late developments in the Arab Spring and early developments in the 99 Percent movement were great examples of too many differences for clear patterns to emerge. In both cases, the energy was clear and the movement was undeniable, but who and what the movement supported was (at least for a time) unclear. On the other hand, the U.S. Congress during the same time was stuck because there were not enough relevant differences. The body was absolutely locked into inaction because the only difference that seemed to count was whether to tax or not to tax the American people.

Finally, the parts of the complex adaptive system have to be connected to each other or nothing will happen. We call this connecting condition "exchange" and represent it with E. An exchange is any connection that transmits information, resources, or energy between or among parts of the CAS. When one part of the system receives an exchange, the pattern internal to the part is changed. When the part changes, it transmits information, resources, or energy back across the exchange, and other parts of the system receive it and are themselves changed. These transforming interactions are the engine for self-organizing change in a CAS. Too many or too tight, and the exchanges lock a system into an unchanging pattern. Too few or too loose exchanges, and the pattern either doesn't emerge or doesn't persist.

When a company considers outsourcing key functions, it is changing fundamental exchanges. Funding, work direction, quality controls, scheduling, communications, and product delivery are all exchanges that shape productivity and satisfaction. When a function is managed in-house, the exchanges are usually consistent and relatively tight. When the service is outsourced, any or all of these exchanges are weakened, and a contract may or may not tune the exchanges to the optimal levels.

Technology has had a tremendous influence on social, economic, and political patterns in recent years because of the many ways it has shifted patterns of exchange. In some ways the exchanges have become weaker (from face-to-face to virtual meetings), in other cases they have become stronger (social networks connecting friends around the world), and in some cases they have cut key players out of the exchange altogether (online commerce and the decline of the local retailer).

Container, difference, and exchange are the conditions that influence a self-organizing process and shape how quickly the process moves forward, how messy the path is, and how clear the resulting pattern is. You can use the CDE to see the pattern as it emerges and understand how the conditions shape the emergent pattern. The CDE Model can help you recognize and name conditions of systems, but intentional action requires more than just recognition. Conscious influence over self-organizing patterns requires an intentional process for seeing, understanding, and influencing the conditions that shape change in complex adaptive systems. We call that process Adaptive Action.

Adaptive Action Defined

Adaptive Action is an elegant and powerful method for engaging with dynamical change in an ever-emerging, always self-organizing world. As represented by Figure 2.3, the Adaptive Action model consists of three questions:

What?

So what?

Now what?

What? What do you see? What changes have occurred? What is the same as before? What is different? What containers are most relevant? What differences are emerging or disappearing? What are the current exchanges, and how strong are they? What is the pattern of the past? What desires are there for patterns in the future? *What?*

So what? So what surprises you? So what do your observations mean to you? So what do they mean to others? So what might you expect in future? So

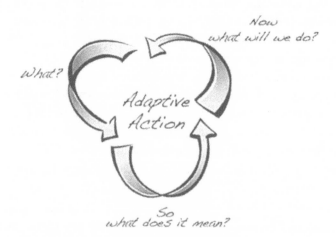

FIGURE 2.3. Adaptive Action.

We use iterative cycles of data collection, analysis, and action to see,
understand, and influence patterns in our complex systems.

what assumptions or expectations were confirmed or denied? So what contain-ers are open to change, and what might those changes mean? So what differ-ences are open to change, and how might new or more effective differences be infused into the system? So what options are there for building new exchanges, changing existing ones, or breaking ones that are not helpful? *So what?*

Now what? Now what will I do? Now what will you do? Now what will we do together? Now what messages should we send to others? Now what out-comes might we expect? Now what will we do to collect data for our next and emerging cycle? *Now what?*

That's it! After framing such an enormous set of overwhelming challenges as those we face in the world of today and tomorrow, it is a bit surprising that we would offer a solution as simple as the CDE Model coupled with Adaptive Action. How can such a simple method prepare individuals and groups to thrive in response to such complex challenges? How can such a simple method help us leverage the uncertainty that plagues complex adaptive systems? The answer is not so simple.

First, Adaptive Action is a variation of a very old idea. Similar processes show up as the scientific method of building and testing hypotheses; PDSA (Plan, Do, Study, Act); learning cycles; action research; and diagnostic proce-dures. From records of ancient warfare to the latest scientific treatises, we see the steps of data collection, analysis, and action repeated in an infinite num-ber of ways. The reason it keeps showing up is that it works. When adaptation is called for, seeing, thinking, and acting in iterative cycles is exactly the right response. Adaptive Action is a slightly adapted version of the age-old process. We have altered the process to account for the openness, high dimensionality, and nonlinearity of dynamical change in complex adaptive human systems by stating it as a series of inquiries and by embedding into the process the condi-tions for self-organizing.

Second, Adaptive Action is a cycle. Every ending action makes the next beginning question necessary. Complex systems of all kinds—from fractal mathematics to genetic biological systems—are driven by iteration. A short, simple process is repeated over and over, at different times and speeds, and with different raw materials. The result is a highly diverse, but fundamen-tally coherent, pattern. You find examples of iteration leading to coherence in every facet of human activity. Practice makes perfect for the musician and the athlete. Reliable processes produce consistently high-quality goods. Behavior that is modeled and practiced is embedded in habit. Rituals build community.

Good manners encourage respect. Saturation advertising seduces consumers. Once you begin to see them, you find the examples of simple iteration and complex results everywhere.

Third, Adaptive Action is framed as a series of questions. An adaptive actor is always standing in inquiry. In times of uncontrolled and dynamical change, inquiry is absolutely necessary. The greatest risk is allowing assumptions of the past to dominate expectations for the future. The only way to avoid this dangerous path is to ask questions—clearly and perpetually.

Fourth, Adaptive Action is simple enough to be flexible. It can be repeated by anyone or any group, in any place, at any time. It may be explicit or implicit, solo or shared, public or private. It may deal with patterns in physical, conceptual, emotional, social, or political reality. Formal groups and informal ones can engage in Adaptive Action. Cycles can be as short as a second or as long as a lifetime. In any variation, it supports effective and efficient engagement between people and their environments.

Fifth, it is the only way to reduce the risk of uncertainty in dynamical change. Under conditions of extreme unpredictability, it is impossible to know ahead of time what will happen. It is impossible to know which is the good choice and which the bad, before you make a choice and see the results. All you can do—the only way to mitigate risk—is to try something, quickly and carefully assess how the system responds to your action, and take another action in mutual response. Adaptive Action leads you to *adjust* and *correct* when it is impossible to predict and control.

Sixth, there are millions of tools, models, and methods to support each step. You can even use the ones you already know to fill in the blanks of *What?*, *So what?*, and *Now what?* In the following chapters, we will share with you models and methods we find helpful. We'll also share stories of how our HSD Associates have used Adaptive Action in their lives and work. Ultimately, though, we hope you find ways to create an Adaptive Action toolkit that fits you and your complex environment.

Seventh, Adaptive Action cycles can be embedded inside one another to build a network of inquiry and action. While you explore any large adaptive challenge, you will also encounter smaller ones. Sometimes these smaller challenges are closely connected together, and sometimes they may be loosely connected. Planning a presidential campaign is a long cycle of Adaptive Action, but within it there are other adaptations: selecting staff, setting and testing strategy, reviewing poll data, deciding where to spend time and where to dispense the message. As any political operative can attest, there is no end to the numbers and levels of Adaptive Action cycles that inform a political campaign. Each one can stand alone, and all of them are intimately connected to each other, so you can choose to deal with one at a time or any combination of a group of them. The trick is to choose a sufficient number to do the work well, and few enough to do the work efficiently.

This book itself is a laboratory in Adaptive Action. Think about what you have read so far. *What* are the containers, differences, and exchanges that shape this approach to change? *So what* do they mean to you and your changing environment? *Now what* can you do to influence them?

As you explore the rest of this book, you will find many other examples of Adaptive Action. You will also see for yourself why the simplicity of Adaptive Action is so powerful and why the power of Adaptive Action is its simplicity. Ultimately, we hope this book becomes an integral part of the Adaptive Action cycles in your own world of work and life.

3

WHAT?

No matter where you go or what you do, information surrounds you. Television in airports, music in elevators, handheld games, and movies on phones feed out steady streams of noise. Every item of information must be filtered, focused, decoded, and stored before it can be used to inform action. Your organization seeks and consumes competitive intelligence. Your team collects and reports performance data. You pick up subtle cues in intercultural encounters. Evolving rules, regulations, and expectations demand your attention in the course of the day. How do you know where to start making sense of the mess? How do you know where to focus? How do you sort the important from the interesting from the merely distracting? Asking *What?* is the first step in the Adaptive Action journey toward understanding a complex world that may not make sense on the surface, a world in which every thread of meaning seems to be tangled with many other threads.

The complex patterns created by this messy and overwhelming flow of information require that you see and understand what lies under the surface of your day-to-day chaos. If you see the relationships and dynamics that drive change in complex human systems, you can influence them intentionally and creatively. The *What?* step of Adaptive Action uncovers the dynamics of change as they emerge around you. During this step, you mine clarity out of confusion; you make sense of the complexity in your organization.

Asking *What?* helps you set your sights and know where to look, understand what is there, see what is important, and ignore what is not. When you ask *What?* you open up the opportunity to see beyond confusion and understand beyond complication. When you see clearly, it is easier to understand complex situations, imagine innovative options for action, and take decisive action—even when you cannot predict or control what happens. In short, seeing patterns in the complexity around you prepares you to adapt to the most complex challenges and opportunities. This chapter provides the foundations for seeing beyond the confusion and "busy-ness," to appreciate the opportunities that emerge from complexity. In this chapter you will:

- Use a simple model to see patterns in the midst of chaos
- Spot patterns of the simple in the complex
- Explore multiple perspectives that shape complex realities
- Recognize and respond to three kinds of change

Finding *What?* to Get Unstuck

If you are faced with the complexity of change in any facet of your work or life, you need simple and powerful ways to see and understand changes as they emerge. The only constant is the requirement that you collect information continuously, because you never know when change will emerge. People who have learned to navigate successfully in complex landscapes intuitively know what to examine and where to go for information. They spend their time observing in ways that may not seem useful from the more traditional perspectives of change. When you ask *What?* in the course of Adaptive Action, you become conscious of how best to collect and sort through data to distinguish the information from the random noise.

You also learn to use simple models and methods to collect and analyze data. We believe that if you're dealing with a complex situation, the last thing you need is a complicated model. You don't need a tool that makes your work more difficult; you need something that clarifies and simplifies a mess of data as quickly and clearly as possible. For this reason, all of our Adaptive Action models and methods are surprisingly simple. One of the most powerful is, indeed, the simplest. We call it Same and Different, and it mimics the most fundamental of all seeing and thinking systems: your own brain. You begin by drawing a simple t-shaped framework. An example is in Figure 3.1. You and others, if you are working in a group, brainstorm similarities and differences you observe emerging from the complexity. The "sames" go on the same side; the "differences" go on the difference side. That's it.

You can certainly see from this why it is the simplest (but it may not be obvious why this is one of the most powerful) of our models that help you identify patterns. It is powerful for many reasons. Because it is so simple, it doesn't ask you to interpret or distort the data any more than is absolutely necessary. The analysis process is fast and simple—no special instruction or fancy preparation required. The simple decision—Are these same or different?—is easy

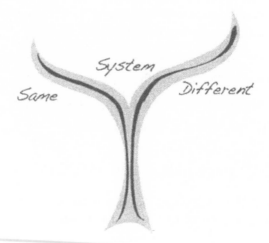

FIGURE 3.1. Same and Different.
We identify patterns as we look for similarities
and differences in our complex systems.

for even the most conflicted groups to make in unison. Of course a discussion ensues about why our pictures of same and different are same or different, but it comes in curiosity and openness, rather than in defense and posturing. We can do it in a group or individually. We can use it to inquire about individuals or groups, processes and procedures, pictures, products, locales, business models, political parties. Anything that might interest us opens its hidden and complex patterns in response to this simple method.

We find that a whole range of *So whats?* and *Now whats?* emerge spontaneously as the Same and Different brainstorming develops. Groups ask:

Why do you see it differently than I do?

Are these similarities or differences serving us well in our work, or not?

Do we focus more on the similarities that bring us together?

If we focus on the similarities, are they stifling us or giving us strength?

Do we choose to focus on the differences?

If we see the differences, are they inspiring us or distracting us with pointless conflict?

What might we do to amplify the similarities or differences that are serving us?

What might we do to reduce the power of the differences that distract us?

In our experience with business, community, individuals, and groups focusing on personal or professional issues, it doesn't take long with the Same and Different before the conversation turns to thoughtful and authentic discussion of the most daunting "undiscussables."

Once we were working with a group of midlevel managers from a large food manufacturing company. Almost two years before we arrived, the group had received a mandate to "become a team." They had met monthly and tried every team-building approach they (or their consultants) could imagine. Still, the group was nothing like a team. Across the midmanagement level of the organization, there was a high need for cross-functional interaction and collaboration; teamwork was a success criterion. Unfortunately what existed was siloed competition and underlying conflict. The top leaders in the organization had done all they could think of to break down the silos and increase collaboration, but they were stymied. They called us in to facilitate what they saw as yet another in the long line of teaming rituals.

What we found was a room full of individuals who were politely cold, and clearly not interested in becoming a team. So Glenda drew a "T" form on the white board and asked them to start naming similarities and differences in the room. Slowly people started naming some—mostly superficial differences, such as age or the cars they drove or how many children they had. They even got a bit silly and boisterous, creating a long list of differences. Then one person named "Where we went to school" as a difference, and the whole room went quiet. We continued the brainstorming until the group was played out, then we returned to that problematic item: school.

Glenda asked the group to explain what that one was about. After a moment or two of uncomfortable silence, someone pointed out to her that some of the people in the room had studied agricultural economics at the central university campus, while others had studied breeding and nutrition at the "aggie" campus—two very different cultures. So she engaged them in some activities that amplified the difference. She asked them to line up on opposite sides of the room depending on their alma mater. The lines were about equal, and everyone was quite uncomfortable making this particular difference so obvious in the room. Next she asked each side to list everything they thought the other group said about them. Again the room was full of laughter over bovine butts and bookworms. About halfway through that activity, one person said, "If you didn't do what you do, I would have to do it." And that statement broke the tension in the room. From that point forward they were able to talk about how to work together and share information and show respect for each other's work. At the end of the day, the whole group left with a plan for moving forward together.

Same and Different works because it uncovers one of the basic conditions for self-organizing: difference (D). It invites you to explore differences in the context of the similarities, rather than damping or ignoring the differences and focusing only on the similarities. It recognizes and facilitates the full pattern by shining a light on both the differences that spark change and the similarities that build stability.

For the rest of this chapter, we explore three other, somewhat more complicated models and methods for collecting and understanding complex systems as you take the *What?* step of Adaptive Action:

- Inquiry
- Patterns
- Perspectives

Three Kinds of Change

As you step into the *What?* cycle of Adaptive Action, stand in inquiry to identify and name patterns across your system. Pay attention to the patterns of interaction and decision making, noting the degree to which they support or detract from the system's full functioning. At the same time, access a variety of perspectives to gather a wide range of data to create a rich, full-dimensional picture that will inform decision making in the later cycles of Adaptive Action.

Inquiry

"It depends" is the only real answer to any question in times of complex change because every situation, every moment, is unique. What is best practice at one place and time might be a complete mistake in another. For example, you might think that transparency is always a virtue, but there may be times when other values (courage, care, confidentiality) become more important. Speaking an opinion strongly is great after you know enough, but it can be risky if your opinion gets ahead of your information. High expectations, fast turnaround times, low-cost bids, habits of mind and body, assertiveness or aggression, silence and speech—either extreme of any interdependent pair can be the right or wrong answer, depending on the complex patterns of the present, the historical context, and hopes for the future. On a complex landscape, you simply cannot know for sure. Every answer has a short shelf-life. Questions, though, last forever. Only the good questions that result from disciplined inquiry remain helpful wherever you are and whatever you are doing.

In a complex system, inquiry helps you make sense of the system's conditions and provides data for your decision making and planning. You use questions to examine the environment in the context of its history over time, its performance in the present, and its purposes for the future. Looking at individuals and groups, you identify system requirements, explore unspoken rules and expectations, and capture the rhythms of interaction that characterize your experience. You explore network connections and multiple perspectives to help you use your knowledge of the system to inform the next cycles of Adaptive Action. Inquiry in Adaptive Action helps you see the openness, explore the diversity, and learn from the nonlinear causality of your complex adaptive system.

Inquiry means remaining open to the unknown and to asking open-ended questions for which you don't already know or cannot anticipate the answers. To stand in inquiry is to be open to surprises and to engage in ongoing cycles of exploration. When you remain in inquiry, you're never finished; you continue to question and seek new information. In this dialogue with reality, the closure of one Adaptive Action generates the question that triggers the next inquiry.

Standing in inquiry requires a particular way of being.

- Know your "stuff," but remain open to and actively engage in learning more.
- Be comfortable with the ambiguity and vulnerability of holding questions.
- Ask questions more than you give answers.
- Turn judgment into curiosity.
- Turn disagreement into mutual exploration.
- Turn defensiveness into self-reflection.

We have borrowed a set of thinking prompts from soft systems methodology[1] that help make sense of a complex system and dynamical change. We call them *pattern spotters* because they open the system to allow us to see essential patterns that we might overlook otherwise. These statements inform your inquiry to help you sort through and see more deeply into the simplicity that lurks inside chaos. The pattern spotters are five incomplete sentence stems that invite individuals or groups to explore emerging patterns. They ask you to explore and express:

> *Generalizations:* "In general I noticed . . . " (Example: "In general, I noticed that the team was productive.")

Generalizations allow you to look broadly across the system to identify themes and patterns that cover the whole landscape. They enable you to engage in conversation about what you see and what it means to you. When things are in flux, it is sometimes difficult to focus on what stays the same. But the things that are similar across a system are important because they can be stable markers to help track change, a safe haven in times of stress, a place to stand when action is required, and sources for ideas about sustainability.

We use generalizations to great advantage when we consider cultural change in organizations. Once we recognize values or interests that are held in common across the organization, we can leverage them as a launch pad for the future. Generalizations help focus attention on the most pervasive and potentially powerful levers for change.

> *Exceptions:* "In general I noticed . . . , but. . . . " (Example: "In general I noticed they started meetings on time, but Jake was often late.")

Asking about exceptions forces you to look for the gaps in the generalizations and explore them for further insights. In traditional change theories, exceptions were often ignored as aberrations or one-off situations. In fact, many organization development practitioners refuse to use "but" because it excludes rather than including. In complex systems, by contrast, the exception is often a powerful marker for future change. When you work in a dynamical environment, anomalies can signal an impending change in a system's structures or patterns.

We focus on exceptions when a team needs to become more innovative. Rather than focusing on the same-old, same-old, we ask them to collect as many exceptions as possible. In discussion, then, they discern patterns that might draw them into creative and unexpected solutions.

> *Contradictions:* "On one hand I noticed . . . , and on the other hand. . . . " (Example: "On one hand, he makes it on time to most meetings; on the other hand, he is always late for this team meeting.")

Contradictions in the system help point to important differences that offer leverage points for change. As you learned in Chapter 1, differences create the tension that drives complex change. The work of Barry Johnson (1992) and his polarity management approach and our discussion of interdependent pairs from the last chapter clearly explain the role of contradictions in unsolvable, complex problems.[4] This simple question about contradictions encourages group members to put their finger on the factors that drive complex dynamics.

This question is quite helpful in interdisciplinary teams. Rather than focusing on their "common ground," it is often helpful for them to identify their differences. Together, they can mine their contradictions for the opportunities for creative collaboration.

Surprises: "I was surprised that. . . . " (Example: "I was surprised when Jake came to the meeting on time on Tuesday.")

The surprises you identify point to the unexpected emergent information that comes with dynamical change. In static and dynamic change, surprises are not supposed to happen. When they do, someone is at fault. In times of complex change, surprise is a gift. It opens new opportunities or uncovers unseen challenges.

If you cannot watch everything that is happening at the same time, focus your attention on surprises. When change is most turbulent—market shifts, natural disasters, political transitions, pending reorganizations—this focus collects the raw data from which a realistic picture of the future may emerge. You are surprised when something happens that is "out of the ordinary"; when an extraordinary future is emerging, surprises give you hints about what might lie ahead.

The 2011 riots in London were surprising to many around the world, but what smaller surprises came in the preceding weeks and days? What were early warning signals that could have drawn the attention of the community to take action before the system erupted in destruction and violence? In what ways might the rest of the world use this news from the United Kingdom to anticipate disruptive changes in our futures?

Puzzles: "I wonder. . . . " (Example: "I wonder what was different on Tuesday that set conditions for Jake to be on time.")

Finally, the "I wonder" stem points you more deeply into your reflection to identify your own next questions. Puzzles lie at the center of inquiry. On the basis of all you see, from similarities and differences, you are prepared to ask meaningful and powerful questions. That is what the "wonder" statements are about.

This statement is often a breakthrough moment for groups experiencing conflict. The earlier observations (generalities, exceptions, contradictions, and surprises) set the stage for conflicting parties to ask each other meaningful questions that move toward shared understanding and action. Imagine how different the U.S. political landscape might be if elected representatives were asking probing questions (rather than collecting poll data), and their constituents were responding with thoughtful answers.

We live and work in complex systems that are characterized by unpredictable and unending change. Taking Adaptive Action in those systems requires that we explore our world through questions that help us see the complexity around us. All five of these inquiries—these pattern spotters—help discover and articulate the patterns that inform your picture of the present and paint your possible futures. They help us make sense of the complexity we encounter day to day.

Patterns

We have used the term *pattern* liberally in our conversation so far, and you will hear more of it before our work is done. The word has many connotations, drawn from art, design, sewing, dancing, cognition, computer modeling, neuroscience, genetics, mechanical engineering, architecture, and still other disciplines. Understanding patterns—identifying and naming them, coming to understand their source and their impact, and influencing them—lies at the heart of Adaptive Action. Its core role requires that we use the concept in a way that is the most general one you can imagine and yet also the most precise.

In general, a pattern is whatever you perceive in the complex landscapes around you. You scan for patterns of behavior and decision making that show up in the data and information you collect. Patterns appear over time and space, in particular times and places. They show up in social interactions, physical environments, emotional experiences, conceptual models. They may be simple and predictable, as when a recipe becomes a cake. They may be complex and predictable, as when a blueprint is transformed into a skyscraper. They may be simple and unpredictable, as when a group of children play with a ball. They may be complex and unpredictable, as when those same children learn to read and write. In its most general sense, human systems dynamics is concerned with all of these patterns and how they shape your ability to influence your emerging future.

We also depend on a very specific definition of pattern to help people get unstuck from the problematic patterns that constrain them. We define *patterns* as similarities, differences, and connections that have meaning across space and time. Patterns, defined in this very specific way, are the *What?* you look for to begin Adaptive Action. What are the similarities that give coherence and meaning? What are the differences that exaggerate points of interest or generate tension in the present? What are the connections that resulted from the past and set conditions for future transformations? These three conditions, and their relationships to one another, set the stage for meaning making because they articulate reality in a way that is conscious and can be shared. This mode of thinking about patterns gives you a subtle and simple way to capture and reflect on the complex. They also provide hints about actions you can take to break patterns that constrain you, and help you get unstuck from situations where you feel helpless and frustrated. Every human system generates (and is predetermined by) patterns.

When Glenda worked with the group of middle managers who were from such vastly different learning settings, she helped them define new patterns of interaction by talking about how they were similar and different and how they might connect to each other more effectively in the future.

In the following examples, consider how the ongoing patterns of interaction and decision making are, in essence, predetermined by the patterns already in play across this organization. In a highly competitive organizational culture, you see certain kinds of patterns. People share organizational goals of high performance and being the best (similarities). They perform in an environment where they work independently on their own ideas and for their own good (differences). They choose not to share information or resources to maintain their competitive advantage (connections). When this is the mode of working over a period of time, it becomes the expectation and shapes the behaviors of new people who enter the workplace.

In organizations that are warm and friendly places, you will see a focus on shared goals (similarities) as they do their individual jobs (differences) in an atmosphere of engagement and mutual support (connections). Again, these are the patterns of expectations that influence behaviors and decisions of new people as they enter the organization. Think of organizations you know that have these and other patterns, and you can see more deeply into the dynamics of interaction and decision making that shape the experiences of customers, competitors, and staff.

Individual personalities, communities, nations, families, and teams can all be understood in terms of the patterns they create and the patterns that create them. In every case, similarities give identity and stability, differences inspire characteristic creativity or dissension, and connections bring possibility into reality. Recognizing patterns in the *What?* step of Adaptive Action provides system intelligence to inform later meaning making (*So what?*) and action (*Now what?*).

In times of chaotic change, it may be difficult to see patterns as they emerge. As you try to make sense of the chaos that is your world, you look for similarities and differences among parts of the system, observing how seemingly disparate parts of the system connect. Similarities dissolve before your very eyes as markets change, technology evolves, organizations merge, and product lifecycles shrink. Rapid change also makes it difficult to see differences that matter. Amid a flood of information, how do you select the most significant messages? How do you know what to watch for? Finally, in times of change, connections may be fleeting and tentative. Shifting connections leave you without familiar supports and with the risks of isolation at a time when relationships may be vital.

Groups gradually build habits of similarities, differences, and connections that you recognize as organizational "culture." You interact with the same groups and individuals, and those interactions eventually come to characterize your relationships. For instance, living and working in highly competitive environments, you connect with others who are most like you; you focus on differences of performance and power; and you connect so as to protect your own competitive advantage. New people who enter your system soon adapt to those patterns as they learn to behave similarly. Ultimately they learn to reproduce the pattern, and they become as competitive as others who have been in the system for a long time.

Looking for patterns can be as simple as identifying behaviors or cultural activities that characterize a group. For example, in addition to competition you and your work groups can also reinforce the differences, similarities, and connections that create patterns of cooperation, productivity, avoidance, learning, groupthink, and other styles of working together. Cultural and ethnic groups are often characterized by shared patterns that emerge as they engage in common behaviors such as honoring their elders, celebrating national and religious holidays, participating in government and governance, and expecting commitment to family and community.

Looking for patterns can also be as subtle as being open to the nuances of interaction and behavior that may not be obvious on first observation. You may not have immediate access to various hidden agendas or political alliances that shape patterns you encounter. To see these more hidden patterns, you often need to be aware of history and the context of differences that may not be apparent on the surface.

Understanding patterns is central to understanding human systems, which is why *What?* is the first step in the cycle of Adaptive Action. How well you can see, understand, and influence those patterns determines your adaptive capacity, your ability to adapt by shifting and generating new patterns in a balanced dance of self-organization toward fitness and sustainability. If you want your system to move toward greater health and strength, you can shift your interactions to change the similarities, differences, or connections that influence patterns toward greater adaptability.

In a human system, patterns across the whole are never exactly the same, even when they appear to be highly similar. For instance, in an innovative system risk taking may be commonly encouraged across the whole, yet risk-taking behaviors may be celebrated differently from place to place. But it may be that slight differences exist in the degree of risk that is acceptable. Even these slight differences in similar patterns create less certainty for the individuals who must figure out new rules, expectations, and activities as they move from one part of the system to another. The only way to make those adjustments effectively and efficiently is to engage in Adaptive Action.

Differences in systemwide patterns make the overall culture less coherent. The more similar the patterns are, however, the clearer they are; the more likely they are to sustain themselves. *Coherence* in a human system is the degree to which patterns across the whole are similar, without losing the richness of difference at the same time. High coherence means that individuals experience similar expectations and patterns as they move through a system, even as they realize subtle, small differences across the whole. Low coherence says individuals experience patterns that are dissimilar, even contradictory, as they move from one part of a system to another. Highly coherent systems are usually more efficient and adaptable than those that are less coherent. However, a system that is too coherent, too focused on homogeneity, may be unable to innovate or adapt to changing circumstances. Again, the focus is on inquiry. It is most important to ask, "How much coherence serves the current purpose?" The answer will depend entirely on the situation.

Seeing patterns is a fundamental survival skill in times of rapid change. Adaptive Action consists of seeing and responding to patterns in the environment by taking action to strengthen or change patterns in human systems to seek greater fit. Adaptation means reinforcing similarities to make coherent patterns emerge, or to spark diversity in a pattern that is too coherent; amplifying or damping differences to encourage learning and change; and building or breaking connections, according to their usefulness in the system's adaptability.

One challenge to pattern spotting is that, in complex systems, many patterns exist at the same time. No one pattern is so dominant that others disappear. A competitive organization may include some highly collaborative teams, and a relatively homogeneous culture might include a few mavericks. The patterns you are aware of depend on many factors: where you stand in the organization, data you have available, your experience or expectations, your hopes or accountabilities. With all these pattern possibilities, an effective *What?* cycle must consider multiple perspectives and stay in perpetual inquiry, without losing the capacity to act.

Perspectives

Your ability to see and understand patterns contributes to greater adaptability. It appears as simple as looking around and remaining aware of your surroundings. It is not so simple, however, because you live and work in complex systems that always generate multiple patterns at the same time. The more deeply you discern the patterns around you, the better you understand the complexities of the system; but there is no guarantee that you are "seeing" the same system as others are. It is a maxim credited to a number of individuals, but it is true nonetheless that in complex systems "what you see depends on where you sit." Two people can look at the same situation and see contrasting details, depending on their experiences, interests, and contexts. In complex systems of many individuals, those differences become greater in both number and size.

Every complex system depends on multiple perspectives. It's why we offer many ways to see through others' eyes to gain access to patterns that may enhance or detract from options for action. We recognize that divergent perspectives can emerge from a number of sources in the system. Where people are sitting can depend on their worldviews, how they see and understand the reality in their lives, and the degree to which they share those views with others. Where you are sitting also has to do with your proximity to the given patterns. Are you an active player in the system? Are you a casual observer? Are you looking at small parts of the system, or viewing it at the more global level of the greater whole? Are these your own patterns, or are they someone else's? We offer suggestions for considering patterns you see so as to help you talk with others about the patterns they may be seeing, and to work with them to build shared understanding and action.

Four Truths   The first question we consider in talking about the impact of perspective on seeing and understanding patterns has to do with the question of how an individual thinks about and describes the reality of his or her own experience. In multidimensional complex systems, the diversity of thought and action that is possible can present a variety of perspectives about any one event. Ask a group of people who have gone through a collective experience to describe what happened, and you are likely to get as many stories as you have people in the group. It's also highly likely that the more complex the experience is, the greater the differences in the stories. Any of these perspectives can be called evidence, and as you collect data in the *What?* step of Adaptive Action it is important that you can sort out the differences and understand them for their underlying meaning. Figure 3.2 represents our model and method for understanding how people make meaning of their individual and shared realities.

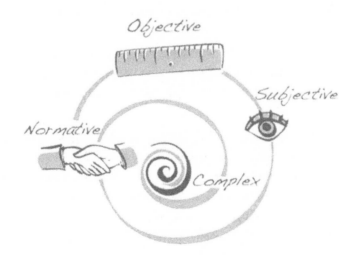

FIGURE 3.2. Four Truths.
We recognize four ways of knowing that shape
perspectives in our complex systems.

In an open, high-dimension reality, multiple views of a shared event can all be true and yet differ greatly. It is the nature of human beings. Every person brings a unique history and set of lenses to see and interpret things idiosyncratically. Sometimes that makes events richer and more engaging. Sometimes it causes conflict and discomfort. Borrowing from the writings of Jürgen Habermas,[2] we created a model with which one can think about the multiple truths that may derive from multiple perspectives. We work with people to understand and accommodate this phenomenon by talking about four ways truth can be known in any group.

As you look at the model and read through the descriptions here, keep in mind that there is no real order to working through the truths. There is no hierarchy or value to be inferred from these examples or from the diagram. Although an individual's own personal means of coming to know generally start at the heart of the spiral with subjective understandings, this is not to imply it is the most important. The following development of the definitions of the four truths reflects an entirely different approach to working through the connections between and among the types of truth.

First there is *objective truth*. This is what is observable, evident, and present. It is outside the group; it's what we refer to as the "facts."

> Here on Earth, we experience cycles of light and dark that last approximately twenty-four hours each. This is objective truth because it is observable and present in the same pattern across groups, cultures, and locales.

The second kind of truth is *normative truth*. When any group comes to agreement about what is true, that is normative. It belongs to the group; much of what we call culture is made up of normative truths of a given group of people.

> Humans who speak English have agreed that the lighter part of the twenty-four-hour cycle is called "day," and the darker part of the cycle is called "night." Other languages have their own words, but those words are generally accepted as normative truth across any group that shares a language.

The third way of knowing is *subjective truth*. This type of truth belongs to the individual. It is based in personal beliefs or convictions, perspectives or opinions any person holds, as a lens for seeing and understanding the world.

> As individuals experience their days, they each form opinions about the quality of that experience. For instance, on days when my clothes fit right, and my

hair looks good, and the traffic is light, and people are smiling at work, my own subjective truth is that I am having a good day. At the same time, another person may set a separate standard for calling a day "good." His or her subjective truth may be that it is enough to have gotten to work safely and without incident. Another subjective truth may say that any day at work is not a good day. All of these can be simultaneously true because they represent the subjective truths of the individuals.

The final way of knowing is referred to as *complex truth*, which Glenda defines as acknowledging that all three of the other truths are equally valid. No one of the truths takes precedence over the others all the time. With differing times and circumstances, one or another of the truths is more relevant than the others, but another can become relevant at any moment.

> At any moment I can go with my own decision that this is a great day; I can respond to my boss's interpretation of a bad day; or I can look at the clock and see that the day is almost over. I get to choose whatever works in the moment. This is what makes it the complex truth.

No group can function effectively when all the possible truths are in play and conflicting with each other. When a group recognizes the equal validity of all the truths and comes to an agreement about which truth serves them best in a given situation, they are working in the realm of complex truth. The agreement may be implicit or it may be explicit, but the agreement provides the basis for a shared perspective from which a group can focus on the most important patterns. They use one of the truths for their decision making and interaction, while holding the other truths in abeyance for the moment in service to the group.

A high-performing team is able to depend on complex truth as the members shift easily from objective data to subjective perspectives to shared norms of expected behavior. They do not always require objective data to validate one member's hunches. They do not require complete agreement on every point. They do not succumb to conflict on the basis of differing opinions. In short, they match their truth tests to the purpose at hand, whatever that might be.

It's important to realize the impact these four truths can have on how a group sees, understands, and takes action in a situation. Though the examples used here are simplistic, there are many ways the four truths can be useful.

In conflict situations, unbraiding truths can help clarify reality (objective truth) from the story that individuals may be telling themselves (subjective truth). The individuals in conflict may develop an agreement (normative truth) as an explicit plan about what to do, or they may use complex truth to step into alternative stories to move forward.

In culturally or socially diverse situations, knowing the various normative truths is very helpful in creating understanding and increasing productivity. Even knowing that there is such a thing as normative truth allows people in a high-dimension, complex system to stand in inquiry with each other, rather than in judgment of opposing beliefs and behaviors.

In sales and marketing, knowing the normative truths for various demographic groups is critically important. A strong marketing campaign can, in fact, develop the complex truth that becomes the normative truth for much of a population. Think about the power that sports events have in shaping the behavior of entire countries during the final, championship events. The World Cup in soccer, the Super Bowl in American football, the Americas Cup in sailing . . . each is marketed to shift from subjective truths for committed individuals to normative truths that bring people together across traditional geographical or cultural boundaries.

We don't know and can't say whether marketing or other professions consciously use this understanding of four truths to extend their influence. What we are proposing is that their reach is extended because their practices manipulate and influence the underlying dynamics around the types of truth. Consider how much more effective and powerful your own work could be if you intentionally use this understanding of the types of truth to solve problems and influence patterns in your life.

Even in the realm of personal experience, the four truths can be powerful. A professional disappointment or a personal conflict resolves itself most easily when one is able to sort out the subjective from the objective and normative truths, and to address each most appropriately. As we work with individual leaders who are stuck in conflict, we coach them to express and understand their own powerful feelings, while they acknowledge the normative rules of the road and collect and analyze hard facts. Out of such a four-truths analysis, appropriate, creative, and Adaptive Action options emerge.

If you are aware of these four truths, you have new insights and find more creative options for action. If you approach your world through a stance of inquiry, you can understand and accept others' truths as well as your own. This understanding helps you build a common foundation and work more coherently, in spite of the diversity you encounter in your complex systems.

With others you are better able to establish conditions for productive, generative relationships that move you toward common goals while sustaining individual identities.

Questions you can ask yourself to gain clarity about the four truths help you see where you stand and how your own perspective is shading your vision:

Is my perspective based in what I can see, hear, feel, or touch?

Is my perspective based in what I feel or believe about what is in front of me?

Is this something the group has agreed to, or is it something that I alone perceive?

In this immediate situation, which truth will help us find the best fit and most effective options for action?

Even as you see and understand that multiple truths are possible, other variables emerge to influence or distort observable patterns. Another variable has to do with your "distance" from the action itself.

Near and Far   The source of information, and its relationship to you, can also be an important factor in collecting data and understanding patterns as they emerge. *Near* and *far* perspectives become important when you consider these factors in your system.

Situations that are familiar or that are close to you in time or space are near. If you are too close to the situation, you will see patterns through a filter of expectation. You know the people involved, so you think you can predict or even influence how they are interacting, without really watching for their behaviors. Similarities will be obvious as you draw on your historical experience. Differences may be uncomfortable as they disturb your assumptions and expectations. Traditional connections will be comfortable and strong, while new ones may seem uncomfortable and threatening, or different and stimulating. It will be difficult to discern the patterns objectively and clearly, because the patterns you know and the ones you expect will dominate your view. Being on the inside of a situation gives you access to understand the patterns as they emerge. Differences you might not even see from the outside are visible and meaningful. You are in the loop for patterns of communications and connections.

Situations that are unfamiliar or distant from your observation in space or time are far. They pose difficulty because you have little or no contextual knowledge on which to build. Your distance or newness to the situation means you may miss subtle aspects of a larger pattern, or you may even miss patterns altogether, if they are too subtle or your time to observe is too short. Your knowledge of the connections may be limited, your understanding sparse. At the same time, distance gives you an opportunity to see a situation, sometimes even more clearly or more analytically than can someone who is close to the situation. You may notice and track differences and patterns of connection that have become routine to them. Your distance may offer the clarity of a more objective view.

As with the four truths, there is no "naughty or nice" in questions of proximity. Sometimes near is better; sometimes far is better. Always you should ask: "What is my distance from the pattern of interest? So what does my current position add to or detract from my ability to see clearly? Now what should I do to stand in the best place to see what I think is most relevant and ignore what is not?"

We have observed how this dynamic of proximity can impede innovation in organizations. People who are inside a situation are attached to successes of the past, winning strategies, and what they understand to be high-quality products. They can grow blind to emerging patterns that challenge expectations. Those who are far from a situation can miss the nuances that might trigger real innovation. In the examples of senior management and national law makers, we often see the danger of distance in decision making. Standing far away from constituents or market interactions, policy makers may miss important patterns and base their decisions on incomplete or biased views of the world. Changes in technology in recent years have relied on perspectives from inside and outside multiple aspects of life. Standing only inside corporate or business applications ignores the multiple ways technology can contribute to leisure and personal productivity. The proliferation of Apple as a brand that permeates home, office, work, and schools is an example of how staying near all markets can support innovation.

This new technology called for significant changes in skill sets, expectations, and work styles. For some, these new, emergent patterns of high-volume information, email communication, and instantaneous connections are stimulating and exciting. Moving from email to blogs to Twitter to Facebook, these individuals stay connected and constantly get new perspectives on the world—from both near and far. This level and speed of connectivity creates differing patterns in ever-expanding containers, and they require new patterns of work and attention. Organizations and individuals who have adjusted most effectively to these new patterns take advantage of those connections to build their businesses, enhance their brands, and bring innovation into their workplaces. Organizations and individuals who continue to cling to more traditional, less technical connections are hampered in their efforts to keep up with current patterns of information and relationship that lead to success.

Changes in organizational culture also fall prey to the domination of the nearby pattern. You live in patterns that you understand and know, so you miss the important signals when patterns change. Older workers in today's workforce have had years to create comfortable patterns of interaction and decision making, and younger workers tend to disrupt those patterns. Younger workers may hold very different values and perspectives from the older employees they are replacing. This clash of cultures can be very difficult to navigate. People get comfortable with what they know, and it is difficult to see the subtle shifts that occur as a culture changes. At some point an unexpected event "suddenly" moves patterns from the distant landscape into one that is near and dear. Patterns that were irrelevant yesterday are crucial today and into the future.

Looking at the near and far perspectives in our work allows us to explore the open nature of a complex system. In our day-to-day interactions, we are introduced to, bombarded with, and influenced by messages from countless sources that are both in our immediate sphere as well as quite removed from our local awareness. We see and hear our own immediate impressions, or what we see and hear is filtered through the perspectives of those who carry the messages. Our systems are so wide open that unless we seriously consider the near and far perspectives, we miss important dynamics of the patterns that surround us. Such a gap in seeing can severely limit our options for effective, productive action.

Questions you might ask yourself to help you see into this perspective have to do with your own familiarity or lack of it, and how that influences what you see:

What am I not seeing because I am too close to this situation, and who can help me know that?

What history of this unfamiliar system will help me know it better and increase the chances that I will see what I need to see?

How do the others who are close to this system see the dynamics?

How can I draw on a network of diverse perspectives?

The challenges of near and far perspectives are similar to, but different from, another way of understanding perspectives. We call it "yours and mine."

Yours and Mine   From one point of view, a particular similarity in a pattern may appear to be a benefit, a difference can be an opportunity, and a connection could form a lifeline. The value of the pattern depends on whether it is your perspective or my perspective. From another point of view, the same pattern may present boring similarities, delightful differences, and connections that impede rather than encourage. Again, the distinction depends on whether it is your perspective or mine. The significance of point of view is well known in twenty-first-century business and community, and it opens doors of innovation and action in complex systems.

Mergers and acquisitions encounter many challenges, but none so powerful as the dominance of one organizational pattern and blindness to the strengths and opportunities of the other. This represents a classic case of "yours and mine" perspectives. That's because each group in the merger has its own set of patterns of operation and interaction. Each side comes into the merger with its own organizational culture. When the two come together, there is no way to predict how those patterns will collide or combine to generate new patterns. Much of the work of the change manager focuses on supporting people as they transcend their own perspectives, build empathy with the other, and generate a new and more resilient point of view that encompasses the whole. Individuals and groups who accomplish this adapt to new patterns and learn to work together to generate productive patterns for the whole.

The nonlinear systems in our lives use what we know and experience today to inform our actions tomorrow. If we are unable to differentiate between what is "yours" and what is "mine," we may not harvest the real learning from a situation or satisfy our questions before we move to action. But if I fail to put "yours" and "mine" into a pattern of shared similarities, differences, and connections, no generative relationship can emerge. I may hear of your experience and think I know how it will or should influence my action, without really knowing the fullness of what you have learned. At the same time, I may make assumptions about what you know because of my own experiences and learning. I face two risks: ignoring relevant differences between us, or focusing only on differences between us. Either way, we lose the opportunity to create something new out of an emerging mess.

Questions that help us differentiate and set relationships between "yours and mine" are critical in the *What?* step of Adaptive Action:

> What do others see or experience, and what can they tell me about their learning? Given what I know today, what of this information is from my own experience, and what of it is from others' experiences?
>
> How can I benefit from their learning as I gather data?
>
> What assumptions do I hold about the patterns I see?
>
> What assumptions do you hold about the pattern?
>
> How do those assumptions align or conflict with each other?

Too often, differing perspectives we encounter seem to be irreconcilable with our own. Parties in a relationship agree to disagree, and they disengage without ever really entering into Adaptive Action together. HSD offers an alternative by giving a concrete and analytical definition of pattern and opening dialogue in which we can explore and learn from the patterns that each of us sees. One example from our consulting practice offers specific insights into the idea of perspective, using the concepts of four truths, near and far, and yours and mine in action.

A three-party coalition, made up of researchers, clinic administrators, and the quality enforcement team, was in charge of occupational therapy in a Canadian province. The researchers saw a pattern of academic rigor (similarity), innovative findings (difference), and opportunities to publish and present their findings (connections). Their partners, the clinics, focused on patterns created by consistent treatment protocols (similarity), health outcomes (differences), and doctor-patient trust building (connections). Finally, the official quality enforcement team was preoccupied with patterns of health outcomes (similarities), statistical variability (differences), and reports to the government regulators (connections). These three groups had to work together, but each was seeing and responding to its own pattern.

Once we helped them make their contrasting patterns explicit, they were able to generate an overarching pattern that incorporated the insights and needs of each group. They considered one another's truths, they could consider perspectives from near and far, and they could discern between their own views and those of others. They built a pattern of the whole by exploring how their three patterns were similar, different, and connected. Using these applications of perspectives helped them see into the dynamics of their whole system and beyond the dynamic or static views they were used to looking at in their own limited portions of the system. In the end, the groups created a shared pattern—an annual conference—in which they were able to make their own patterns manifest, engage in meaningful dialogue, and teach and learn together. Over time, the diverse patterns did not disappear, but they did become parts of a larger and more productive pattern that improved quality for all.

Three Kinds of Change

The world is full of words and images, messages and stories, data and information that can change in a heartbeat. In the midst of the chaos and confusion, islands of order exist, where change is moving more slowly or not at all. No two situations are the same, so reactions to change will be most effective when they are adapted to fit each immediate situation. Sometimes change comes so slowly that you can hardly see it. Sometimes it rushes in a straight and somewhat predictable path. Sometimes it comes in unpredictable bursts and breakthroughs. As we discussed earlier, all these kinds of change are visible in human systems.

Adaptive Action helps you see and understand the many kinds of change that surround you. It helps you recognize where the patterns come from, anticipate what will come next, create the most effective response, and then assess and adjust that response over time. As described in the last chapter, physics has offered three ways to think about change, and all of them can be useful as you start to understand the complexity that surrounds you and your team. The next section explores the risks of assuming any one approach to change, and the benefits of engaging with each kind of change in human systems. As you read, refer to Table 3.1.

Static Change   Static change is easy to see and understand, even though it is difficult to depict in a set image. Usually static change refers to change in space, moving from here to there, without considering the movement from one place to the other. It's a before-and-after picture that ignores the forces of change. We use it to refer to the same kind of changes in other contexts, including time, quality, competitive position, expertise, power, and any other relevant dimension. A single situation might include change in many measures, but all of the important dimensions are known, or at least they are knowable.

In day-to-day talk, we use ideas of static change metaphorically to describe things that do not exactly fit the description. For example, you can think about employee motivation, individual and group learning, or succession planning

	Performance Appraisal as Static Change	Performance Appraisal as Dynamic Change	Performance Appraisal as Dynamical Change
Frequency	Annual "snapshots" of performance are used to formulate evaluation and feedback	Periodic feedback based on expectations around cycle time of a project, projected completion dates, or agreed milestone of completion	Ongoing conversation and formative feedback built into day-to-day inquiry in the Adaptive Action cycle, with at least annual documentation and summative feedback
Unit of Measurement	The difference between this year's snapshot and last year's snapshot Based on static measures such as output, time use, resource allocation, or usage	Performance measured against established milestones or certified, standardized measures Performance measured against established standards or competencies relative to job assignment	Ability to engage in Adaptive Action to influence patterns in the system
Definition of Success	Work was completed on time and under budget Output this year exceeded last year Amount of savings or profit	Achievement of established milestones Meeting or exceeding standards of certification Exhibition of a given rate or percentage of competencies relative to job assignment	Ongoing performance and movement toward increased sustainability and fitness across the system
Rewards and Incentives	External, disparate awards of money, prestige, privilege based on narrowly focused measures External or extrinsic enticements for engagement with the system (Casual Fridays, etc.)	Awards of increasing levels of certification Awards for achieving established levels of performance according to milestones or competencies Awards for reaching disparate levels on individually set goals (customer satisfaction, performance objectives, etc.)	Increased autonomy and authority in the work Personal accountability and recognition for contributing to the success of the greater whole

TABLE 3.1. Characteristics of Types of Change.
This table reflects how a common organizational activity
(performance appraisal) might look different, depending on the type
of change you use as a screen for planning and carrying it out.

as static change, though it is clear the system is not totally at rest either before or after the intervention. In each case, it can appear that the individuals or groups are simply moved by an outside force. For example, motivational practice talks about the carrot and stick that move people forward from one position to another. Individual or group learning can appear to happen as new information or meaning is "put" into someone's field of knowledge.

Succession planning "puts" people in line for the next job opening that fits their skills, abilities, or aspirations.

Even when everyone knows the idea of static before-and-after change is just a metaphor, it can inform (or misinform) theory and practice. Expectations of static change lead us to believe that a shared adventure will fix an underperforming team. The theory is that the results of the program will be predictable, and when the program is over, employees will retain the team spirit they developed during the event. Our experience, however, is that except in rare instances this is not the case. The belief in the power of static change is so strong that it informs theory and consultant advice, even when the theory fails repeatedly in practice.

When you use money or power as a reward, you assume static change. People will work harder, we tell ourselves, if they receive stock options or quarterly bonuses. The proverbial corner office or the newest technology or telecommuting from home or Casual Fridays all represent the types of motivators that have become part and parcel of life in organizations. Yet we know they don't necessarily elicit the motivation they are intended to provide.

When individual or group learning is considered as static change, it is treated as a simple exchange of information. Online learning is static when it just presents new information, without modeling or coaching. Some of the most basic aspects of organizational life are often shared as though learning is static change. Traditional approaches to human resource policies and procedures, equity and diversity training, and fundamental skill development are examples of learning that is delivered as if the intended change were static. The benefit to treating learning in this way is that it is efficient. Large groups of people can be presented with great amounts of information in a relatively short time—or simultaneously—at low cost to the organization. The risk is that it is not an effective way to ensure that people grasp complex concepts and apply them in diverse work assignments.

In some cases, "static" is an important and useful way to think about change. Logistics and manufacturing cycles depend on static change as raw materials move through production and toward delivery to customers. Trip planning and global positioning systems (GPS) mapping are representative of static change. Sometimes they even acknowledge the limitations of their static views by providing disclaimers about the road and traffic conditions and other complicating factors they exclude.

Thinking about a change intervention as static can be helpful if you:

- Have successfully made the same change before in similar circumstances
- Know that there are few complicating factors
- Believe you are in complete control of the environment
- Consider a change that is short-term or limited in scope

It is relatively simple to gather information about static change. You consider the situation before and after the intervention and measure the change. You can say how much change and in what direction; you might even be able to name a force that caused the change and replicate the change at another time and place. The problem is that even if you are lucky enough to replicate the change, you may not know why your efforts worked or what will make you successful in the future.

When you deal with static change, questions help you gather information and understand the depth and scope of the impact of the change on the system.

What is the situation immediately before and after the change?

What is the direction of change?

What is the time of change?

What is the force that drives the change?

What is the impact of the change?

Static change cannot help you think about how a change happens or what bumps and surprises might happen along the way. To understand those dynamics you have to think about change in other ways.

Dynamic Change   Dynamic change, like static change, can be predicted and controlled. Dynamic change occurs when multiple forces cause movement along a smooth trajectory toward a predictable endpoint. If you want to change that endpoint, you can manipulate one or more of those forces. Think about how water flows out of a garden hose. You don't even have to know details about how much water is flowing or the amount of pressure being applied; you simply know how to change the arc of the flow to aim at a specific plant. In soccer, if you know the angle and force of the kick (and you are Beckham), you can pretty well predict the flight and path of the ball. In driving, if you know the speed, direction, efficiency, and weight of your car, you can pretty well predict the amount of gas you will use driving along an unimpeded path toward a destination. Not only do you know the outcome of these change processes, but you make some assumptions about what happens during the change. The progress should be smooth, predictable, and replicable.

We draw on assumptions of dynamic change when we think we can predict the path and outcome of a change process. Weight management approaches such as Weight Watchers and Nutri-Systems promote change by advertising that if you just follow their program you can have the same results as described in the testimonials on their commercials.

Moral development, social development, and other progressions through life are described as dynamic change. Developmental approaches to change and growth refer to stages or phases of change or learning, complete with smooth and predictable transitions from one stage to the next, as though there are absolute points of reference to describe how change happens. Any change management approach that has stages or phases is based on a view of change as dynamic. In organizational change theory, John Kotter describes eight stages or phases of change and makes recommendations about leadership activities that can move a system through those stages safely.[3] In 1965, Bruce Tuckman described how teams progress through a series of relationships as they "Form, Storm, Norm, and Perform."[4] Traditional models of strategic planning are designed to present a dynamic picture of change where you can predict what the world and your organization will look like in five years and develop your plan today to move toward that vision over time. Most leadership development programs are designed around the assumption that if a group of "students" goes through a series of classes and activities, each person will emerge as a leader, ready to take on a position of authority and accountability.

None of these images is inherently evil or bad; they are just incomplete. Managers and other leaders often find their organizations don't progress directly through prescribed stages of change. Groups and teams find that even as they perform at a high level, they may have more norming to do as new situations emerge. Organizations at any point may or may not be able to move forward as the strategic plan has outlined. In fact, the sneaky truth is that planned change processes seldom go according to plan, because of multiple and entangled forces that cannot be considered when planning according to a dynamic change perspective.

Each metaphor and its application to change in human systems was developed at a time when "dynamic" was the best we knew about how change happened. Everyone knew that paths for human endeavors were never that clear and unambiguous, yet they didn't have models of change to help them understand or design change efforts in any other way. They simply integrated random elements and agreed to act "as if," ignoring the unpredictable and uncontrollable patterns of the reality of their situation. What these theories did for us was give us some semblance of choice in a time when control seemed a more possible and appropriate response to change. They worked satisfactorily in a time when the world moved slowly enough that the models appeared to fit. They worked perfectly in finite games with clear boundaries, few influences, and one-way causality. Those theories helped us prepare for a future we thought we could predict.

In today's open, high-dimension, nonlinear landscapes, we know we cannot always predict the future, and we cannot always control what happens. Most of the change we encounter is simply not dynamic, but dynamic change is still an occasionally useful model. Metaphors and descriptors based on dynamic change give us points of reference about general expectations, even as we know they cannot be specific applications. New groups coming together will need to do some storming and norming as they work out their relationships and standing in the group. Plans for change over time help coordinate group action and expectations. Leadership development programs do teach important skills and ideas. Knowing this can help us recognize smooth and predictable change when it happens, and take steps to try to mitigate the impact of the real, unpredictable change that occurs in the long run. To take advantage of our understanding of dynamic systems, we learn to ask specific questions.

What are the forces at work, and what are their relative strengths?

What is the most likely path of change?

Where are we now, relative to the starting point, the final point, and the predicted path?

How far along the path are we?

Are we moving toward the goal?

Understanding dynamic change helps you address the "average" needs of individuals and groups. You can develop approaches and responses that work moderately well for a wide range of individuals when you act as if you can control and predict. What you don't get in these responses are extraordinary results. There is no way to generate the high-functioning, adaptive responses that are needed by unique individuals dealing with a variety of unpredictable challenges and opportunities. You don't get individuals and groups who are able to respond quickly and move toward fitness in their own local landscapes. That level of response requires that you operate according to a totally different understanding of change in human systems.

Dynamical Change   To gain the level of responsiveness that addresses individual needs and abilities in a highly diverse, quickly changing environment, you have to understand dynamical change. Dynamical change is complex change that results from unknown forces acting unpredictably to bring about surprising outcomes. Complex systems, like those where you live and work every day, are massively entangled and interdependent.

Dynamical change is characterized by periods of relative inactivity and quiet as the tensions and pressures in the system grow. These quiet periods are followed at unpredictable intervals by brief periods of cascading change, when the accumulated tensions and pressures are released. Dynamical change can be seen when patterns emerge to dissipate random activity. Dynamical change is what happens when differences in the system become strong enough to cause a breakdown of boundaries as two systems emerge from one or when one system splits into two. Dynamical change is unpredictable, yet recognizable patterns of activity and decision making emerge to decrease the tendency toward chaos and entropy and set the conditions for self-organizing change.

You experience dynamical change every day. Multiple events, factors, and perspectives that are far removed from the day-to-day events that create your local field of experience and knowledge influence all that happens to you in one day of work. You wake up from sleep that may or may not have been restful, to launch your day of work and activity. You travel to work on highways and streets that may be busy, or you board crowded, rush-hour mass transit. As you get to work, you hear of events around the globe that may have an impact on your organization. You engage in problem solving, exploring a variety of options for action, depending on and responding to the actions and flow of other businesses, organizations, and communities that influence the performance of your local system. You work with other individuals who experience their own versions of professional life—buffeted by external forces, driven by internal needs and attitudes, and presented with varied choices. The life you experience every day is open, high-dimension, and nonlinear, and the kind of change you experience under these conditions is very often dynamical.

In the midst of all these interactions and unpredictability, you can identify patterns in how people around you make decisions and interact with each other. Individuals have their personalities and moods, so even though you cannot predict how they will behave in a specific instance, you can guess how they are likely to respond to changes in general. Seasonal cycles of buying and selling, organizational behaviors, and functional expectations repeat throughout the life of an organization. Patterns of behavior and interaction create the organizational culture you face every day. These types of patterns emerge because of the dynamical nature of change, and they come to characterize the systems where they manifest.

This understanding of change recognizes that, in reality, you can neither predict nor control the paths or outcomes of complex change in human systems. Dynamical change is what you experience when

- Boundaries are open
- Many factors influence events
- Causes are effects, while effects are causes

Dynamical change is the result of open boundaries. Whatever happens "here" influences what happens "over there." Dynamical change emerges when systems are highly diverse and multiple factors are present to influence what is going on, either by their direct action or by our consideration of potential impact on them. Dynamical change is nonlinear, meaning there is no single and identifiable root cause for what happens. Whatever is happening now contributes to whatever happens next. Change occurs as an iterative process of outcomes triggering the next cycle of action. Whatever you might try to assign as the cause of a change can always be tracked back to an earlier triggering event or series of events, which were influenced by events that happened even earlier.

These spiraling, iterative cycles of cause and effect contribute to a system's complexity because it means you can never "treat" the root cause to solve challenges or issues. It means you cannot predict the specific outcomes of a chosen intervention. It means you cannot control the actions you put into effect because you cannot know what other actions will feed into that effort. It means you must depend on Adaptive Actions and pattern intelligence to inform effective action.

As you deal with dynamical change, the best you can hope for is to influence the emergent patterns that characterize your system. Only Adaptive Action can prepare you to be successful in dynamical change. Using Adaptive Action, you engage in ongoing cycles of seeing, understanding, and influencing the conditions that generate patterns in your system. In the first step of an Adaptive Action cycle, you stand in inquiry. You step into the *What?* by formulating questions that will help you see the patterns surrounding you. As you seek to make sense of dynamical change, your questions can emerge from any understanding of a complex environment, including:

- Distinguishing the same and different
- Spotting patterns (generalizations, exceptions, contradictions, surprises, puzzles)
- Looking for similarities, differences, and connections that mark patterns as they emerge
- Considering all four truths
- Taking into account diverse patterns from near and far
- Acknowledging the difference in my patterns and yours
- Exploring the risks and benefits of seeing change as static, dynamic, or dynamical

Adaptive Action: *What?*

Complex systems are open, highly diverse, and interdependent. They are iterative and dynamical. The most effective way to influence complex systems and work in dynamical change is to use what you know about the underlying dynamics—the patterns—of the system. Through inquiry you collect data and information in such a system to examine the patterns that emerge through ongoing processes of self-organization and adaptation. To identify and understand those patterns, you examine similarities, differences, and connections that have meaning across space and time.

Standing in inquiry as you collect information about the patterns that surround you, it is critical that you attend to the perspectives you might take as you look at those patterns. What forms of truth are informing the patterns you see? Are you seeing the situation from the near perspective—inside the system—or far removed from the system across space and time? Are there perspectives that separate groups into yours or mine? How do people perceive the types of change they need and how that perception matches the types of change they experience? These perspectives are critical to how you see the patterns around you.

In the first step of Adaptive Action, you see beyond confusion into the complexity in your system. Massive amounts of information are filtered and focused to separate simple structures from the surrounding chaos. Recognizing essential patterns and sharing your recognition with others prepares you for the later steps of Adaptive Action. The next step of Adaptive Action is *So what?* In it, you will consider the meaning of the patterns you observe and explore the possibilities of nudging the patterns forward. Then in *Now what?* (the final Adaptive Action step) you will select and implement one action that seems likely to shift the pattern toward greater productivity and coherence. In future cycles of Adaptive Action you will repeat the process of seeing, understanding, and taking action. You will continue to move forward, and you will avoid getting stuck in complexities you neither predict nor control.

With these insights and perspectives gained from looking at the emerging patterns of your system, you are now ready to begin working on the *So what?* step of Adaptive Action.

4

SO WHAT?

It is easy to access data in today's complex human systems. In fact, the greater threat is drowning in available data. Retail businesses have daily sales reports; nonprofits have donor commitment measures; Google can tell you everything you want to know about who visits your website when and where; and Twitter puts people and their 140-character insights at your services whenever and wherever you find yourself. Getting information is not a problem; filtering the important from the trivial, assessing contradictory messages, and making meaning to inform action is not so easy. The second step of Adaptive Action helps you separate signal from noise. It focuses on answering the question *So what?* and leads you to confront questions that challenge you.

So what patterns emerge from this deluge of data?

So what are the most important patterns I'm seeing?

So what contradictions drive this change?

So what matters to me, to us, to them?

So what opportunities might emerge from the current patterns?

So what surprises or puzzles me?

So what are my options for action, given patterns uncovered?

Meaning making has been a core theme of management and leadership literature for a decade. Peter Senge[1] focused on shared dialogue, systems modeling, and archetypal patterns to make sense of complex data. As early as the mid-1970s, Karl Weick[2] opened the door to our thinking about meaning that emerges only in the interaction between knower and known. For him, it is in action that meaning is ultimately made. Dave Snowden,[3] John Kotter,[4] Dick Axelrod,[5] Ralph Stacey,[6] Brenda Zimmerman,[7] and others have explored how to make meaning of the patterns that emerge and dissipate in chaotic human systems. Their tools support decision making for individuals, teams, organizations, or communities. We embrace all of these perspectives and encourage you to use them when they work in service of your meaning-making processes. What we offer in Adaptive Action is a way to bring all of these rich tools, models, and methods together into a coherent and powerful process of inquiry and action.

In this chapter, we explore how individuals and groups make sense of emergent patterns and how those patterns can inform choices about action. As a result, we hope you will approach your own sense making to stay conscious of dynamical change around you and multiply your options for making a difference.

Adaptive Meaning Making in Chaos

Joe and Jane walked toward the meeting, each dreading and preparing for their next encounter. Joe just wanted to get the team meeting over so he could get back to real work. Jane was committed to building an excellent team that could work together creatively. But every meeting of the team resulted in frustration, sniping, or outright conflict. Jack, the team leader, dreaded the meetings, too. He saw wisdom in both points of view and didn't want to show preference for one over the other. Couldn't these two people just get along and move the work forward?

Usually such conflicts are seen as personality conflicts: the one likes to go fast by himself, the other wants to pause and go carefully with the group. Other members line up on the basis of affiliation or empathy, and the team is stuck in a pattern that seems irreconcilable. One or the other is often banished to another team, to become the lightning rod for the same patterns in a new place and time, earning a reputation that may or may not be an accurate portrayal of his or her contributions.

Adaptive Action leads in a different direction. Drawing from the complex capacity of the environment, and the rich and diverse observations of *What?* the second step of Adaptive Action helps you generate many potential options for action. During this step, you consider the current patterns that are emerging; you consider your purpose, intended outcomes, and desired path; and you imagine many ways to influence the pattern as it emerges. Sometimes you will choose to interrupt an emerging pattern; sometimes you will amplify it.

Sometimes you will choose to collect more data and move into the *What?* of your next Adaptive Action Cycle.

During the *So what?* step, you will ask, "So what are the patterns that influence the group? How are they manifested in the actions of and relationships between Joe and Jane? So what is the manifestation of those patterns within each team member, at the self-organizing level that underlies the team's interactions? So what relationship does that pattern have to the perspectives of others? So what does that pattern reveal about the work of the team, at the higher level of self-organizing? So what relationship does that pattern have to the attitudes and actions across the organization?" And ultimately you ask, "So what are the multiple options for action I might take to influence the pattern as it emerges?"

Let's look at an example of how Adaptive Action multiplies your options for action. In *So what?* one of the things you might consider are the patterns that appear at the most obvious level of the problem. You can see how they play out at less obvious levels, and generate many options for action from which you can choose. Consider the example of Joe and Jane.

At the level of the part . . .

What might we see if we consider the personal pattern in this process? What might be the source of Joe's impatience with the group processes Jane uses? What might he need that the meeting time and activity are not giving him? What might Jane be trying to accomplish by gathering the input and engagement of team members in the meeting? How do the personal and professional ambitions for the two generate the patterns that disrupt the team? What is common in the needs and perspectives of the two? So what options for action would emerge from this perspective?

At the level of the whole . . .

What other patterns influence the team? So how might the meeting agenda set the stage for emotions to flare? So how can perspectives and expectations of other team members influence interactions? So what formal and informal norms shape behavior? So what is the clarity of the purpose of the team and the tasks of members of the team? So what are others willing or able to do to influence Joe's and Jane's behaviors? So what options for action would emerge from this perspective?

At the level of the greater whole . . .

So what are the larger tensions that influence the work in the organization? So what is the relationship of this team to others? So what evidence of similar behaviors shows up in other teams, other parts of the organization, and other levels of management? So what might you learn about the organization-wide challenges by exploring the conflict between Jane and Joe? So what options for action would emerge from this perspective?

At first glance, this process of meaning making may seem to generate only questions, and those at more and more complex levels. When tensions run high and conflict appears unavoidable, it seems answers would be more helpful than more questions. What this exploration does, though, is leverage the current conflict into better understanding of patterns that are endemic across the complex system. This new perspective generates options for action that transcend the usual personal coaching and restrictive interventions that are the most common response to such team-based conflict. It allows you to see beyond the conflict to make sense of the patterns that hold the conflict in place.

In this chapter, we will explore models and methods to support sense making in complex systems. They include ways to:

- Design actions that shift patterns
- Play with the stability of a human system
- Understand and influence complex decision making

The next chapter, "*Now What?*" will give you some guidance to help winnow down a long list of powerful options into one action that is the best fit for your purpose and the current state of your complex system. But before you select, you need a range of options from which to choose. The *So what?* step, along with the models and methods introduced here, will help you generate creative, surprising, elegant, and powerful options for action. The more options you see available to you, the more likely you are to find an approach that addresses underlying dynamics of the situation. You will shift the pattern, rather than responding to the superficial symptoms that arise from the apparent chaos.

Shifting Patterns

In the last chapter you learned about patterns and how to use them to seek clarity in chaos. You can use the same pattern analysis model as a method to inform action. It is pretty simple.

When you see a pattern as similarities, differences, and connections, and you want to change the patterns, all you have to do is change the similarities, differences, or connections. Yes, it is as simple and profound as it sounds. We will say it again: if you want to change a pattern, all you have to do is change the similarities that give the pattern coherence, the differences that articulate the pattern's shape and potential, or the connections that hold together the elements that affect (or are affected by) the pattern. Let's revisit Joe and Jane for a practical example of using shifting patterns for change.

The pattern of conflict that held Joe and Jane and all the other team members depended on similarities, difference, and connections. A change in any one condition has the potential to shift the pattern.

Shifting Similarities

Any human system is characterized by innumerable similarities, and any of them can be used to shift a pattern. Similarities that are recognized can be reinforced to shift a pattern. Those that are not visible can be uncovered. Similarities that are problematic can be deemphasized by moving them into the social background.

The Joe-and-Jane pattern emerged from a variety of similarities. A change in any one might change the pattern overall. Imagine the possibilities.

Joe and Jane live in the same neighborhood. Their relationship might be transformed if they shared rides to the office or worked together on a volunteer project to benefit the neighborhood and their families.

They are about the same age. Their relationship might be transformed if they engaged in a conversation about music and memories, or if they planned a way to engage together across a generation gap by setting up mentoring programs with people older (as mentees) or younger (as mentors).

They are both parents of young children, athletically inclined, members of the same professional discipline, working in the same part of the building, and interested in the same movies, books, and wines. Any of these (or an unending list of other) similarities might be leveraged to build bridges between the two and make it easier for them to work together more effectively. The point is not to throw the two together and expect them to play nicely around their shared interests. It is to recognize similarities and work opportunistically to leverage them into moments of coherence.

Other possibilities emerge at subtler, and perhaps more powerful, levels. For example, Joe and Jane both hate the team meetings. They might be engaged to work together to design a standard agenda that could meet both of their needs, or they might agree to alternate among approaches that satisfy the one or the other. They are both bright and articulate, so they might be invited to work together to represent the work of the team to senior management.

Any similarity that can be discerned in the Joe-and-Jane pattern can be leveraged to shift the unproductive pattern that has developed and gotten locked in over time. The trick is not to find the "best" similarity to accentuate; it is to look for and touch on as many similarities as are relevant. The more similarities leveraged, the more likely the shift.

The same method works with patterns in human systems on all scales. I can shift patterns of understanding by looking for similarities. This is how metaphors and similes work. Teams or departments can overcome silos by focusing on similarities, even ones that appear trivial. Street gangs, collaboratives, interdisciplinary teams, all will be more coherent if similarities in patterns are recognized and amplified.

Shifting Difference

Like similarities, an infinite number of differences characterize any human system. Each can be reinforced, bridged, attended to, or ignored in an effort to make a pattern more coherent or productive.

Another set of options for action emerge from the differences that make up the pattern of conflict between Joe and Jane. The different genders might invite (or at least allow) private restroom conversation with other team members in the middle of particularly difficult meetings, where they can develop strategies or understandings to share with the larger group later. Their differing hobbies and interests might encourage conversations that are not associated with work. Opposing preferences for email versus phone contact might inform better communication practices. Complementary sets of skills might build productive collaborations. Cultural differences might open the door to conversation about perceptions of reality and behavioral expectations.

Again, subtler differences might be leveraged to change the system. They might be given team roles that fit their own abilities and interests. In a conversation, one might be invited to take the role of the other and represent the contrasting point of view. In the course of a team conversation, they might be asked specifically to contrast their two unique views.

Any difference that can be observed can open an option for constructive action, and every constructive action carries the potential to shift the pattern. The power of difference to incite change works at all levels, too. We have used this strategy to approach issues of conflict, racism, dissension in religious communities, and challenging collaborative relationships. Some differences are obvious and block engagement, but others exist that might open doors to interaction. For example, when a conversation stops being about group characteristics such as race and focuses on individual differences in interests or concerns, the pattern of interaction shifts and new opportunities for action emerge.

Shifting Connections

Finally, patterns in human systems are influenced by the nature of the connections. A pattern can be changed when new connections are created or when old ones are strengthened, weakened, or broken completely.

Joe and Jane dealt in isolation with their frustration with the meetings. A conversation between them about improving the quality of meetings could accomplish more than just generate ideas for action. It might also build a connection between the two under new conditions to shift the perceptions and behaviors of both. Increasing the number and types of interactions between them may allow a new level of understanding and emerging empathy. Introducing new modes of communication either during or between meetings could also improve their relationship. They could be encouraged to leave voice mail messages rather than emails, or post written messages on a bulletin board, or engage in online chats, or use drawings or photographs to illustrate their key messages to each other. Any shift in connection or communication can open the door for new patterns to emerge. They might also consider their group norms and use the conversation about, as well as the emergence of, new agreements to move their work forward.

Connections at any level can shift the patterns at all levels. Once leaders engage differently, patterns of interaction shift across the organization. When processes are improved to make connections between functions faster or more reliable, patterns of performance change unpredictably and powerfully.

None of these potential interventions suggested by similarities, differences, and connections is shocking by itself. Certainly you have tried one or another of these approaches to resolve an interpersonal conflict. The difference is that you can generate more options and understand their possible influence better if you recognize that what you are doing is shifting the conditions to change problematic patterns into productive ones. And this understanding can make you more intentional and effective in seeing and influencing the patterns around you. That is the purpose of consciously completing the *So what?* step of Adaptive Action.

Generating Options for Action

When a dysfunctional pattern emerges in a human system, it is possible to recognize the similarities, differences, and connections that shape the pattern, and to imagine various actions that could leverage the potential of the current pattern to generate patterns for the future. A simple process can support this work.

1. Define all the similarities, differences, and connections you can observe in the current pattern you want to change.

2. Consider how you might uncover new similarities, or amplify or destroy existing ones. Write down all of these possible options for action.

3. Focus on the differences and consider increasing or decreasing current differences, or shifting attention to new ones that might tip the dynamics in a new direction. Add these options to the list.

4. Locate all the current connections that influence the pattern. Consider making the existing connections stronger or weaker, breaking them or adding new ones between parts of the system that are currently disconnected. Expand the list of options further by adding these exchange-based options for action.

In this way, the *So what?* step of Adaptive Action leads to many new options for action while it builds your sense of confidence to influence whatever the current system pattern is. It is important to remember, however, that you cannot reliably predict the behavior of complex human systems in response to your action. Actions that influence the pattern may generate a new and more adaptive pattern, they may be damped by other system dynamics so no change occurs, or the system may shift in new and surprising ways. The worst and most common mistake in dealing with human systems is depending on the delusion that you can predict when or how a human system will respond to your efforts to influence the patterns. You can never be sure about the impact your actions will have, but you can engage in Adaptive Action so that whatever happens, you will be able to see and respond to new patterns as they emerge.

Playing with Stability

Another factor that influences the ability to anticipate and influence system behavior is system stability. Our concept of "stability" is derived from the technical meaning of the term in physics. If you disturb a stable system, it will return spontaneously to its original position. Pendulums, marbles in round-bottomed bowls, bureaucracies, and spoiled children are all stable systems; it takes energy to disrupt them, and as soon as you let go they return to their initial state. Unstable systems, on the other hand, tend to keep moving once they are displaced. A pencil balanced on its point, a car on ice, a person under stress, an economic bubble, a culture—all encompass large disparities. Each of these systems is unstable because any small push can send it careening off into new and sometimes unpredictable directions.

As you can imagine, recognizing this aspect of human systems is critical in the *So what?* step of Adaptive Action. If a system is in a stable state, then a large investment of energy over a long period of time might be required to sustain change. In an unstable state, by contrast, a tiny push may generate an enormous and systemic response. Of course the world, and especially the world of human systems, is not so black and white. Between stable and unstable lie a variety of systemic responses.

We use a simple model to inquire about and describe the current and desired stability of a human system. We call this model the Landscape Diagram. It was first described by Ralph Stacey[6] and then picked up by many others, notably Brenda Zimmerman, Curt Lindberg, and Paul Plsek.[8] The Landscape Diagram has emerged as one of our most effective and efficient tools to inform *So what?* for us, for our Associates, and for our clients.

The Landscape Diagram

The fundamental assumption of the Landscape Diagram is that two factors influence the relative stability of a human system. The first relates to how much agreement there is among the individuals who influence system patterns. Sometimes a group is close to agreement; for example, everyone assumes that paychecks will be distributed on the same day and same time. Or groups can be far from agreement, even on important issues such as climate change, market investment, and future innovations in technology. On the Landscape Diagram, the level of agreement in a system is charted on a vertical axis, with "close to agreement" closest to the bottom and "far from agreement" at the top.

The second factor on the Landscape Diagram is based on the certainty of the environment in which the decision will be made. Sometimes the system is close to certainty: if paychecks don't come out, employees will be angry. Sometimes the system is far from certainty: if we invest in a particular technology, we may or may not get our money back. The diagram locates conditions "close to certainty" on the far left end of the horizontal axis, and "far from certainty" on the right-hand end of the horizontal line. Figure 4.1 depicts these axes and their relationship.

Within the space defined by degrees of agreement and certainty, you can locate various stability zones. In the lower left, where both agreement and certainty are high, the system is very stable. Payroll variation in one month is likely to be resolved quickly because both agreement (on the time of payment) and certainty (the response if payment doesn't arrive) are high. This system is considered to be in a *stable* state. At the opposite corner of the diagram, where conditions are far from agreement and far from certainty, system behavior is *unstable*. For example, a new technical innovation can disrupt the market unexpectedly and permanently.

In the space in between the easy-to-describe corners lies a world of emergent complexity. Some agreement leads to fruitful, but unpredictable,

FIGURE 4.1. Landscape Diagram.

We map levels of stability in our complex systems, which
informs our action as we influence patterns around us.

engagement. Some certainty inspires action but does not allow for simple lock-in and repetition of yesterday's successful strategies. We call this zone of the Landscape Diagram *emergent stability*.

The Landscape Diagram supports *So what?* in two ways. It can help you recognize and describe current stability, and it can also inform options for action to shift the system toward greater or less stability.

Seeing the Current Stability   In a given situation, you can gauge the levels of agreement and certainty and use the Landscape Diagram to see the relative stability, and the likely response, of the system. For example, team members are in agreement that Joe and Jane will disrupt the meeting, and the meeting agenda makes it certain that a conflict will arise. If these conditions exist, then the current dysfunctional pattern is stable, and it will resist efforts to shift to a more productive pattern.

At the same time, some other facet of the system may be unstable. Imagine that the agenda includes a new item. No one knows how Joe or Jane will respond (far from certainty), and opinions differ about what to expect (far from agreement). From this perspective, the situation is unstable, so action in this moment may radically shift the pattern.

As this example demonstrates, the same situation may be stable in relation to one pattern, while it is unstable with regard to others. No one of these perspectives is better or worse than any other. Given the Four Truths, in fact, we know that they are all equally valid at the same time. The important question is how well the stability of the system, as we understand it, fits the current reality and intended purpose. Is the system more, less, or perfectly stable compared to an ideal state for the situation of the moment? If it is not fit, then how can we influence a shift in the emerging pattern?

One purpose of *So what?* is to address this concern by asking three questions: Where are you now? Where do you want to be? How do you get there? These questions invite you to focus on the pattern that reflects the stability that best supports the current purpose of work. You can then use this system description to inform the most powerful options for action. For instance, you may want to move the system toward emergent stability to set conditions for creative responses and full engagement, or you may want to move the system toward a stabler state to conserve energy or reduce risk. You might even want to push the system toward an unstable state to explore the unknown, which would inform your actions very differently.

It is important here to share one of our fundamental assumptions. Royce calls it "Ain't no naughty or nice." What this means is that neither stability nor instability is a preferred state. A group that strives to become more innovative will thrive in instability, far from certainty and far from equilibrium. But work that must be replicable and reliable belongs in the stablest space: close to certainty and agreement. Neither is by nature preferable to the other, but one level of stability will be more fit to purpose than others. Deciding what is most fit is a key part of the *So what?* step of Adaptive Action.

Influencing the Current Stability   The same simple set of three questions converts the Landscape Diagram from descriptive model to action-oriented method. You won't be surprised to see that these questions are closely related to the three questions of Adaptive Action. The three questions help you recognize other options for action.

Where are you now? This question invites you to analyze the current stability of the system from various perspectives. It also facilitates shared meaning making when a group engages in a conversation about the current state of their shared system.

Where do you want to be? This question focuses on the purpose of the work and the future patterns you would like to encourage. This question too focuses a group and helps uncover important agreements and disagreements that influence the pattern of shared meaning making and action.

How can you get there? This question invites you to take action to increase or decrease agreement or certainty in the system to shift the pattern toward greater or less stability. Finally, such a process of analysis, especially when differences of opinion are uncovered, sets the stage for options for actions that are clear, intentional, and understood by all.

"Getting there" deserves more attention. After you have decided where you are and where you want to be, how do you explore options for action for making the shift? Again, the approach is surprisingly simple: shift the level of certainty to move to the right or left, or shift the level of agreement to move up or down. Whatever you do to shift either of these systemic variables will automatically shift the stability of the system.

If the current purpose calls for more stability, you can increase certainty by collecting data, consulting with experts, running a pilot, or shifting your system view to focus on more certain aspects of the system. Increase agreement by encouraging conversation, focusing on common ground, or reducing the number of people involved in decision making. In the end, it doesn't matter which of these actions you choose; any one of them will influence system stability in some way.

If the current purpose calls for less stability, you can decrease certainty by exploring new issues and questions, considering longer-term impacts, and focusing on more systemic factors. Decrease agreement by enhancing the diversity of the deciders, asking provocative questions, collecting individual perspectives, encouraging individual reflection, and growing networks.

Whether it is your intention to raise or lower system stability, the Landscape Diagram can help you make meaning from your *What?* while preparing you for the action of *Now what?*

Complex Decisions

Stability may be a sufficient description of a physical system in motion, but though helpful it is far from a complete description of a human system in change. The Landscape Diagram is a good start, but other, more sensitive, models are frequently required to capture the critical dynamics of the complex human system. In these cases, we sometimes depend on the Decision Map, which appears in Figure 4.2.

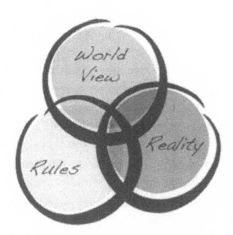

FIGURE 4.2. Decision Map.

Our decisions are shaped by the worldview we hold, the rules that are important to us in that moment, and the evidence we see around us.

Points of Interest

Neither individual nor group decision making is a simple, linear process. Though we talk about basing decisions on reliable data and logical processes, the reality frequently tells another tale. Many sophisticated models have been developed to explain or simulate a process of decision making, and they often succeed in their mission. Those models, however, are not very helpful to individuals or groups making day-to-day decisions in organizational life. Ironically they are both too complicated and yet not complex enough to handle real-world problems of real people. Most decision-making models depend on sophisticated mathematics or arcane computer programs, neither of which is accessible to support real-time decision making. Even if they were simplified or made available, they still wouldn't be very helpful. Regardless of their sophistication, models depend on assumptions about closed, low-dimension systems driven by linear causality. They are good for playing finite games, but as we have pointed out many times, human systems are open, high-dimension, and nonlinear. They are infinite games, and no matter how sophisticated a decision model is it will be insufficient to support play in the infinite game.

When we focus on Adaptive Action, influencing patterns in complex adaptive systems, decisions emerge from the complex interactions of multiple patterns of thought. Though it is simple and straightforward, the Decision Map helps you describe factors that influence a decision and become aware of their interdependencies. As a method, the map opens new options for action in the *So what?* step of Adaptive Action. The Decision Map includes three interdependent factors that shape decision making as it happens in offices and board rooms, as reflected in Figure 4.2.

Worldview represents the patterns of assumptions and values. Developed through cultural interaction and life experience, worldview represents the way things "should" be, according to the individual or group. These factors, collected over a lifetime, influence what is considered to be possible or preferable. In the Decision Map, worldview correlates with subjective truth.

Rules represent the world of social expectations, standards, and guidelines. Rules may be formal laws and regulations, informal cultural norms, or personal ethical guides. Some rules are explicit and others are implicit, but all of them inform decision making in a specific, personal way. Rules correlate with and hold the substance of normative truth.

Reality is the realm of observation. We don't worry about the existential questions of whether or not reality exists. This point of the map merely focuses on data that is accessible and how data shapes this decision at this place and time. Reality correlates with objective truth, and the three points of the Decision Map open the door to a practical application of complex truth.

Emerging Decisions

These three contexts (worldview, rules, and reality) are not independent. Each one shapes the other two in a complex fashion. What you expect—your worldview—shapes and is shaped by what you observe. What you observe informs the rules you honor; the rules you follow influence how you see what you observe. Rules derive from worldview and culture, while they also shape how you see the world. Because of these complex interdependencies, the Decision Map is a complex adaptive system in itself, so it can represent and help us understand the complex nature of individual and group decision making at all levels. Also, because it is so simple, it is easy for individuals and groups to use in support of everyday decisions.

In the previous chapter we defined dynamical change. Now we can point out that complex interdependencies such as those described here create dynamical, emergent patterns of understanding that in turn generate dynamical and emergent decision-making processes, adaptive decisions, and effective action. One function of the *So what?* part of Adaptive Action is to pause long enough to consider forces that shape each point of the Decision Map. The reflection can reveal how current conditions interact. It can also suggest actions that might resolve internal tensions among the three conditions. Finally, *So what?* reflection can uncover unexpected opportunities to shift external patterns to relieve internal tensions. Let us reconsider the situation with Joe and Jane, using the Decision Map.

Decisions for each individual emerge from internal tensions among worldview, rules, and reality. In this case, Jane believes that professionalism requires creative thought. She follows a cultural code that demands respect for and attention to individuals' needs, and she has observed how uncomfortable people have been in meetings in the past. Joe, for his part, believes that time is money. His code of conduct demands clarity and precision, and his perception is that the team has already wasted too much time in beating around the bush and avoiding real work. On the basis of these maps, of course Joe and Jane will come to very different conclusions and pursue strongly divergent paths of action.

Three pathways emerge to resolve the conflict between Joe and Jane.

First, Jane could shift any point in her Decision Map to come into more alignment with Joe. For example, she might recognize greater time pressure for the work, and see that personal interactions were not the most critical consideration for the team at this time. She might be led to understand and accept the disciplinary constraints that rule Joe's behavior and expectations, or she might do some research to widen her observations about the correlations between building personal relationships and doing high-quality work.

Second, Joe might change any of his Decision Map points to align with Jane. He could reflect on his most productive times and recognize how his creativity increased when he spent time in reflective thought. He could become more sensitive to others' feelings and observant of cultural norms. He might pay close attention to the people in the next meeting to observe how they react to suggestions from Jane and him, and consider shifting his behavior to influence those reactions.

Third, Joe and Jane might consider, together, how to converge on one or another of the Decision Map points. A conversation in which they disclose their own worldviews, rules, and realities might lead them to create numerous options for action to resolve their current tensions and set the stage for future collaboration.

Any of these three paths can generate multiple options for action. All are possible, but only one—any one—is required to shift the pattern. Why? Because the points of the Decision Map are connected to each other within the pattern of the individual's decision making. A change in one changes all, so the overall emergent pattern is transformed. Likewise, Joe and Jane's decisions influence one another, so when one of their shared points adjusts to new tensions, all of their other shared points of the Decision Map become more coherent, too. And because they are members of a team, a shift in their individual or shared patterns will reframe teamwide patterns as well.

Across settings in organizations, we see examples of how Decision Maps influence individual behavior and team interactions in situations like the one represented by the Jane and Joe story. We also see how an organization's Decision Map can influence the patterns of performance and interaction of the whole system. Think of the worldview represented in highly innovative companies such as Apple, Sony, and Google. They are built in a worldview that says anything is possible if you just figure it out—if you can dream it, you can do it. When you have such a wide open, exploratory worldview, you establish and live by rules that support and reward innovation and creativity. When you own or run a company with such a worldview, you create policies and procedures around performance management, compensation and recognition, hiring, promotion, and planning that reward your people for their individual and collaborative innovation. You seek data and information in your world that feed your employees' need to know what's new in technology and public trends.

By contrast, say you purchase a company that has a traditional, more conservative history, and you want to encourage risk taking and innovation. You might go in and change the organizational worldview by sharing multiple, powerful messages that describe this new perspective. Alternatively you might consider establishing new rules and expectations around creativity and innovation. Finally, you might bring in data and information that support your new and preferred view. As we said earlier, any one of these can, in fact, have the potential to shift the old patterns. On this scale, however, working on all three points of the decision map builds the coherence you need to bring about a systemwide culture change, and it may accelerate the rate of change. But without a careful analysis of the Decision Map, there is a good chance that you will implement multiple interventions at the same time and find out that some of them contradict or neutralize others.

Teams or departments can also establish shared Decision Maps that set their own internal cultures. In a large government human services agency we work with, we see this in the behaviors and interactions across various departments. Social workers, medical personnel, and compliance and enforcement agencies all have their own approaches to the services they provide. Driven by general descriptions of the work they do, they develop Decision Maps that govern their very different roles. Social workers tend to look at individual needs from a psychological and emotional, needs-based worldview, while nurses and doctors approach their work from a medical model that is about finding what's wrong and fixing it. Compliance and enforcement agencies work from a worldview that calls on them to be sure people do what they are supposed to do. Each group serves a critical role in meeting the human services needs of their clients. The various Decision Maps that guide the work of those groups can lead to misunderstandings, distrust, and conflict, if people are not aware of the specific ways in which they differ from one another.

We worked with an agency of this kind where they were moving all the human services toward a one-stop-shop model that would enable clients to enter the system through a portal and get whatever services they needed. Immediately the organization encountered difficulties in sharing data and information, in tolerating work habits and expectations of groups outside their own, and in understanding the variety of problem-solving approaches they might take in a given challenge. By facilitating conversations based on the Decision Map, we were able to help them "see" into the worldviews of the others and come to some agreements about protocols and expectations, as well as about the data they collected to measure their progress.

Whether you work at the level of the individual, the team, or the whole organization, understanding the prevailing Decision Map (or maps) is critical to making sense of the patterns of interaction and problem solving that emerge in a complex human system. And good sense making in the *So what?* step feeds into good action taking in *Now what?*

Adaptive Action: *So What?*

The purpose of the *So what?* step of Adaptive Action is to make meaning and generate options for action. In this chapter, we introduced three models to see and make sense of patterns in human systems; each model becomes a method for generating options for action. Similarities, differences, and connections of emergent patterns provide options for shifting the immediate pattern. The Landscape Diagram helps you assess the stability of a system, consider the best fit, and take action to shift toward greater or less stability to fit the purpose at hand. Finally, the Decision Map articulates three factors that shape decisions, and it allows you to see and influence those factors to reduce tension within and between individuals and groups.

So what? generates as many creative options for action as possible, to help you imagine the most efficient and effective ways to move forward. In a complex system, however, multiple actions are not required to bring about change. The massive entanglement of the system leads to sensitive interdependence among the parts, so that a small change in one might result in a large change in others. For this reason, a single action has the potential to bring transformative change. This situation sparks two challenges for the next and final step of Adaptive Action, *Now what?* In that step, you will (1) select the "best bet" action and (2) make plans to observe and respond to results in the next Adaptive Action cycle.

NOW WHAT?

Lois, an HSD Associate and one of our anthropologist friends, told us about the difference between description and explanation. A description focuses on what happens and what is observable as a result or an outcome. An explanation, on the other hand, tracks the underlying dynamics and gives a sense of why or how something happens. This distinction shows up in our consulting practice frequently. A client will call us in to "improve communications" or "increase innovation," or "enhance quality." They are describing their problems, not giving explanations. Our first job is typically to search for the underlying patterns to find a possible explanation for the source of their problems, and then we can help the client take action to shift the dynamics. Saying they want to "improve communications" is a description. In looking for an explanation, we might find a power imbalance, or lack of time; or use of jargon may be the real reason for ineffective communications. Aversion to risk or organizational constraints or lack of diversity might explain lack of innovation. Low quality might emerge from poor motivation, lack of training, or insufficient feedback mechanisms. One description may lead to many explanations, but intentional and effective action relies on evidence-based explanations that emerge from exploring and articulating patterns of behavior.

This distinction between description and explanation is particularly important in step three of Adaptive Action. Unless you know something about the mechanics that lead to an outcome, it is impossible to know how to take action to influence the next outcome. Given that Adaptive Action involves *action*, it requires an understanding of relationships and some inkling of dynamics that shape patterns as they emerge from self-organizing processes. In this chapter, we explore explanations for complex phenomena in human systems and share some models and methods you can use to explain complex dynamics to inform wise action, even when you cannot predict or control a situation.

A word of warning is appropriate here. An explanation in a complex system is not the same as a "cause" in a simple one. A cause lies in the high-certainty and high-agreement part of the Landscape Diagram, while an explanation can be in any part. It can give you ideas and possibilities of the genesis of a pattern, but it may not give you a definitive cause. In most parts of the Landscape Diagram, an explanation does not imply certainty, but it can suggest promising opportunities for action in any situation.

Many complexity-inspired approaches to organizational change are great at description, but they fall short of explanation. You can think of a description as listing symptoms of complex change. Just as I might say, "My nose is running, my head hurts, I'm sneezing, and my throat is sore," to describe the symptoms of my cold, we can point out fractals or attractor patterns or scale-free networks in complex human systems. Although descriptions help communicate about patterns, they cannot really lead to sustainable and meaningful action to change or maintain existing patterns. Only explanation can do that. An example from our practice might help illustrate this distinction.

One of our clients wanted to strengthen a national network. They could see that the network had emerged over time; they could describe their network. What they wanted, however, was to move their network toward more coherent action. We drew from theories about scale-free networks and the CDE conditions of self-organizing to explain the underlying dynamics of what they wanted. Then we could use that explanation to work with them to shape an intervention. Because they could explain why their network was "stuck," we could help them set conditions to encourage their network to move to the next level of maturity and coherence. This is how an explanation can lead to wise and elegant action in a complex system.

Because it involves conscious engagement, the *Now what?* holds the payload of Adaptive Action. In this step, the data collected in *What?* and the analysis and explanation that emerged in *So what?* are invested in planning and executing real action. This step depends on the accuracy and usefulness of the explanation of how change emerges in a complex system, as well as humility in knowing the power of uncertainty.

Essence of Change

The fact that we focus on the action step of Adaptive Action distinguishes HSD from many other applications of chaos and complexity to human systems.

Glenda tells a powerful story about the source of this focus in HSD, in her own voice.

When I began working in this field in the late 1980s, we all used the language of complexity to describe the emergent patterns that shaped our experience in society and business. We combed through case studies to find butterfly effects, we deconstructed time series to find attractor patterns, and we found and named fractals. We became quite adept at describing the symptoms of complex phenomena. Many practitioners and scholars of complex human systems still pursue this approach, but stopping with the *What?* and *So what?* of a method. Their work relies on description; it does not dig into explanation. As a result, they can give eloquent descriptions of emergent phenomena, though they are not so good at informing wise action to influence complex change. In human systems dynamics, we have chosen a different path. Well, in truth, the other path chose us.

When I first found out about complexity, I was stuck in a business challenge bigger than any I had ever dealt with. I was running a software documentation and training company. Our business model, reputation, and profitability were based on the predictability of our process and products. We grounded our work in an engineering paradigm that was perfectly predictable and controlled. It was so under control that we could take an external design from the technicians and build training and documentation while they built an application. Seventeen months later, we would deliver the training, test it against the application, and implement with few changes if any. Nothing significant would have changed in business, technology, or policy in the time it took to create a suite of documentation and training to support the business need. We could predict and control and deliver on schedule and under budget. Those were the days!

In late 1986, that way of doing our business no longer worked. Our clients all went unpredictable at the same time. One moved to client-server infrastructure. One went global. Another implemented total quality disciplines. Another began a series of reorganizations that threw the whole company and all its vendors (including us) into radically emergent space. I recognize now that even my descriptions of the experience are grounded in an expectation of static change: from this to that, with no messiness in between.

In that time of turbulent change, our tried-and-true methods were suddenly causing problems rather than solving them. Not only were our projects in trouble, our client relationships were affected, and our internal processes and team dynamics were disturbed. We desperately needed a new way to think about our clients, their products, and how we did our work. We were drowning in uncertainty. We were stuck.

In an effort to escape from the stress of a business going down the tubes, I dove into an exciting and (I thought) distracting book: James Gleick's *Chaos: Making a New Science.*[1] I intended to lose myself in the history and philosophy of science and avoid thinking about the challenges of my day-to-day world. Imagine how surprised I was when I found my messy business world reflected in Gleick's stories about research in fluid dynamics, ecology, thermodynamics, cosmology, and meteorology. Yes, the descriptions of those complex patterns matched the symptoms of my business challenges. For example, I could see our quality control processes as shaped by point attractors, while our client needs were shifting into strange attractor patterns. The dysfunctional problem-solving patterns of our clients' organizations showed up in fractals among our teams and individual team members. I felt myself moving through a phase shift from the solid, structured solution space of the past into the more fluid (and sometimes gaseous) problem space of the future. I could see business challenges appearing as structures that dissipated entropy, and I recognized the short lists of simple rules that set the cultures in client organizations. Everywhere I looked, Gleick described my problems. Maybe he could also help me find solutions.

Perhaps the patterns and processes described in these nonlinear sciences could help me see and understand what was happening in my business context more clearly. Even more importantly, I thought the explanations of those complex dynamics might provide insights to inform my action as an entrepreneur, manager, consultant, and writer. And so the final step of my own personal and professional Adaptive Action process began to emerge as I came to see the conditions of self-organization now known as the CDE Model.

In this chapter, we explore how the CDE Model[2] is an explanation rather than a mere description of complex dynamics. We also share two other models and methods that are particularly helpful in the *Now what?* step of Adaptive Action: Generative Relationship STAR, and simple rules.

Conditions for Self-Organizing (CDE) as Explanation

From the beginning, I tried to reach past the descriptions of complex phenomena to find the explanations that drove complex change. The frustration was that every scientific and mathematical discipline dealing with chaos or complexity brought with it an explanatory theory base of its own. Though the superficial descriptions of all were similar, their causal explanations derived from the unique models of each discipline. Predator-prey models explained emergent population dynamics. Computer algorithms explained nonlinear simulation models. Molecular bonds, quantum mechanics, psychological archetypes, and asymmetrical and high-dimension geometries produced explanations for complex, emergent phenomena. Though the descriptions of symptoms of self-organizing were similar across all these contexts, at that time there was no generalizable explanation that was both rich enough to be true and simple enough to inform rational action.

For about a decade, I was satisfied with the patterned descriptions of symptoms that were helpful for my own work and meaningful for others. My first book, *Coping with Chaos: Seven Simple Tools*,[3] described the patterns that resulted from complex dynamics and suggested how individuals and groups could respond to those patterns as they emerged. This approach proved helpful to many, but it did not satisfy my desire for explanation to inform wise, flexible, and robust action. Explanation, I believed, required research, and for me at the time, research meant the focused work of a doctoral program. So another stage of my Adaptive Action journey began.

In my research, I explored a range of disciplines that had recognized and were exploring complex and chaotic dynamics: thermodynamics, ecology, chemistry, computer science, and mechanical engineering. In these diverse methods and models, I was looking for the similar "causal mechanisms" that lay at the core of all of them. There was no question in my mind that causation was different in these emergent systems, but I believed that some meaningful pattern, some shared explanation, had to exist. This, I believed, would be the explanation of complex dynamics that would be clear, reliable, and robust enough to inform wise action in complex human interactions.

What I found in every discipline, model, and method I examined were conditions under which coherent patterns emerged. It did not matter whether the conditions were set in mathematical algorithms, scientific laboratories, analytical frameworks, open prairies, or bits and bytes of computer programs. Whatever the underlying medium, self-organizing patterns emerged only under certain conditions. Sometimes conditions were set naturally, so the patterns emerged spontaneously, as they do in whirlpools of mountain streams. Sometimes they moved spontaneously when conditions were set intentionally, as in the beautiful Belousov-Zhabotinsky (BZ)[4] reaction where chemical changes generate symmetrical patterns of color. And sometimes the conditions had to be carefully set and completely controlled, as in the nonlinear interactions that generate laser beams. In every one of these diverse, nonlinear environments, coherent self-organizing patterns emerged only when the conditions were "right."

At the same time, as my consulting practice continued I saw how we set conditions for human systems to self-organize. Sometimes a group moved smoothly and quickly toward a shared goal, sometimes they wandered, and sometimes they never arrived at all.

I examined conditions for self-organizing in a variety of contexts and classified all of them into three categories that were based on function. I called these categories meta-variables and named them *container*, *difference*, and *exchange*. For me, the conditions—container, difference, and exchange—both described the emergent patterns and explained the dynamics of the self-organizing processes that generated them. As an explanation, the CDE Model could form the foundation for a theory of action.

Adaptive Action emerges from this theory of action, in which change is driven by accumulation and resolution of tension within the system. Tension emerges wherever variation of any kind (difference) exists within a bounded space (container). Change occurs when some means of interaction (exchange) releases the tension, and the boundaries and variations shift. Examples are myriad. A market (container) evolves because of tension between demand and supply (difference) in which there is some means of transactions (exchange) between buyers and sellers. Individual learning (container) resolves the tension between theory and practice (difference) when inquiry (exchange) supports mediation of the known with the unknown. Culture (container) changes when differences in beliefs or practices (differences) generate dialogue (exchanges), and the dialogue enables new, shared patterns of social interaction to emerge. A team (container) becomes productive when members with differing points of view and areas of expertise (difference) engage in shared work (exchange) to complete tasks and pursue goals.

This same theory of action provides an explanation of change in every human endeavor, at any level, and in any context. The influence of and interactions among these three conditions explain why Adaptive Action is the only effective and sustainable way to play the infinite game of the future. To influence change, you must be aware of tensions as they accumulate within a context and make or break connections so as to increase accumulating tensions or else release them. You must see the patterns formed by the CDE in this moment, consider how the patterns support or distort your purpose, and take action to influence one or another of the conditions in hopes of shifting the pattern to a more useful configuration of containers, differences, and exchanges.

This theory of action and the practice of Adaptive Action within it have inspired the field of human systems dynamics and a collection of models and methods to simplify how individuals and groups consciously engage with change. Let's take a moment to think about the categories of conditions captured in the CDE Model as an explanation rather than a mere description of a complex pattern. Then we will be able to see what the CDE means for the *Now what?* step of Adaptive Action.

For a complex adaptive system to generate coherent patterns, *diverse* (D) agents have to be *held together* (C) in a group and *connected to each other* (E) transformatively. It is also true that if diverse agents are held together and connected in transformation, systemwide patterns emerge. The conditions that make such emergence possible are the conditions that hold the system together (C), that differentiate one agent from another (D), and that transmit information or energy between the agents (E) to rearrange the differences and transform patterns within and between agents over time. Though this explanation of emergent complex dynamics is simple, it is a powerful path toward wise action.

If you want to change a complex pattern, you can do only one of three kinds of things.

- *Change the container* that holds the similarities by making it bigger or smaller, by breaking up large ones or introducing small ones

- *Change the differences* by incorporating new ones in or excluding old ones from the current container, or ignoring or focusing on differences that exist within the current container

- *Change the exchanges* by breaking existing ones, by altering them (making them stronger or weaker, wider or narrower, longer or shorter), or by adding new connections where none existed before.

That is it. Those are your only options for influencing the emergent patterns in complex adaptive systems. In fact, it is even simpler than that. You only have to change one of the conditions at a time, because they are so interdependent. A larger container introduces more differences and weakens exchanges, while a smaller one tends to reduce difference and tighten exchanges. Additional differences tend to stretch a container and challenge exchanges, while fewer draw the container and the exchanges closer. Tighter exchanges tend to shrink the container and reduce difference, while looser exchanges allow both the container and the differences to increase. In this way, a CDE explanation directly informs action.

Consider the example of a dinner party about to go down the drain.

The place and time were announced well in advance (C), you thought you invited all the right people (D), and many of the guests could speak easily because they already knew each other (E). The emergent pattern should be perfect. Early in the party, you notice that the conversation is slow to get started—obviously an E problem, right? If so, then you would simply announce that everyone should talk to the nearest person, and the evening would be off to a great start. You have probably never tried such an intervention, because it obviously would not work. On the other hand, it isn't so different from the management consultant who claims to improve communications by telling people to talk to each other.

From a CDE explanation or your own experience of trial and error, other more powerful and innovative options might occur to you. You could change the C by taking everyone on a tour of the garden or inviting some of them into the kitchen to help you with final preparations. You could reshape relevant Ds and see new patterns emerge if you point out that some of the guests have lived abroad. You could also make a political or sexist joke to provoke difference and instigate more E, but this is not recommended for obvious reasons. You could prompt new Es by asking a question (low risk) or inviting people to dance (high risk). Any of these interventions is a potential *Now what?* Any one of them will influence the dynamics and shift the pattern. All of them might be wise, effective actions that emerge out of a simple explanation of complex dynamics.

If you choose to use all of these options at the same time, people are likely to be confused. The pattern will seem random, and it will be incoherent until new conditions are established, and a new pattern emerges. That, too, is a possible but not very rational *Now what?* Change consultants and traditional strategic planning processes often lead to this result. They generate a long list of actions, each of which may shift conditions in a particular way, so chaos results. Some complexity-inspired gurus recommend total disruption as a path to change. It is not hard to see why such interventions seldom result in sustainable transformation. When all the conditions change at the same time, there is no stable point around which the new pattern can coalesce. The obvious result is that the system returns to the stability of previous patterns.

At this point, everyone always asks the same question: "How do you know which of the conditions to change? How do you know which action is the right one?" The answer is simple: you don't. You can never know how a complex system will react when you change the conditions of its self-organizing patterns. That is why Adaptive Action is the only reasonable choice. After you take an action—any action—you watch to see how the system responds. If the pattern gets better in your judgment, then the action was a wise action. If the pattern gets worse (*What?*), then you need to rethink it (*So what?*) and come up with another option (*Now what?*).

So, with the CDE Model as the explanation for change in complex adaptive systems, and Adaptive Action as a problem-solving procedure, individuals and groups can develop the capacity to take wise action and revise action that turns out not to be so wise after all. These powerful problem-solving partners work at every level of scale in a human system. You can consider CDE for physical health or happiness and shift conditions to improve well-being. You can consider CDE for a partnership and shift conditions to improve success for both parties. You can consider CDE of community or neighborhood and shift conditions to reduce violence or increase civic commitment. You can consider the CDE of national conflicts and shift the conditions to attain and maintain a pattern of greater social and political justice.

In some situations, a thorough CDE analysis is not possible. Often it isn't even necessary to inform wise action. Some situations are rather common, so there is no need to rethink the whole CDE analysis every time. In our experience with a variety of business, government, and community contexts, we have found models and methods that represent recurrent CDE patterns. In those cases, a model or method that can be applied in many similar, but specific, situations. We call these simplified representations of CDE patterns "midlevel abstractions" because they are more concrete and more specific to particular situations and challenges than the CDE, but they are still generalizable across multiple contexts. All the HSD models and methods presented in this book are simply that: midlevel abstractions helping you see, understand, and influence containers, differences, or exchanges in specific situations to shift emergent, dynamical patterns.

In this chapter, we share two models that are especially helpful when you come to the final step of Adaptive Action and you and your colleagues must decide what to do next.

Generative Relationship STAR

In the 1990s, Brenda Zimmerman[5] was working with governing boards of non-profit organizations. She and her colleagues recognized emergent patterns of interaction that were not always effective. She wanted to find the conditions that would establish generative relationships, in which the members of the board were more productive together than they could hope to be individually. She embedded those conditions in a simple graphic and defined the resulting midlevel abstraction as the Generative Relationship *STAR*. We find it a powerful and easy-to-use midlevel abstraction for the CDE, and we have used it to help develop generative patterns with boards, technical and management teams, committees of all types, faith congregations, community groups, and even families.

The STAR, as pictured in Figure 5.1, represents a four-pointed model of the conditions required for generative relationships to emerge and be maintained.

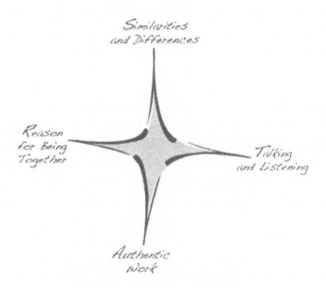

FIGURE 5.1. Generative STAR.

We understand and influence conditions to maintain generative relationships.

S stands for *s*imilarities and differences. This arm of the STAR points to the *D* in the CDE Model, so changing it will shift the pattern of the whole. It is easy to see that a team will be productive over the long run only if its members are different enough to be creative and similar enough to focus on the same work. Too many similarities or too few differences make the group boring, and it will lose energy over time. Too few similarities or too many differences, and the group will find it hard to settle down and get to work. An appropriate balance of similarities and differences set one of the conditions for self-organizing patterns of a generative relationship to emerge.

T in the STAR stands for *t*alking and listening. This part of the STAR points to the *E* in the CDE model and helps a group be conscious of the exchanges that will influence the speed, path, and outcome of their shared emergent process. No matter how bright and creative individuals in a team are, if they cannot communicate with each other they will not be creative as a group. Too much talking and not enough listening exhausts people and fails to build alignment across the group. Too much listening and not enough talking stops the group in its tracks, and they have little hope of finding shared meaning or action.

A of the STAR stands for *a*uthentic work. This represents one kind of *C* in the CDE, as the task is one way to hold a group together to form shared patterns. Real projects and real action plans keep a group moving together toward common ends. Without meaningful work to do, groups sustain energy over just a short time. Individuals lose interest, and group conversation degenerates as the group becomes distracted by differences that really do not matter. Over time people lose interest and wander away from the group, to find another place to invest themselves and their energies.

R, the final condition of the STAR, stands for *r*eason for coming together. This is the second kind of *C* from the CDE. This container is a conceptual one. It articulates the shared meaning and collaborative desire for change. A group that is unclear or in disagreement about its reason will lose focus and pull itself to pieces as divergent reasons drive individuals in sometimes competing directions.

So the STAR is a lovely midlevel abstraction for the CDE because it takes the generalized conditions for self-organizing and focuses on the particular conditions for a particular need—in this case the pattern of generative relationship. We have found this model helpful because it is easy to understand, is supported by common sense, and touches on the most common dysfunctions of groups. We also find it helpful because, like all of the CDE-inspired models and methods, the STAR avoids much of the emotional baggage that so often disrupts or distorts serious conversation about group dynamics. When they use the STAR, the members of a group are talking about patterns, not about one another.

We talk about models and methods in our work because tools that are based on good explanation allow you to see and influence patterns. The STAR model diagnoses a dysfunctional pattern. It becomes a STAR method when individuals assess the STAR for a group (*What?*), share their reflections and insights (*So what?*), and make plans together to strengthen one of the STAR's rays (*Now what?*).

We recently used the STAR with a public-private partnership supporting information technology and emerging markets. The group included small and large consulting firms, hardware manufacturers and retailers, telecommunications companies, and government entities that regulated and supported the IT industry across a Canadian province. It was a diverse group that found it difficult to come together in productive shared work. They had spent a couple of years defining a shared mission, but they always lost direction when they tried to plan or implement collective action toward their shared mission.

This is a very common problem. Traditional methods encourage groups to begin with vision and mission statements. We find that diverse, action-oriented groups not only find it hard to agree on something as abstract as a mission but also get bored with the conversation quickly and drop out of it. Our IT industry group was at risk of just such a fate.

We led a one-day retreat with the organization's board. The purpose was to either come up with an action plan or find a way to sunset the organization gracefully. We began our work with the board by acknowledging their vision and mission statements—the *R* of the STAR—and putting the words aside. Then we asked the group to brainstorm their similarities and differences. During this process, we discovered that the core barrier to constructive action was not the diversity of the membership, as we had been led to believe. Instead, it was the fuzzy relationship between the public and private sectors. After we identified public-private differences as the core *S* issue of the STAR, we moved to talking and listening. We divided the groups randomly into two parts and asked the first half to list what government wanted or needed from private industry. The other half listed what private industry needed or wanted from government. The groups then traded lists, so every person had a chance to consider both questions from both perspectives.

The board was very surprised to find that the needs and wants of the two sides matched perfectly. Government wanted to receive the same things that their private sector partners wanted to provide: data about demand, local markets, and emerging new technologies. Private industry wanted what government needed and wanted to give: information about economic projections, access to development resources, a voice in shaping public policy, and investment in workforce and business infrastructure.

This generative conversation led quickly to authentic work that could ensure every player got what he or she needed, and gave what was possible, to move toward a shared mission. By the end of the day, the board had defined an action plan for the year. They even realized that their new call to action was compelling enough to solve the recruitment and retention problems that had plagued the group over the preceding two years. The STAR informed action in a way that the mission, on its own, never could have done because it provided insights about wise actions we could take to set the conditions for a new pattern of collaboration to emerge.

Simple Rules

Another model or method we find helpful in *Now what?* is the short list of simple rules. The idea is that a diverse and loosely knit group can work as a coordinated unit if every one of the members follows the same set of simple rules. The idea emerged from computer simulation models of birds flocking. If a bunch of birds follow three simple rules (fly toward the center, don't bump into anyone, and match the speed of your neighbor), they move together as a coherent flock (Figure 5.2). In 1986, Craig Reynolds created a computer program based on this assumption. Images representing separate birds move across the computer screen and interact from these simple rules, and they do indeed appear to flock. Reynolds called his simulation "Boids."[6]

Many complexity scholars and practitioners[7]—we are among them—find the idea of simple rules to be quite powerful when working with groups.[8] Sometimes implicit rules establish organizational culture, and when a group becomes conscious of their rules they have the capacity to change them and transform their culture. Other times, a leader frames a set of rules to establish conditions for adaptive diversity and coherence.[9] In still other circumstances, a slight change in the simple rules opens space for cultural transformation, or exploring different rule sets gives insight into persistent conflict.

FIGURE 5.2. Short List of Simple Rules.

Emergent behavior in a system is coherent when interdependent agents use a shared list of simple rules to inform their behavior and decision making.

Although we find them quite useful, there is a good bit of controversy about simple rules among those who apply complexity concepts in social contexts. Some people think simple rules deny free will ("Human beings don't follow rules; they are free to do as they choose"). Others question the relevance of simple rules that emerge from computer simulation modeling ("We don't even know if dumb animals follow simple rules; how can we imagine that humans do?"). Still others fear that such a simple concept might be used or abused to control individuals or groups ("What will we do if a bad rule gets absorbed in the mix, and a whole segment of the population follows it?").[10]

We acknowledge all of these challenges to the concept of simple rules, and we give a single response: we find the concept useful for groups that want coordinated action without sacrificing individual and local decision making. We have used the idea to support integration of human services in government, strategic program execution, program evaluation, corporate mergers, improvements to customer service, education reform, personal and professional development, complex change processes, corporate culture change, quality improvement, and community action. In all these contexts, multiple agents with diverse needs and resources followed simple rules to move into collaborative action without losing their individual diversity. Simple rules help with a flexible balance between the collective systems and the single actor because they support the choice of the individual while serving the shared purpose of the whole. We find them to be a useful CDE midlevel abstraction, because the rules set the boundaries of the system (C), define differences that make a difference (D), and describe acceptable interactions (E). Simple rules are helpful models and methods, whether or not they truly drive individual decision making and action moment to moment.

As an aside, it is our opinion that the worst cases of manipulation by "shorts" and "simples" have already occurred in many cultures. Consumerism in the United States and terrorism around the world, for example, can be understood as dominant and destructive short lists of simple rules. The way we see the real problem in these situations is that we are helpless to counteract a trend because we are not conscious of the simple rules that drive our collective behavior. If we acknowledge our shorts and simples, we may be able to begin shaping our shared social space intentionally toward our common goods.

Not all rules are simple rules, and not everything that's simple is a rule. In our practice, we find that simple rules are most effective when they are created with a few guidelines. We call these our short list of simple rules about simple rules.

- Keep them few in number (three to seven), so they are easy to remember.

- Begin each rule with a verb, so it directly informs action.

- Design simple rules to establish all three conditions for self-organizing (C, D, and E), so the pattern that emerges from following the rules is coherent and stable.

- State the rules in the positive, because *not doing* one thing does not help you know what you *should* do.

- Create simple rules to be more generalizable than simple meeting norms, so they capture the essential patterns of the group in all places and all times.

- Focus on the core patterns to be created, so the list constrains only what is most essential.

- Ensure that simple rules apply to everyone in the system, in every function, and at every level, so the pattern is as seamless and consistent as possible.

- Revisit and revise the simple rules often, because any pattern that doesn't adapt will ultimately fail.

As an example, certified HSD Associates follow a short list of simple rules. The resulting patterns of action that characterize human systems dynamics and our international network are intentional and coherent. Imagine what pattern would emerge from these HSD shorts and simples:

- Teach and learn in every interaction.
- Search for the true and the useful.
- Give and get value for value.
- Attend to the whole, the part, and the greater whole.
- Engage in joyful practice.
- Share your HSD story.

How different would the pattern be if any one of the rules was omitted? What would it look like if we only "give value" or if we only "get value?" What emerges when we consider both the true and the useful? How have you seen these patterns played out in the pages of this book? Perhaps more importantly, how have you seen them *not* played out? Please let us know, because if the pattern is not coherent, then revisions (either to the book or to the rules) will be in order!

You see, we are engaged with everyone in our network, in cycles of Adaptive Action. Our aim is to observe patterns around us as they emerge, to make sense of them in realistic and creative ways, and to take action to shift patterns toward greater fitness for individuals, groups, organizations, and communities. If you provide feedback, you become a part of our network of Adaptive Action. When you observe, decide, and act to respond to us, you benefit everyone in the network, including yourself. As a result, we all leverage uncertainty to our individual and collective benefit.

Simple rules are not the same as values. Values capture what you believe or what you hold dear: honesty, integrity, creativity, adaptability and so on. Those are wonderful descriptions of the patterns you wish to generate, but they do not explain what you have to do to create the pattern. Often, when we work with an organization, we can help convert tired old value statements into compelling and energizing simple rules. In this way, the value word "Quality" might become "Create the best and test, test, test." "Innovation" might become "Leverage surprise." "Honesty" might become "Tell the truth, and expect truth from others."

One delightful aspect of finding simple rules is playing with the verbs. Consider the diverse patterns that would emerge from "Allow surprise,"

"Invite surprise," "Discover surprise," and "Fund surprise." All of these might generate innovative cultures, but the day-to-day decision making and action could be radically different in each case.

We use simple rules both retrospectively and prospectively. A recent retrospective case dealt with a service delivery organization that was painfully siloed. Clients complained bitterly because no one in the company seemed to know (or care) what anyone else was doing. We worked with a cross-functional team and asked them to explore the simple rules of the past that had generated this pattern of disconnection and dysfunction. After some nervous silence, followed by even more nervous laughter, the group named some simple rules:

- Cover your boss's butt.
- Conserve your resources.
- Argue your case.
- Follow the rules.

Any one of these rules could be perfectly defensible, by itself. Together, they generated a corporation-wide pattern of tension and competition, and that pattern generated a larger pattern of client dissatisfaction. By helping the group members reflect on their current rules and the patterns they experienced, we were able to make a minimal change with maximum effect. The revised rules read:

- Cover your boss's butt.
- Conserve your resources.
- Argue your case and pay attention when others argue theirs.
- Follow the rules.

As you can imagine, this new rule set was relatively easy to implement and extremely transformational for internal and external patterns of performance. It was a small intervention that grew into a cultural transformation.

We also have used simple rules prospectively when a client is beginning a new effort and wants to set conditions for future success. We worked with a cluster of federal projects designed to prevent child abuse and neglect. At the first meeting of the group, the members defined the rules they would use in all their interactions with each other. Note how their simple rules follow the guidelines we gave them for creating simple rules.

- Remember the children.
- Implement with integrity.
- Keep it simple.
- Ask, share, listen, learn, and teach respectfully.
- Appreciate similarities and differences.
- Enjoy the process.

Through times of turbulent change, participants in these projects continued to do their work collaboratively and productively. These simple rules helped them build the capacity to adapt.

The process of defining simple rules is rather simple in itself.

1. A group of people consider the patterns they want to establish for themselves and their work.

2. They are given the list of rules for formulating simple rules, so they know what they are building.

3. They brainstorm a list of possible simple rules, making sure they are addressing all three conditions for self-organization (C, D, and E). The group does not need to know about self-organizing conditions, or the CDE. The facilitator can help them watch for and prompt rules that will complete the conditions. Alternatively, once the draft list is finished, the facilitator might ask whether the list is complete to tell the group who we are (C), what is important to us (D), and how we work with each other (E).

4. They refine the list by deleting redundant rules, clustering similar rules, and taking out rules that are obvious or unnecessary because people will follow them anyway. They simplify language and hone the list down to the essential ones.

5. The group agrees to try the rules for a short time and return to review and revise them.

This final step—continual testing and improvement—is a critical step of the process. Not only does it ensure that the rules are practical, it also allows the rules to shift as needed as the group or the environment evolves. You will probably notice that this process of revision, too, is an Adaptive Action cycle.

Sometimes a short list includes two rules that seem to be mutually exclusive. For example, "Respect tradition" and "Welcome innovation" could be in the same set of shorts and simples. This is not bad; it just means that the system will remain in a constant state of dialogue with itself because it must resolve the tension between the competing rules in every new situation. Sometimes such an emergent process is beneficial, and sometimes it is not. The rule makers and the rule users are the best ones to decide whether to include a pair of contradictory rules or to delete one of them and resolve the question once and for all—at least until the next round of revision.

Adaptive Action: *Now What?*

In this chapter, we have distinguished between descriptions of complex systems and explanations of complex phenomena. We have explored how explanations in general, and the CDE Model in particular, inform action to influence the patterns of complexity as they emerge in human systems. We have also shared two of the models and related methods we have found helpful as we move individuals and groups toward effective engagement with complex systems. The Generative Relationship STAR helps a group set conditions so that it can function as more than the sum of its parts. Simple rules provide practical and simple guidance for individuals at the same time they support coherent collaborative action across an entire system.

Both of these tools, and all the others in this book, are midlevel abstractions of the CDE Model. They draw on the fundamental explanation of the dynamics of complex systems, while opening the door to practical and responsible action in particular times and places. All of the models and methods are designed to inform every step of Adaptive Action, but step 3, *Now what?* is the key to making sense of the uncertainty, and to taking action in organizations, communities, families, and relationships of the twenty-first century.

6

NOW WHAT? AGAIN

Adaptive Action is the fundamental building block of survival in a complex adaptive system. As we have discussed in earlier chapters, each step of the process—*What?*, *So what?*, and *Now what?*—focuses on a specific question while contributing to the emerging learning across the entire process. The three steps are perfectly simple. They have been described in various ways and used in everything from ancient warfare to the breakthrough edge of scientific research. Adaptive Action is not new, but its simplicity and flexibility make it perfect for decision making and action taking in the twenty-first century. It is the path for making sense of uncertainty in your organization.

In this chapter, we focus on the features of Adaptive Action that make it both flexible and powerful enough to meet our needs in increasingly complex and unpredictable environments. Earlier, we explained the challenges of tomorrow in terms of global reach, immediate communication, massive diversity, and constrained resources. These realities of the new century challenge traditional problem-solving processes. They even challenged earlier forms of decision making that looked like, but were not the same as, Adaptive Action. Now that we have delved deeply into all the steps of Adaptive Action, we will explore how together these simple steps generate a powerful and adaptive problem-solving method. We believe Adaptive Action is so powerful because it is variable and iterative. In this chapter, we explore the implications of these Adaptive Action characteristics and share a story about Adaptive Action in education reform to illustrate how the features help individuals and institutions thrive in their unavoidable uncertainty.

Adaptive Action Is Variable

Although the three steps may seem simple—or because they are so simple—many Adaptive Action cycles can be happening at the same time, in the same place, and with regard to the same challenge. Computer scientists call this parallel processing, and it is an effective approach for understanding and taking action in the midst of dynamical change. Rather than solving one problem at a time then moving along to the next, parallel processing supports massive numbers of data collection, analysis, and action cycles happening simultaneously. Each variation and every cycle multiplies the amount of information available to inform meaning making and action taking. In parallel processes, there is no natural limit to the amount of problem-solving power that can be focused on a specific question at a specific time. The only challenge is coordinating the many cycles, and that process in itself sparks another Adaptive Action. Parallel processing is one reason Adaptive Action is so powerful at helping individuals and groups make sense of the uncertainty in their complex challenges.

Adaptive Action cycles can happen in diverse timeframes. At the same time that my organization engages in a five-year cycle of Adaptive Action long-range planning, I can complete multiple cycles in a single meeting. Even day to day, I participate in cycles that take seconds (responding to a question in a meeting), hours (writing a project status report), days (developing a new policy or procedure), weeks (preparing a budget), months (implementing a training plan), or years (planning for retirement). All of these Adaptive Action processes, with their own cycle times, happen simultaneously. As a result, I am able to adapt to unpredictable change in my environment, whether it emerges quickly or slowly.

I know that I am not the only actor in a complex system. Many others are engaged in their own Adaptive Actions while I'm doing mine. In a meeting, each participant is cycling through Adaptive Action. On a team, each member is engaged in Adaptive Action cycles. Across a department or in a global market, many Adaptive Action cycles, driven from different centers of action, happen at the same time. Every person's action in any moment has the potential to influence someone else's action at any subsequent moment. With intelligent and conscious decision making at every point, even the most complex social system can adapt to changing conditions.

Scale

Adaptive Action also happens for the whole, the part, and the greater whole, all at the same time. While individuals ask *What?*, *So what?*, and *Now what?*, teams are asking the same questions. At every level of organization, from the front-line worker to the World Bank, every decision-making unit is taking Adaptive

Action. Sometimes one level is synchronized with those above and below, and sometimes not. It is easy to imagine that mismatches in Adaptive Action at various social levels resulted in the worldwide rebellions of 2011. Individual adaptive actions of frustrated teenagers, unemployed workers, and hungry families were totally out of sync with political agendas of their leaders. It is also easy to imagine that coordinated Adaptive Action at multiple levels could be a powerful force for systemic coherence. The most successful points in the evolution of the European Union demonstrated the power of coordinated Adaptive Action.

Scope

Finally, Adaptive Action can focus on various scopes of action at the same time. A military officer asked me once, "This Adaptive Action stuff is fine when you think about one person and one small task, but how does it work when I have to build a new road?" The answer is that it works the same way—and it works very differently.

In both cases, the players collect relevant data during the *What?* step. The difference is what is considered to be relevant data. Road building requires information about terrain, climate, political and social stability, demand, population and economic projections, budget and technical requirements. Personal decisions depend on such information: When was lunch? How much time do I have? What do I remember about this person or this task? What is surprising, easy, hard, funny, frightening? The content of *What?* the time, and tools required differ, but the process is identical.

In both cases, players analyze data and consider criteria in the *So what?* step. The difference is that road construction uses methods and models of civil engineers and economic forecasters, while personal decisions depend on one person's experience, values, temperament, and capacity. In these very different situations of Adaptive Action, the content, risk, breadth, and depth of the *So what?* differ, but the process is the same.

In both cases, *Now what?* leads to action. But options for action play out differently for the road builders than for the lunch eaters. Every specific may be unique, but the overall pattern is the same, so it is possible to build a coherent relationship between what is happening in local, small-scale action and what is happening in global, large-scale actions. This is particularly critical in complex, emergent phenomena such as global conflict, sustainability, or economic stability because the emergent patterns of the whole must emerge simultaneously from personal and institutional choices. Adaptive Action provides a way to synchronize and coordinate shared work, so that individuals and institutions make diverse contributions as they reach for the same shared goals.

So an unlimited number of Adaptive Action cycles are going on at any given moment. They may be connected to the same or different external sources of information as they complete the *What?* step. They may or may not use the same data analysis and decision-making methods in the *So what?* step. The final choices for action in the *Now what?* step will almost always differ radically. This diversity makes adaptation possible for individuals and groups who must cope with complex and emergent environments. But sustainable change requires yet another factor. Our Adaptive Action cycles must be iterative. We, individually and collectively, have to learn from the past if we are to make sense of today's uncertainty and prepare for tomorrow's emergent realities.

Adaptive Action Is Iterative

We talk about the Adaptive Action cycle because every *Now what?* leads to a new *What?* Every action out of a *Now what?* influences a system's conditions for self-organizing. Every choice shifts a container, reframes a difference, and builds or breaks an exchange. Every completed Adaptive Action cycle results in a change to a systemic pattern, so it creates the need for a new *What?* and its subsequent Adaptive Action steps. These in turn necessitate the next cycle. The circle of *What?*, *So what?*, and *Now what?* is not just a coincidence or a convenience. It is the fundamental nature of adaptation. Every adaptive act generates the need for the next adaptation.

In recent years, this adaptive process has appeared in a variety of guises. It was seen through the filter of the Learning Organization.[1] Senge and his colleagues at Massachusetts Institute of Technology explored a range of complicated methods and models to describe the Learning Organization, but building and sustaining an organization that learns has been an elusive goal. The complicated processes have been resource-intensive and dependent on the commitment and strength of powerful leaders.

Seen through the simple lens of Adaptive Action, "Learning Organization" is easy to describe, and as a method Adaptive Action provides an explanation that makes learning possible. A Learning Organization is one that asks the three Adaptive Action questions and answers them over and over and over, at many levels and with many time horizons.

What are we observing?

So what does it mean for us and our organization?

Now what can we do to optimize patterns of productivity and sustainability?

And begin again, with *What* new patterns emerge as we observe the system in response to our action?

The models, tools, methods, and approaches that inform each step of Adaptive Action can be as common as dirt or more sophisticated than you can imagine. In either case, the process is Adaptive Action, and the result is an organization (or an individual) that leverages iterative learning into adaptive capacity to make sense of uncertainty and create the future.

Adaptive Action and Education Reform

All this talk of variability, simultaneity, and iteration may sound quite abstract and heady. We guarantee you that it is not, and a story will help you see the concrete and useful side of Adaptive Action. Beginning in the winter of 2011, Human Systems Dynamics Institute and the Ball Foundation collaborated with the New Haven Unified School District in Union City, a suburb in the San Francisco area. The purpose of the work was to set conditions for the self-organizing process of learning. The project had three far-reaching goals: incorporate diversity across all levels and areas of learning, employment, and engagement; improve learning for students and staff; and assess outcomes to improve learning at all levels of the system. The transformative process at New Haven has been fascinating and powerful. Over time, many stories emerged of students, teachers, administrators, and board members (and their spouses and families) building adaptive capacity for themselves and their students.

Adaptive Action was the core of the intervention. Individuals and teams were encouraged to name a single "sticky issue," which could have been any concern that seemed intractable to them. Sticky issues feel intractable because they are too large to think about all at one time; they keep coming unsolved; or they are just appearing over the horizon. What we have learned is that sticky issues actually name how people perceive and experience the uncertainty in their systems.

Early examples of sticky issues from New Haven included communities of practice that were not productive, long-standing conflicts, lack of collaboration among adults in the district, unfair and unpredictable assignment of students to special programs, underperforming classrooms, and so on. Whatever the challenge, it became raw material for Adaptive Action for individuals and groups across the system.

As people worked on their sticky issues, their questions were transformed. Many realized that their original issue statements were too vague and broad. Through Adaptive Action cycles, their issues became more focused and actionable. Others recognized that stickiness came from issues being entwined in larger, more systemic concerns. When set in context of the larger system, original issues transformed into systemic interventions with clear, actionable goals and outcomes.

Over time, with the diversity of Adaptive Action cycles taking place concurrently, transformation began reaching into every corner of the district. In one fifth-grade classroom, literacy instruction became Adaptive Action dialogue. For a team of middle-school teachers, Adaptive Action was the foundation for a productive community of practice. For the superintendent, Adaptive Action established new relationships with parents and the community and brought additional supports for children in poverty.

None of these changes stood alone. Each one shifted the patterns across the system and inspired a new round of data collection and analysis. Every one shifted patterns that were intimately connected with other patterns. Changes in classroom management unfolded into changes in instructional design. Innovation in the science classroom sparked innovation in language arts. An open conversation between faculties in two buildings brought about change in both. And every adaptation set the conditions for the next.

The complex network of learning became sustainable because it was embedded in policy and practice at the individual, building, and system levels. New Haven is only one school district, and at the time of this writing changes there are in their infancy, but the simplicity and power of Adaptive Action encouraged us to think that these changes are generalizable and sustainable. If we find out they are not, then we will not be stymied by the uncertainty of change. We'll just begin another cycle of Adaptive Action because every *Now what?* breeds another *What?*

The Next *What?*

Adaptive Action works at any level, across any time period, from any point of view, all at the same time. It connects individuals and groups with real-time information about their challenges, encourages probing analysis, and supports courageous action. It is a practice that helps you see patterns emerging from complex systems, make sense of those patterns productively and powerfully, and supports action to engage and change the patterns, even as they are emerging. It provides many ways to get unstuck, or avoid getting stuck in the first place, in complex and unpredictable situations.

Over the past years, as our theories and practices of Adaptive Action developed, there were many a-ha moments when we saw the potential of this work in a new and more profound light. One moment in particular cracked open the power of Adaptive Action compellingly.

We were meeting at a bowling alley with seventy-five Roman Catholics who are committed to reforming their church for the twenty-first century. They support including women and married men in the priesthood. They believe the time has come for laypersons to lead communities of the faithful. They want to root out racism, sexism, abuse, and consumerism from church policy and practice. They call themselves the Call to Action, and the changes they intend could transform the foundations of their religious community and reform institutional patterns that have developed over centuries. They form a loosely connected network of networks focused on an enormous agenda for change.

They asked us to share some insights about how to set the conditions for such a massive and complex change, and this was our first meeting with the group. After we got started, a woman, let's call her Mary Margaret, came in through the side door and took her seat in the front row. Later I was told that she was a member of a holy order, and no one was supposed to know she was with us. Mary Margaret sat quietly through most of the meeting, but her face revealed her mounting excitement and hope. When we finished our description of Adaptive Action, the silence in the room was overwhelming. This often happens when people see the breakthrough potential of the Adaptive Action. A profound silence overtakes them as the breadth and power of such a simple idea soaks in.

Into this hear-a-pin-drop silence, Mary Margaret said, "Does this mean that we never have to be stuck? Are you saying that, no matter what happens, we can always do something that will move us forward?"

Yes, that is what we are saying.

PART II

SO WHAT DOES ADAPTIVE ACTION LOOK LIKE ON THE GROUND?

Uncertainty in organizations is more than speculation, and Adaptive Action is more than theory. We and our Associates use Adaptive Action to respond to a variety of organizational challenges, from improved quality of life for Alzheimer's patients to political power for residents of Washington, DC. This section tells the story of nine complex situations and how Adaptive Action helped make sense of the uncertainty for individuals, organizations, and communities.

7

ADAPTIVE ACTION IN ACTION

A paradigm shift takes place when one fundamental worldview is superseded by another. Paradigm shifts are never easy, even when they are obviously necessary. Joel Barker[1] was the first contemporary business writer to popularize the idea of paradigms. He celebrated the need to shift from mental models of the past to those more fit for the future. He was certainly not the first to explore the concept. Western philosophers since Plato have explored the relationship between the thinker and the world that is thought about. Scientists, mathematicians, psychologists, and painters develop their own ways to think and talk about abstract, concrete, and creative practice where the three intersect. Thomas Kuhn explored the process of changing such a fundamental worldview in his paradigm-breaking book *The Structure of Scientific Revolutions*,[2] now in its third edition. He introduced what have become well-worn clichés about the kinds of change we recognize as paradigm shifts.

Among the most common notions, you will find the following "facts."

Two symptoms precede the emergence of a new paradigm. The first is that accepted models become increasingly complicated as they are expanded, distorted, and adjusted to accommodate new data. The second symptom is that surprises and anomalies become more frequent, as reality continues to generate data that the old models cannot explain. During the paradigm shift, creativity flourishes and multiple new perspectives and potential models vie for center stage as new hypotheses arise and are tested.

To be successful, a new paradigm must account for everything explained in the old one. It also has to explain observations that were surprising under the old paradigm. After the shift from one paradigm to another, it is difficult to imagine that the other world view ever appeared to be reasonable. Not only does one no longer think in the old ways, but it becomes difficult to imagine that anyone else still does. There is no recipe for making the shift.

People and institutions make different shifts at the same time, and the same shifts at different times. For an individual, a paradigm shift can be confusing. For an institution or culture it can be a real mess, and sometimes even a violent mess.

In this book, we make the case for a paradigm shift. Perhaps we are asking for many shifts across many paradigms at once. Since we began to use ideas from complexity to work more effectively in the late 1980s, we have seen individuals, groups, and whole industries move from the dominant paradigm of command and control to an emergent paradigm of complex emergence and uncertainty, in which Adaptive Action thrives. Some of our clients and students have adopted all the habits of thought and action implied in the new paradigm. Some visit the new paradigm and then slip back into their old ways of knowing and acting. Others come over a bit at a time, and still others find the journey virtually impossible. The increasing uncertainty in the world at large has been our greatest ally in this shift. As interactions around the world became more open, more diverse, and more interdependent, people found it more and more difficult to sustain the illusion of the previous paradigm: that they or their institutions were in control.

It has never been easy to make a fundamental change in a worldview or help others do it, but we have learned some lessons about the "other side" of this critical paradigm shift and how to get there. Those lessons are embedded throughout this book.

First and foremost among those lessons is the power of practice. In this section, you will meet ten scholar/practitioners. You will see the theory of Adaptive Action come to life in their stories, but their tales are not just illustrations or examples of the power of Adaptive Action. They are integral to the theory of human systems dynamics, to our core models and methods such as Adaptive Action, and to the continuing evolution of our field.

Indeed, authentic paradigm shifts, at least initially, draw more from practice than from theory. The history of science is full of examples where theory had us stuck, unable to deal with the uncertainty of our worlds. We remained stuck until practice pushed us forward. We will not debate here why that happens, though we do have some hypotheses based on our theory and practice in human systems dynamics. We will, however, share a story that is particularly instructive about the relationship between wise practice and dominant theory. Copernicus will be our informant in this finite game about infinite games.

Practice 1, Theory 0

Ptolemy had a lock on astronomical theory. Born in Greece in 90 CE, he documented a paradigm that explained the motion of the heavens. According to him and his students—including much of the "civilized" world until the sixteenth century—the earth sat at the center of the universe. Some stars (they were called the fixed stars) were etched on a larger sphere that encompassed the earth and formed the sky, like a ceiling. This simple worldview would have been fine, except that the sun, moon, and some of the stars moved across the heavens. To explain this anomaly, the theory included circular, fixed paths along which these special heavenly bodies moved.

This somewhat simple worldview would have been fine, except the timing did not work out right. It took longer for the bodies to pass through some parts of the heavens than others. To explain this anomaly, the theory incorporated the idea that the paths were not circles but ellipses (oval shapes). This even less simple worldview would have been fine, except that sometimes some of the stars moved backwards. To explain this anomaly, the theory introduced epicycles. These were circular paths that some stars took around points that were moving along the usual, elliptical routes. If you imagine the axle of a bicycle wheel moving along a big oval, and then a star riding on the outside of the wheel, you will understand how epicycles worked. That pretty complicated explanation served people well enough. It helped them navigate on the high seas. It also reinforced a religious ideal that God was the center of the universe, so the earth and the people on it, his most prized possessions, must lie in the center of the universe, as well.

This paradigm persisted for centuries. Then Copernicus, a Polish scientist and mathematician, published an astronomical treatise right before he died in 1543. In it, he challenged the complicated geocentric, Ptolemaic theory with a much simpler one.

Copernicus put the sun at the center of the universe. From this new paradigm, it was easy to explain why some heavenly bodies appeared to move while others stood still and why the speed and direction of motions varied. Besides that, Copernicus also explained some phenomena that Ptolemy was never able to account for. Clearly the heliocentric theory gave a superior explanation of observed phenomena, but no massive paradigm shift occurred until a wise practitioner came into the picture.

Tycho Brahe was a Dane who was born in 1546, three years after Copernicus's death. Brahe's contribution to the future of astronomy was that he kept meticulous records. He tracked and recorded the movement of heavenly bodies with amazing accuracy. Ultimately, it was the Copernican paradigm that could explain the details of his data. People came to realize that Ptolemy's explanation was not only more complicated but it was also insufficient to explain Brahe's observations.

It was the data that came from careful practice that successfully challenged the Ptolemaic paradigm, not the introduction of a powerful new theory. It was the sight and insight of the practitioners that supported the world-shaking view of the sun at the center of the universe. Today virtually everyone holds this "new paradigm" view of the universe, but it would never have moved off the page and into cultural acceptance and action unless wise practitioners had tested theory against lived experience and shared what they learned.

In our experience, many social sciences are experiencing a Ptolemaic moment in these early decades of the twenty-first century. Economic, sociological, psychological, political, and educational theories have been built on the faulty foundation of closed, low-dimension, linear paradigms. Over time, layers of complicated adjustments have been added to try to accommodate for observations that challenged the underlying assumptions, until the theories and their related practices are neither simple nor useful. In every discipline, models and methods become more complicated as they try to accommodate observations in reality while holding onto sacrosanct assumptions. At the same time, real practitioners move beyond the theoretical assumptions to derive wise action from continuous engagement with real challenges in real situations. Freed from the old worldview, their experience makes sense of the uncertainty of high-dimension, open, nonlinear systems in ways that any number of theories cannot.

Practice and HSD Theory

Just as those practical people of old had a deep and abiding sense of what truly happened in the real world, we find many practitioners today who act wisely without support from the dominant theoretical paradigms. In business, families, industry, government, education, and community, many people use Adaptive Action (whether they name it or not) to engage with the complex dynamics of human systems. Intuitively they see emergent patterns, make sense of them, and take action to shift them. They work with natural forces to influence conditions so the patterns shift to become more productive over time. Also, as with practitioners among the ancients, widely accepted explanations and theories leave them cold. They find much to misunderstand and confuse, and little to reflect their own experience about what works. The logical texts and complex models of academic management and leadership books seem internally consistent and coherent on the page, but one encounter with the real world, and the theories fall flat. We see these patterns of conflict between theory and practice in many disciplines.

Teachers are forced into instructional practices that they know will hinder the learning of many of their students.

Evaluators construct measurement systems that are practical but unenlightening about the complex nature and far-reaching results of social programs.

Health care professionals work with families and patients to find pathways to comfort or wellness that have little to do with protocols of professional medical practice.

Peace builders use their intuitive sense of tension and resolution, while they write a different story of theory and expectation.

Experienced software designers and project managers break the rules to get the work done.

Effective leaders use their gut reactions more than any textbooks to see, understand, and influence patterns for success.

Even airline pilots respond to an emergency in one way and describe their actions quite differently to match the best practices they learned in school.

To be fair, not all theory-based best practices fall completely flat all the time, but until recently few of them reflected the open, high-dimension, nonlinear intuitive paradigms that drive effective action in our uncertain realities.

We see signs of Kuhn's paradigm shift in organizations all around, as practitioners in many disciplines recognize the necessity to adopt new theory to match their successful practice. Current management and leadership theories are often too complicated to be helpful in times of high stress and little time. Every real person has experienced events, challenges, and opportunities that are not supposed to happen according to accepted theory. So many new and competing theories are emerging that gifted practitioners in many fields roll their eyes and look for the next "flavor of the month." They see the weakness in current theory. They know the power of their intuitive practice. They see the tension between the two and reach out for new and better theory that can inform what they see as effective practice. The problem is that, as long as the old command-and-control paradigm persists, emerging theory will continue to reflect a world that does not exist in anyone's lived reality. Only a move to a new paradigm—one that reflects the complex reality we know—will generate theory that is coherent with practice, and practice that is coherent with real systems change. We believe that the CDE Model and Adaptive Action set the foundation for a theory that generates wise action, and for action that informs evolving theory about uncertainty in organizations.

There is no simple recipe for going from the old view into the new. People who have made the switch to a new paradigm find it difficult to communicate with those who have not yet crossed the theoretical and practical barrier. In reality, many theories claiming the status of paradigm don't sufficiently explain familiar phenomena, and even more of them fail to identify and account for the anomalies that emerged because of the flaws in the old paradigms. To transcend current worldviews, only a paradigm that embraces open, high-dimension, and nonlinear patterns can serve both functions: explain what worked in the past and reach beyond to address the things that didn't. Only such a paradigm shift will support explanations that inform effective action in our complex world.

Earlier, we referred to the Adaptive Action paradigm shift as a move from finite to infinite games. Theory and theory-driven practice of the past named challenges and looked for solutions in closed, low-dimension, linear views. These theories were close enough to reality in an environment marked by local markets (closed), focused only on profits (low-dimension), and driven by hierarchical power structures (linear). As the environment changed and became more unstable, scholars added "ellipses and epicycles" to account for the anomalies people observed in real life. They also blamed their students and clients for failure of implementation, when reality failed to live up to the assumptions of their theories. One by one, wise practitioners abandoned standard models and developed their own home-grown theories to account for what they saw and what worked in reality.

Planning is an excellent example of this tension between what "should" work and what really does. In the early 1990s, we were approached by two professional planners. One had begun her career as an anthropologist and the other as an economist. They were aware that their governmental agencies—local, regional, municipal, state, and federal—completed planning rituals every year that consumed resources and generated reports that sat on shelves. These planning processes became more complicated and consumed more resources every year. But they knew that practical planning happened in a very different way in small and large groups across the organizations. They knew that the ritual associated with planning and the reality of actually developing a plan had little to do with one another. How, they wondered, might we define a formal planning process that captured the power of real planning and avoided the waste of the formal planning processes? Could we build a theory that matched effective action? Those early conversations led to creation of the Decision Map and our earliest explorations into Adaptive Action.

Many of our Associates come to HSD to be certified because they find themselves in the middle of this dilemma. They are successful midcareer professionals in human resources, education, organization development, health care, leadership, government administration, and other challenging disciplines. Over the years, they have developed their own theories, cobbled together from bits and pieces they have read and reinforced in their own day-to-day experience. They are successful, but they miss a reliable, credible, and stable theory base that reflects their lived experience. As successful practitioners, why should they want a theory? These are some of the reasons they give.

Without a theory, the practitioner is stuck being a magician. Your lifelong learning and tried-and-true methods are written off by others in comments like "How did you do that?" "You are amazing!" "I wish I could do that." And "What will we do when you're gone?" The wisdom of practice becomes a performance art rather than an honored professional competency. There is also a risk in being a magician: one misstep or radical culture shift, and your magic tricks stop working.

Without a theory, you the practitioner are stuck essentially alone. You may work with teams and find ways to synthesize and harmonize approaches, but that is rare. More often you find that working with others is difficult if you cannot explain the whys and wherefores of your professional decisions. You are forced either to work on your own or compromise your best in order to work with others.

Without a theory, you and other practitioners are stuck with no exit strategy. As you, a gifted professional, reach retirement age, you will be asked to teach others how to do what you do. Without a language, shared models, or reliable methods, there is no way to orient newcomers or bring aspiring gurus up to speed.

Without a theory, the practitioner is stuck and cannot transcend faulty intuition. Given the rapid and radical change of today, it is common to find yourself in a situation that is absolutely new. When you least expect it, you discover that your natural insight is not good enough, and you are stuck, angry, or frustrated, without reasonable options for action. Or worse yet, you continue to do what your intuition used to tell you, even when the environment is demanding new action.

Finally, without a theory, the practitioner has a limited scope of influence. One HSD Associate said she knew what she did worked when she was in the room, but she wanted to have wider influence. She wanted others to do the same good work she did, and to do it in other rooms.

The people who come to HSD are wise practitioners looking for theory that matches how they work. What they find is a simple and elegant theory that assumes open boundaries, many potentially relevant factors to consider, and causality that goes up, down, back and forth, and all around. In short, in Adaptive Action and in HSD models and methods, they find a dynamical theory that matches their successful dynamical practice.

Today, there is a growing international network of more than 300 Associates who have been certified as Human Systems Dynamics Professionals. Each one of them works in the paradigm that acknowledges stable, unstable, and actively emergent dynamics represented by the zones of the Landscape Diagram. They draw from the HSD theory base and collection of models and methods to observe patterns in the human systems around them, make shared meaning from multiple perspectives and diverse inputs, and act with intention to shift emergent patterns toward greater health and productivity. Not only are they testing the theory with their practice, but their practice is perpetually enriching and informing the theory. In short, their practice of Adaptive Action is real-time co-evolution of theory and practice to meet the unique needs of every Associate and all of their diverse and challenging opportunities for action.

Inquiry Is the Key

How is it possible for a single, simple theory to find use at so many levels of human systems organizations, from personal development through public policy advocacy? How can three steps of Adaptive Action successfully address so many apparently intractable challenges? How can a single paradigm be useful and meaningful for theory and practice in any academic discipline or any organizational role?

The answer is that HSD informs inquiry; it does not provide answers. In fact, we believe that answers have very short shelf lives in complex adaptive systems. An answer that works in one place and time may be irrelevant or destructive at the same place and another time, or at a another place at the same time. Good questions, though, can last a lifetime. They can adapt to even the most extreme situations. They leave any emerging theory open to challenge by emerging reality. Tycho Brahe spent his lifetime asking questions about the relative positions and movement of the heavenly bodies, while others relied on answers from theory that were becoming more complicated and less explanatory.

The role of inquiry is easy to understand when you consider the fundamental structure of a paradigm that embraces open, high-dimension, and nonlinear relationships. What answer can be reliable when a system is open to any external influence at any time? What answer will be as true tomorrow as it is today when an unknowable number of factors influence the emergent causal network? How can a final answer emerge in a system where every answer spontaneously generates its own question in nonlinear cycles of causality? In short, what would it mean to hold onto answers when self-organizing patterns reshape reality unknowably at every moment and at every level of organization?

On the other hand, questions like those captured in Adaptive Action— *What? So what? Now what?*—establish a generative relationship between the knower and the known, between the actor and the acted-on, as well as between the knowing and the acting. Answers may be perfectly reliable in short time, close proximity, high certainty, and close to agreement. Under any other circumstances, answers become barriers rather than bridges to effective action. Making sense of the uncertainty of complex human systems requires that we stand in inquiry and explore our worlds with authentic questions, rather than answers.

Adaptive Action Stories

For all these reasons, we believe that inquiry is the only path to rigorous and coherent theory and practice over long periods of time and across diverse environments.

Over the years with HSD Associates, students, and clients, we explored our own practice, delved into theory of complex dynamics, compared and contrasted our emerging theory of practice and practice of theory. This section of *Adaptive Action: Leveraging Uncertainty in Your Organization* applies the rigor of this inquiry-based practice as it draws on the real-world Adaptive Action experiences of Associates of the Human Systems Dynamics Institute. This section tells some of those stories.

Chapter 8 demonstrates how Adaptive Action has influenced learning and capacity development for Alzheimer's patients, creative learners and scholar practitioners, and masters of quality and performance improvement. Chapter 9 presents stories of courageous leadership from inside organizations, from external consultants, and form one creative woman exploring new ways to integrate life and work. Chapter 10 includes a cluster of stories about Adaptive Action in political and social settings for teams, culturally diverse communities, and public policy advocacy. In all of these cases, you will learn about practical examples where wise practitioners and seasoned professionals use Adaptive Action to improve their games (both finite and infinite varieties). Regardless of the game you are playing, we believe you will find many lessons in these stories and how the Associates responded to the uncertainty in their own situations.

8

CAPACITY BUILDING

Adaptive Action may be simple, but the adaptive capacity to complete the cycles is anything but easy. Every step of the Adaptive Action cycle requires its own Adaptive Action. Individuals and groups must decide how to focus, what questions to ask, who to include in dialogue, and how quickly or slowly to observe, analyze data, or take decisive action. In the following stories, HSD Associates share their experiences of supporting others as they develop the capacity to adapt to diverse, complex challenges.

Janice Ryan tells a tale of developing adaptive capacity in patients suffering from Alzheimer's and in the institutions that support them.

Larry Solow and Denise Easton share their experience of theory and model development for professional trainers who prepare staff to engage in complex systems.

Brenda Fake and Larry Solow talk about how they used Adaptive Action to support individuals, teams, and institutions through successful implementations of technologies that are intended to improve performance.

Each story is unique, but all of them outline practical methods for using Adaptive Action to build adaptivte capacity, to respond to uncertainty, and to get people unstuck from their most difficult and complex challenges.

Knowing Through Context:
Improving Life for Alzheimer's Sufferers

The Story of Janice Ryan

In many ways, the current health care system finds itself stuck. After successfully curing infections and shifting some destructive patterns in public health, the field is left with problems that are apparently unsolvable. Examples are challenges in end-of-life care, preventing lifestyle illnesses, avoiding hospital-borne infections, and treating chronic degenerative diseases such as Alzheimer's. This last challenge is the focus of Janice's Adaptive Action story.

Traditional medical models have solved the problems that are based on static and dynamic change in simple systems, but they now face complex issues that seem to be beyond the reach of current theory and practice. These most challenging problems elude practice because the problems emerge from self-organizing complex adaptive systems that are open, high-dimension, and nonlinear. If we are to overcome these issues, we will have to engage in Adaptive Action as individuals, institutions, and social groups. In the following story, HSD Associate Janice Ryan demonstrates how she has used Adaptive Action and built adaptive capacity for her patients, professional colleagues, and institutions.

Janice is a certified occupational therapist who went through the HSD certification in 2008. In her research and practice, she focuses on improving the quality of life for patients who experience dementia, most as victims of Alzheimer's. In one aspect of her work, she contracts with care facilities to develop environments and interactions that support patient functioning. As she develops theory and practice for her unique approach, she also teaches at her local university, where she engages students as partners in ongoing Adaptive Action research.

What?   In 2005, Janice joined a team to develop a quality-of-life program in a long-term assisted care facility. The project was intended to operationalize a service model for people with dementia who are typically found in skilled care facilities. The ultimate goal of the project was to assure personal freedoms for these patients in an assisted living model. The owners of the care facility were just starting to consider quality-of-life services, anchored in a deep connection with what people needed and wanted. Their priorities were to offer a high level of safety and services but within a comfortable, "homelike" environment. Although an assisted living community designed especially for people with dementia requires more supervision and accommodations than one for a typically aging population, the owners wanted to modify the physical environment and the role of skilled care providers so that independence and quality of life could be preserved.

Through her work, Janice was asked by the owners to design the social model, including the physical space and occupational model, to serve these clients. Approximately twenty people took up residence in this "memory care" community, and families were invited to play a role in developing a personalized memory care program for their resident. Janice based her work on patterns of doing and being that clients had developed in their earlier lives. Her goal was to continue those old patterns in this new life in a new home. A key role for families in this process was to furnish information about the resident's lifestyle, history, and interests, drawing from their own memories and from others who might have known the patient in those earlier stages of their lives.

Her approach was based on occupational and social science research that says an individual establishes life patterns such as habits, routines, and rituals that create the experiential landscape of the world in which he or she lives. These patterns become stronger as the individual continues to participate in them. As we get older, the patterns become even more deeply engrained, and it requires a great deal of effort to change them. An individual who is under stress tends to be even less able to change life patterns. Alzheimer patients are both older and under high stress as a result of the dementia, so it is very difficult for them to change their patterns of thoughts, feelings, and behavior.

Janice noted that traditional approaches to dementia care were based in a medical model that treated only the symptoms of the disease and did not accommodate the dynamics of changing patterns. She knew that many in the long-term care industry wanted to overcome the quality-of-life constraints that resulted from this medical model, which was developed out of a need to "get things done" when caring for medically ill patients. How can care be both efficient and sensitive to the life patterns of residents? The long-term care industry wanted to move beyond patterns of practice that required people with dementia to spend years living in a social environment that treated them as if they were sick. Although resident independence was recognized as best practice in the assisted living industry, the realities of service delivery often made this goal difficult and stressful to achieve.

Janice theorized that decreasing the patient's stress within the boundaries of a realistic long-term care model would enable residents to adapt more easily to other changes and to participate more effectively in their own care. Grounded in that hypothesis, Janice developed a programming protocol designed around the understanding that each resident needed an environment that reduced stress and supported quality of life, and that caregivers must be given opportunity and responsibility to know their patients well before they can create such an environment.

Janice developed a simple training exercise for caregivers to help them recognize the personal, social, and resident-support benefits that come from knowing the habitual lifestyle patterns and interests of their residents. They experience role playing in which caregivers interact as both themselves and the residents to develop authentic awareness of the positive differences two-way interactions and pattern sensitivity can make. Janice described this process as developing mindfully interrelational patterns.

These new patterns of Adaptive Action can be recognized as preserving two-way exchanges of information that increase the residents' ability to say what they need and the caregivers' ability to react more intuitively to resident actions or nonverbal communications. In this exchange, caregivers will gain needed clues to create a landscape of life and activity to engage and support the patterns that mean so much to individuals. She saw this use of HSD in her description of seeing, understanding, and influencing patterns. Janice knew that she could find ways to influence the patterns of these clients' lives if she could understand the patterns that had been important to them at the height of their own life's activities and interests.

She worked with the care facilities to set conditions for Adaptive Action as she created areas of activity in the facilities that replicated some typically familiar activities for most of the residents. The owners of the facility where she was working allowed her to design the space she needed. She took radical steps to create environments that helped the patients recognize and engage in the patterns of the lives they had known prior to the onset of their illnesses. Knowing that people with dementia depend on physical and visual cues, she designed one activity space to look like an old school classroom, creating a more comfortable space in which people could engage. She designed another area to replicate an old garage and found that male patients often chose to hang out there, rather than isolating in their own rooms. Additionally, she created an area that represented a home space where residents could go to connect with their patterns of meaning through family and home routines. For one retired minister, she even turned a broom closet into a tiny place of worship so he could reexperience the familiar pattern of standing in and serving from a pulpit.

Because the patients connected the locations and situations with the patterns they knew before they became ill, some eventually developed a habit of stopping by a place and engaging in more lucid social activity than they did before the setting was made available. There is, of course, variability in how the strategies work from patient to patient and from space to space, but the critical discovery was that there definitely were improvements in patient functioning as the patterns around them shifted. The results were significant enough, in fact, that she has replicated her work in communities across six states. She has trained staff in each location and has coached and monitored for success.

One tool she developed was a short list of simple rules for how to influence patients' social involvement. She taught staff members to use a set of simple social rules designed to influence their everyday decisions to complement more traditional pattern rules of the medical model. By integrating her own adaptive approach with the medical model rules of engagement, she identified a list of simple rules.

- Consider safety first.
- Watch for changes in health and wellness.
- Report all changes to nursing staff.
- Use personal meanings.
- Encourage current abilities.
- Learn to speak nonverbally.
- Use the power of first impressions.
- Use simple language.
- Stay observant, to respond quickly to change.
- Be in joyful relationship.

All levels of staff were taught the rules, while caregivers received experiential training to embed the rules into daily activities. She also provided additional training for the life enhancement coordinator in each facility, who is in charge of establishing and running the system. Rather than focusing on the self-developed calendars of a typical activity director, a life enhancement coordinator is taught to be an expert in operationalizing mindfully interrelational care. By teaching all staff to connect with residents' lifelong meaning-making patterns, life enhancement coordinators can positively influence the quality of life and daily routines of everyone in the community. The use of these simple rules ensured that as the patients interacted with staff, they experienced a familiar and more comfortable pattern of exchange, which further decreased their stress and heightened their level of functioning.

Over the past five years, the model program has grown stronger and continued to expand and improve. In that community, Janice sees powerful two-way exchanges that reflect engagement between caregivers and patients to create familiar environmental patterns of being and doing that are based in the residents' healthier, earlier lives. Two-way exchanges can elicit a shift in pattern variables, such as a sense of personal control and safety, interest in performing daily routines, awareness of spatial cues for finding one's way, and motivation for activities. Where those exist, observations of patient behavior reflect less of the stress reaction than is typically seen in traditional long-term care. The quality of these exchanges is critical. Today Janice knows that even how direct care providers greet a patient in the morning influences that patient's functioning throughout the day.

Working in multiple settings, Janice realized that the engagement and commitment of the administration was as critical to success as were the individual care providers' abilities and skills in establishing the two-way exchanges with the patients. This realization, along with other insights led her to the *So what?* step in her Adaptive Action to make sense of her inquiry.

So What?   Janice realized she had created a different paradigm of service that depended on relationships and connections—very abstract concepts. They found places where the staff changed the language and routines of working with the patients but seemed unable to establish those more abstract characteristics that created the necessary quality of relationships and connections. She found that as those staff members changed only what they could see—language and routines—they found only short-term changes. Her findings pointed to the need to change staff and administrator understanding of their own behavior to be more consistent and authentic in connecting with the patients deeply and more meaningfully. She needed to make Adaptive Action a conscious and chosen act to get its greatest benefit.

As Janice worked to change the context in the places where the approach was being less successful, she realized that neither staff nor administrators were ready or able to establish deeper understanding of behavior and the human capacity for change in the resident or themselves. They continued to offer a level of care seen as efficient and complete on the surface but lacking the thought and behavioral flexibility required to move beyond more impersonalized approaches. Over time, Janice recognized that intervening in a person's total environment supports felt-sense awareness, interrelationship building, and capacity for experiential learning. Those staff members unable to enter relationships with residents in this adaptive way were less able to create familiar patterns of interaction and opportunity for client engagement. They failed to grasp the power of this more mindfully interrelational approach to enhance patients' meaning making in their narrowing worlds.

She has come to realize that to help people learn about this model of client engagement, she has to consider two things. First she has to enhance the immediate shifts of patient engagement, which she does by changing the environment, creating the familiar patterns that contribute to reducing stress of patients as they deal with their disease in the context of an unfamiliar environment. Second, she has to teach staff how to engage in two-way exchanges as they watch for and support patients' meaning-making processes. The adaptive capacity of the patients must be accompanied by the adaptive capacity of the staff.

As she continued to learn from and about the implementation of her ideas in these care facilities, she began teaching occupational therapy students at the university level about this approach and how best to implement it at other facilities. What she has learned through the *So what?* step of her inquiry has helped her move to dissemination and teaching of her ideas as a part of the *Now what?* step of her Adaptive Action cycle.

She has developed a complementary treatment approach using an enhanced environment to facilitate positive qualitative changes in behavior patterns of hospice clients with advanced dementia, partly as a strategy to make the abstract concepts of her original model more visible for student learning. By first observing videotapes of clients making the more dramatic shifts in awareness and engagement facilitated in her treatments, students are learning to recognize the subtle changes that occur over time in her original program. She has become convinced that she has to pass on this new way of thinking about dementia care to the next generation of occupational therapists to influence this slow-moving process of paradigm change in the culture of care. Her approach is adapting as she helps professionals adapt to build environments that support adaptation for patients and their families.

Now What?   Because of what she learned in her *So what?* step, Janice engaged her students in multiple ways to help them experience the application and meaning of her innovative treatment model. Three considerations she identified about implementation of the model are critical in their instruction.

First, they have to understand the importance of the physical environment as a landscape of interrelated multisensory experiences that contributes to lifelong meaning making. Second, they need to recognize that transformative change of all human behavior occurs largely on the unconscious level of the meaning-making process. Third, they must understand the role that stress commonly plays in shutting down this open exploratory learning process for the clients.

As she worked with students to develop and administer assessments of patient functioning, Janice saw another, and sometimes more difficult, challenge in developing caregivers' awareness of the subtle changes in patient meaning making and engagement. Students had to learn to recognize hidden thought-behavior dynamics, while preparing to work in a health care system that was only beginning to develop means to recognize and measure these types of qualitative change in behavior over time. They had to learn to see shifts in patterns in the *What?* step before they could plan and take action in the rest of their Adaptive Action cycles.

She used videos of patient interactions, training students to conduct assessments and observations with fidelity. She taught them to see the differences in stress, meaning making, and engagement by looking at qualitative changes in patients' behavior. They learned to observe slight shifts in visual attention and scanning, auditory awareness and localization, reciprocal patterns of social and emotional information exchange, occupational complexity, and awareness of personal identity.

She saw this level of development as a necessary step toward her next *What?* which was beginning to emerge in the interplay between her program advances and ongoing developments within the current health care paradigm. She began work on a community partnership in which her program and treatment ideas would be researched as a preventive intervention for adults with special needs, including those at risk for Alzheimer's.

Janice's Conclusion

At the same time as she was working with patients and their caregivers, Janice was contributing to the good of the greater whole. At the time of this writing, Janice saw herself on the fourth iteration of her Adaptive Action inquiry into changing life experiences of dementia patients in care facilities. She experienced migration of her understanding first from her own, personally held beliefs, observations, and learning to influence her practice. Her practice then informed both her research and her teaching. Finally, her own personal

Adaptive Action cycles generated new options for action in the broader health care system.

The first iteration was about looking at the day-to-day patterns for clients and identifying how to make those patterns familiar and comfortable. For her, the *What?* question pointed to the high levels of stress and disengagement among patients. It also pointed her toward research into the impact of familiarity and comfort on an individual's stress level. In her *So what?* step of that first iteration, she realized that creating greater familiarity in the social and emotional patterns of the patients greatly reduced their stress. This led to radical change in the physical environment in the care facilities, creating communal settings that replicated classrooms, kitchens, garages, even places of worship.

Iteration number two led her to understand she had to get past the barrier that prevented professionals from changing their behavior. Having staff and administrators use these new approaches of life pattern change required that they experience the changes for themselves and reflect on their learning. So the *Now what?* step of this iteration led to new approaches to staff training, and to working with people to experience and reflect on the environments she was asking them to create.

In the third iteration, she launched a network of people to examine how well she has taught staff members and students to observe patients and engage in their own meaning making to create a more supportive environment. The testing and evaluation at this iteration helped inform her theory and her complementary experience of teaching her theory to others brought broader understanding. Research on her applications of an enhanced multisensory environment to treatment of clients with thought-behavior challenges furthered her awareness of the need for abstract concepts to be developed into experiential models to facilitate the understanding of others. These lessons have contributed to her latest *Now what?* decision.

In the fourth iteration, a community partnership developed around her next *What?* question; it includes district support from the Alzheimer's Disease Association and involvement of the director of a local center serving special-needs adults as well as the president and CEO of a large assisted living and memory care provider in her community. Her student groups remain involved in developing a grant proposal to support the further research and program development capacities of this new community partnership.

Her work in HSD has helped her develop three-pronged support:

• Meaning making includes both a person's intentionality and what makes things meaningful to the person. Individuals have a deep intentionality that makes them move toward what is meaningful, and that is what drives learning.

• Social and group interactions are crucial to meaning making and patient intentionality. Finding means for two-way exchanges to occur on this scale within a social group and in educational settings makes people better able to engage with and respond to the patterns around them.

• Social interaction is a two-way process, and individuals can be shut down by what comes in. People must engage with others so as to allow them to tap into the thoughts and meaning making of the other.

Janice believed that an individual's ability to see a transformation and reflect on the response to that transformation enables patterns to change. Her Adaptive Action research to help caregivers understand how to treat patients with dementia continues to inform her practice, research, and teaching. She believes that as caregivers reflect on their own patterns of change and understand their own responses, they will be better equipped to support their patients.

Likewise, she believes that teaching must be approached as a two-way exchange of information. Research studies designed to follow the logic of Adaptive Action inquiry can create two-way exchanges of information between what we know as qualitative change and the conceptual link between thought and observable behavior. In her current iteration, Janice believes that Adaptive Action can support research partnerships between professionals who follow various meaning-making processes and contribute to breakthroughs in the science and practice of care delivery.

Adaptive Action to Design Process Consulting: Redesigning Design

The Story of Denise Easton and Larry Solow

There is no shortage of recommendations about learning, innovation, or product development. Some are complicated sequences of steps based on engineering methods and models. Others leverage the artistic facet of creativity, encouraging divergent thinking activities and apparently random exploration. Sometimes these processes work, but quite often individuals and groups get stuck before they reach the final product. Every experience of being stuck may be unique, but the patterns of getting stuck in these processes are relatively common. The engineering model includes so many steps and so much formal activity that the energy and excitement of the creative effort wears out before the end. The creativity model asks people to step into a completely new way of thinking and being that may become a major barrier for some teams and some people.

The Landscape Diagram (Chapter 1) explains the limitations of these two approaches: the one demands too much agreement and certainty, and the other offers too little. What is needed is a creative process that sits in the emergent space of the landscape and leverages the adaptive capacity of the team. In this story, Denise and Larry share their experience of using Adaptive Action as a path to discovery and product development and how it guided them through a complex process without getting stuck.

Denise Easton and Larry Solow became HSD Associates in 2008. They soon began a business collaboration centered on a shared interest in integrating the principles of HSD to define a more dynamical approach to process consultation. Denise is a "serial entrepreneur" who pioneers in virtual learning and collaboration space. She founded an e-learning design, production, and consulting firm focused on professional development for individuals and organizations. Larry is a longtime corporate consultant who has worked in both internal and external capacities and is recognized for his creative integration of people, process, and strategy improvements. At the time of the writing of this chapter (in 2011), Denise and Larry were piloting their new ideas to gather data and fine-tune their work in the field.

Unlike Janice's story of what she saw emerge in her Adaptive Action, the story Larry and Denise shared focuses on the history or the "how" of their collaboration. Their story provides a map for how they were committed to using Adaptive Action to define, track, and enhance a process of innovation. This shared commitment to acute awareness of the emergent patterns through the process has helped them in several ways. It has informed their insights about the complexity of co-creating intellectual property. They have come to think more clearly about how and where to change the patterns they see. Finally they have identified new methods to influence patterns of adult learning behavior and its impact on organizational change.

Their first Adaptive Action challenge was to identify what it was they wanted to create collaboratively.

What?   Their initial conversations about their "same and different" business experiences and perspectives framed the collaboration. After several extensive conversations, they engaged in a number of *What?* questions:

What were their shared passions and professional interests?

What did their interests have to do with HSD?

What was the "itch" they believed they could scratch in this shared space of exploration?

Over the course of several weeks of online and telephone conversations, they considered the patterns formed by their individual and shared responses. Each time they cycled through their core questions, they reviewed their explorations through a lens that integrated HSD principles and tools along with the more traditional process patterns of their current consulting practices. Finally, they sought clarity about how these questions would or could shape their new, shared business model.

Those conversations coalesced in March 2009 as they settled on a three-part question to explore: What do we want to do together to (1) help the field of HSD, (2) meet our personal objectives, and (3) offer a product for clients? One significant discovery was the number of times they went through this part of the cycle. They documented between seventy and eighty starts in their earliest conversations, which served to build a solid foundation based on these seemingly "simple" questions and reaffirm a commitment to their joint work.

So What?   Over their next exchanges, Larry and Denise would individually answer questions, and then share those responses with one another. A common thread that emerged during many of the conversations was recognition of the need to address adult learning behavior in an HSD and complexity-based consulting process. This topic offered a clear contribution to expand the field of HSD into new applications. It offered an opportunity to address questions that were important to both of them in their separate careers. It also held the promise of a commercial product, as it became their shared question: "How can we design learning experiences that meet both the specific needs of adult learners and the broader needs of any organization?" This focus had the potential to generate a variety of products through consultation, coaching, and direct services as they co-created learning and change processes for their clients. Working together to create a dynamical approach to learning and change was a very clear answer to their shared questions and pointed them toward action.

Now What?   When they came to the *Now what?* step, their process slowed again as they took more time to explore and identify next steps. They were aware that answers to the *Now what?* question could have significant impact, both individually and collectively, on their lives and work. They reviewed their initial conversations to ensure coherence between current responses and original questions. They confirmed their shared desire to have an impact in the field and agreed the product they would create had to yield a "positive return" on the time and energy they were investing in its development. Larry and Denise, both prone to move quickly to action, supported each other in the need to stay in the *Now what?* step for a period of time and avoid coming to closure too soon. It felt like the right thing to do at the time, and they trusted the Adaptive Action process to know that they were in the right place. After several more *What?* and *So what?* iterations, they came to agreement and were able to step confidently into the *Now what?* step of the cycle, designing a suite of concepts and tools that met their three stated goals.

Denise trusted the Adaptive Action process to allow them to leave a "trail of breadcrumbs" through the three questions, providing a path for them to follow backwards as they needed to confirm or challenge earlier thinking. She felt comfortable wandering around in the questions, exploring numerous concepts and options for action because she knew she would be able to find her way back to the path and eventually to an informed way to move forward.

The language of the process—naming the cycles as *What?*, *So what?*, and *Now what?*—was less important to Larry. His work style was more intuitive and less specifically framed by the language itself at the time. On reflection, he grasped the match between his own, more intuitive exploration process and the structure provided by the Adaptive Action model. This match is one often recognized when wise practitioners begin to use Adaptive Action and come to appreciate its familiarity.

Begin Again . . . and Again . . . and Again

As Denise and Larry continued their design efforts, they used the frame of Adaptive Action to evaluate both their existing and emergent theories and models. This reexamination enabled them to put aside any question that moved them too far out in front of their current work. For instance, at one point early in the *What?* step of development, they began telling stories about piloting and managing their work after the design was complete. Rather than table the conversation as not relevant to the current phase of the work, they were able to make a note of those questions and "put them in the parking lot," knowing they would supply valuable guidance later in the process.

They continued to develop their model, flowing through multiple iterations of the Adaptive Action process. As they finished design of one element (*Now what?*), they returned to a *What?* question to define their current state. On the basis of the answer to that question, they identified implications for the next phases of development (*So what?*). Through this shared reflection on the process, they challenged each other to move from discussion to action, agreeing on the next element of the process to be designed (*Now what?*). Adaptive Action established a framework for creating the time and space to accomplish their work at a deeper level. Their shared inquiry process allowed them to share individual ideas, go off in different directions, and return, ready to share their learning and create shared meaning.

The net result of their continuing use of Adaptive Action was creation of the Complexity Space Framework (CSF). To see their model and learn more about their approach, visit http://thecomplexityspace.com/.

Once they felt they had a product to share, they used Adaptive Action again, this time explicitly inviting and exploring new perspectives. They engaged other learning and change professionals in dialogues that centered on three sets of Adaptive Action questions:

"What are your questions about the purpose or details of this model?"
     (*What?*)

"How does this fit with your models of learning and change? Does it make
     sense? Do you see value in its contribution to the field of adult learning
     and change?" (*So what?*)

"How might you use the model in your practice? What might we do to
     make the model more useful, valuable, etc.?" (*Now what?*)

They incorporated the feedback to identify what patterns in their shared work contributed to desired end results, how they could make those patterns stronger, and how they could eliminate patterns found to be less useful.

Larry and Denise's Shared Conclusion

Larry and Denise reflect on how their story relates to the bigger question of the role HSD can play in change management. They see how the three Adaptive Action steps helped them make sense of their own learning and experiences in a process of innovation. Their product benefited from their commitment to use Adaptive Action intentionally as a part of their development process. In addition to aiding in creation of the CSF, the Adaptive Action process also furnished a framework for testing and responding to the multiple and varied environments and systems where the CSF will be used.

Use of Adaptive Action produced some unintended consequences as well. First, even though they collaborated across time and distance (they seldom met face-to-face and had no formal working structure), they were never disorganized thanks to the strength of a shared sense of their approach to the mission. Second, use of this adaptive, flexible process created a safe space that invited them to share their intellectual excitement, doubts, and accomplishments with one another. These outcomes generated greater appreciation and a deeper relationship than either was expecting when they began their collaboration using Adaptive Action.

The Human Side to Quality: Recovering Investments in Lean and Six Sigma

The Story of Larry Solow and Brenda Fake

Around the world, many organizations are stuck in efforts to implement Six Sigma, Lean, and other techniques for quality improvement. Masters are trained, processes are put in place, and investments are made in changing organizations and processes. After an initial burst of improvement, systems often settle back into old habits and wasteful ways. As a result, the benefits promised by these technologies are seldom, if ever, fully realized. The following stories share insights about how Adaptive Action and HSD models and methods set conditions for sustainable implementation of these and other performance improvement approaches.

Brenda Fake became an HSD Associate in 2004. She had worked much of her career in supporting change in manufacturing and service corporations. She and Larry Solow realized a shared interest in the impact of Lean and Six Sigma processes on the human side of organizations and began a conversation about how they could use HSD to address those challenges. Their conversation eventually emerged into a collaborative effort in the form of their book *What Works for GE May Not Work for You: Using Human Systems Dynamics to Build a Culture of Process Improvement.*[1]

In our interview with Brenda and Larry, each used a story from research and practice to reflect how they used Adaptive Action to build capacity in organizations. Rather than a story about knowledge development, as Janice used Adaptive Action, or as a story about using Adaptive Action explicitly as a framework for action, the stories from Brenda and Larry tell how they used Adaptive Action to make sense of their own role and contribution to addressing the challenges their clients faced.

Larry shared his story of Adaptive Action first. He described an Adaptive Action process from the point of view of a manufacturing corporation that wanted to increase its capacity to build quality products and find solutions to business issues.

What?   The company Larry discussed was a manufacturer of plastic vials and bottles for the cosmetics and pharmaceuticals industries. There were ongoing challenges in both process and quality measures. The company had committed to quality products to the point that any failure to deliver quality product on time could, by contract, lead to rejection of the latest six months of deliveries. Although this company recognized the importance of a quality management system, they relied on end-of-line inspections to measure defects, using rudimentary statistical controls, depending on visual inspection in the process. Although they noticed increases in customer complaints, concerns were not (yet) at a critical level. About five years earlier, the company had implemented a total quality management (TQM) program. This effort had yielded some initial success, but it had fallen into disuse over time.

Sensing the need to make some changes, management approached a local college to partner in obtaining a customized training grant to fund implementation of Six Sigma training. In their grant request, they specified the same top-down, classroom-based, standardized training approach they had used in implementing TQM. Their theory was that if everyone had the same knowledge, they could support each other in applying it. Top leaders would support the training. Middle managers would be trained first, with the expectation that they would then train their staff members and set the expectation for full implementation.

So What?   Larry was hired to design and lead the training effort. After requesting a meeting with the senior leadership team, he described Six Sigma as a different way of running the business and what full and effective implementation would mean in terms of time, energy, and resource requirements. Reminding the leaders of this organization of the earlier path they had taken to implement TQM, he noted it had not worked very well over time. He asked them what the senior management team was prepared to do differently how, to change the pattern and reach a more sustainable outcome. After extended discussion, senior management chose not to begin implementation just then. Members of that team recognized they were not ready or willing to make the changes and investments needed to ensure its success. The session ended amicably, with Larry telling the client, "Call us when your business situation changes, and you're ready."

Now What?   Twelve months later the client contacted the college, saying they were prepared to move forward. They explained they were now ready to discuss changes required throughout the organization to accomplish sustainable results. As a leadership team, they saw they needed to do it right, and make it stick this time. They realized the need to change behavioral and leadership patterns as well as build the infrastructure required to move forward.

Stepping into the Next Adaptive Action

The leadership team met with Larry to talk about their current situation and future needs, and to explore what had worked in the TQM implementation. As a result of those conversations, the team worked with Larry to create an implementation plan that incorporated the best of the earlier approaches, while avoiding the pitfalls. A series of two-day workshops was designed, conducted once a month over eight months. Prior to the start of the training, the organization identified real business issues and created cross-functional teams to work on them. Those issues became the application base for the new learning. They engaged Larry to provide coaching between sessions, rather than expecting management to have the competence and confidence to do it on their own. Larry included the managers in his coaching sessions, modeling how another set of questions could offer new possibilities for action.

As a result, the teams were successful in addressing their assigned business issues, and the company elected to expand Six Sigma deeper into the organization. After another internal iteration of *What?* and *So what?* the top management team moved into a *Now what?* step to create an internal black belt process. As a result, the company was able to become less dependent on external consultants.

As Larry concluded his story, Brenda moved into telling about an experience where she used Adaptive Action in her planning and support of an aerospace company as it built capacity to support their quality efforts.

What?   This Fortune 100 company had an internal consulting group that offered process improvement across a number of services in the aerospace division. This group functioned as an independent company in many respects; its focus was to use the discipline of Six Sigma to improve processes related to areas such as training, certification, business analysis, and project management. The consulting group's objectives were to introduce and help apply Six Sigma principles in the work of this aerospace division. Six Sigma was seen as the silver bullet to reduce costs and waste by increasing efficiency across the business functions. The internal consulting group adapted Six Sigma theories, methods, and tools for application across the five strategic business units (SBUs) in the aerospace business division.

Like many systemwide improvement initiatives, the work of this group was imposed by the top leader without a great deal of input from the SBUs or other organizational leaders. In a short time, however, the top leader who had championed the effort left the organization, turning over the job of implementation to the new leadership.

As the new CEO stepped in, his vision and direction for the business called for a stronger focus on new product development, tracking data and process from the point of customer input, to design, to full execution, to market. The new CEO also envisioned a shorter response time in getting products to market by reusing existing technology in new markets and for new products.

The emphasis on and interest in Six Sigma shifted with the arrival of the new CEO. The organizational leaders, along with the Six Sigma leader of the internal consulting group, found several patterns at play across the organization:

- Leaders were using Six Sigma to market to stakeholders.

- Some people in the organization embraced Six Sigma theory, methods, and tools and used them well to produce high-quality products.

- Factions formed among those who used Six Sigma, those who didn't use it, and those who used it in an adapted form to suit their own purposes. Overall this pattern revealed a great deal of inconsistency across the system.

- This inconsistency increased over time, as some tools were used with little or no fidelity to their original applications or specificity in their contribution to efforts toward quality.

- Organizational structures that had been established to compensate and reward those who had earned Master Black Belts in Six Sigma created conflicts within the organization. The perception of elitism around the focus on Six Sigma triggered a negative view of the actual added value of the program.

So What?   Eventually the company set the Six Sigma program aside, taking the focus off of that initiative as the CEO began to talk about Toyota's Production Systems (TPS). Borrowing concepts from Toyota's practices in the area of quality production, he created a process improvement initiative he dubbed "Velocity Product Development." VPD was designed to permit some flexibility inside the more rigid Six Sigma quality process, with a clear focus on improving product development.

The aerospace group decided to continue with the internal specialist team rather than integrating the process improvement talent into the respective businesses. Their rationale for this shift was to ensure that the VPD team remained focused on longer-term critical projects that would shift how new products were introduced and implemented across the aerospace business division.

Over time, the organization went through a great deal of turmoil as the VPD group tried to work with engineers on product development using both the Toyota Production System and the Six Sigma and Lean theories, methods, and tools. The multiple expectations and commitments of the two approaches created confusion that overwhelmed the team as well as the internal clients they were trying to serve.

On the basis of the ten years of lessons learned with Six Sigma and the initial efforts to implement VPD, the group agreed to hire an organization effectiveness leader who specialized in change management. This person would be dedicated full-time to the team and initiative.

The Company's *Now What?* Becomes Brenda's *What?*

Subsequently, Brenda was hired as the organization effectiveness leader to manage the change process and support the team in this initiative. She began by looking at their artifacts of processes, their change management material, and a highly complicated process map that was truly understood by only the handful of team leaders who designed it. Brenda quickly realized she needed to help them see the complexity (open, high-dimension, nonlinear) rather than the complications (inconsistent and incoherent diversity) in the system. She started with a more simplified model based on common theory that everyone agreed on.

Additionally she found that the VPD team members were set up to consult with and influence new product development processes on both the engineering design and the manufacturing side. She recognized that a schism emerged between the disciplines, most markedly between the mechanical team ("Gear Heads") and the electronics team ("Sparkies") within the engineering groups. Across all the teams, individuals were experiencing varying degrees of change. Inside the VPD group she found people who knew they needed change and others who didn't like change. Adding to the complexity, little clarity existed about how the VPD team should be working and where they should be investing their time.

Brenda quickly identified a number of patterns that needed to be addressed:

- Some VPD members imposed their expertise, telling consulting clients what to do and how to do it.

- When the VPD clients were unable or unwilling to implement VPD effectively, the VPD members were often blamed for lack of improved performance.

- There was also a lack of alignment around the discipline of VPD within the team itself. Team members were using a variety of problem-solving approaches. Some imposed their approaches; others engaged in shared problem solving; and still others used a strong consultative approach, recognizing that the internal customer had ultimate responsibility for doing the work.

- The VPD staff tended to make the process, explanations, and improvements much more complicated than they needed to be. Not understanding the implications of the complexity they faced, team members had to make their work more concrete and applicable to the real-world challenges their clients faced.

Now What?   Brenda decided to try to shift the patterns in the system by conducting a team effectiveness assessment among the VPD team and customers. She believed she could help the VPD team members identify their challenges by sharing data with them about how customers valued their work and approaches. The data painted a bleak picture but did help the team see the gaps and discrepancies in their work. She followed up with two brief presentations, to share HSD principles with the team members. Her goal was to help VPD members see the value of simple models and methods that would help them see, understand, and influence the patterns of complexity in their clients' challenges. She made it clear that her intentions were not to replace the VPD approach, but rather to enhance and complement their effectiveness.

In hindsight, she saw that the HSD models and methods supported the socio-technical theories deeply embedded in the Toyota Production System and the foundations behind VPD. VPD leaders and their key customers immediately grasped the importance and value of the HSD models and methods and began to change their initial questions as they engaged with new customers. The behavioral shift was evident when VPD members shifted their consulting stance as they engaged in Adaptive Action with their customers by saying "we discover together how to solve the problem." Even many working relationships that had been problematic in the past began to shift toward greater productivity.

As the key team members received more training and became certified in the use of HSD, people started to select HSD models and methods as their tools to bridge the multiple engineering, TQM, and VPD approaches. They continued to engage with one another and with clients using the HSD models and methods as a complement to VPD. Brenda then realized her role could shift toward greater engagement as she worked directly with the VPD team members to design services and approaches for various client challenges. The team's conversations shifted from shallow discussion of applying specific tools for immediate fixes to deeper discussion of their own dynamics and the impact on their projects.

Larry and Brenda's Conclusions

As they worked together to describe and use the lessons from these challenges, Larry and Brenda came to recognize positive consequences. They continue to use HSD approaches without specifically naming them as something special. They believe this helps their clients engage with the processes, models, and methods in the short run, building skill for their clients to use them after support and coaching is removed. They continue to see heightened capacity in the organizations where they work as they use Adaptive Action to help groups explore how to address their complex issues.

Larry and Brenda see their next *What?* questions focusing on how best to serve organizations, given what they are learning.

What difference does it make when technical experts among their clients apply the models and methods in ways Larry and Brenda didn't expect? Does this create an additional line of sight for the two of them to watch over time?

What is the contextual impact of this work? As various cultures come together, how can they be blended and accommodated in the organizations where they work?

What is the impact of the HSD language? Both Larry and Brenda believed they had to adapt the language according to their initial impressions about who would or would not embrace the theory and who would just take the tools and move forward.

These questions and others guide the next levels of exploration as Larry and Brenda work independently in their own consulting practices and as they work together to pursue their shared interest in helping corporations develop, produce, and market high-quality goods and services.

Chapter Conclusions

The stories differ, yet the underlying message comes through: Adaptive Action offers benefits in all stages of our work to understand and respond to the turbulent and surprising landscape of the twenty-first century.

The *What?* step can and will help us see the underlying explanations and dynamics that make our systems work—or not work—as they do. Adaptive Action helps us make sense of our systems as we come to understand the *So what?* questions that emerge as we engage with our human systems and the world around us. We use those understandings to inform creative and effective action as we move into the *Now what?* step and ultimately into the next *What?* question as we gauge the impact of our actions.

Janice gathered data about dementia in general and about her own patients in particular to understand the social, emotional, and physical impacts of losing contacts and connections to the reality of the world around them. Then, in iterative cycles of learning, she created new spaces for her patients, trained others to engage with dementia patients caringly and productively, and invited partners in to engage in the next cycles of learning and service.

Larry and Denise used Adaptive Action as an intentional guide to understand adult learners and responses to change, and they incorporated that learning into their growing theory and practice. At the same time, they used Adaptive Action to set the stage for their own shared exploration into collaboration.

Both Larry and Brenda collected impressions and data from multiple perspectives to inform their Adaptive Actions and the Adaptive Action of the clients they served and the roles they needed to play in providing most effective services. Independently and together they made sense of their work, sharing it with the world in the form of a book that described the human systems side of Lean and Six Sigma.

These three stories reflect the value Adaptive Action offers as it builds capacity on all scales of human interaction, from individual learning and growth to supporting full implementation of systemwide initiatives that move toward fitness and sustainability. The next chapter presents stories of three HSD Associates who used Adaptive Action to manage change for themselves and their clients.

9

LEADING CHANGE

The roles of the leader in situations of static and dynamic change are pretty clear. In static change, the goal is to move the system from one state of rest to another. To lead this kind of change, one needs to have a vision of the end state, know the resistance that is likely to emerge, and marshal sufficient force to overcome it. Dynamic change leadership is a bit more nuanced. In dynamic change, the system moves along a smooth path from a known beginning, through known forces, to a known end. The dynamic leader must get a picture of the current situation, understand all the forces at work in the system, plan a trajectory that will propel the system forward, and then drive the system toward that desired end. These leadership processes may be difficult, but they are not very complex. And sometimes they even work. More often, leadership strategies such as these leave an organization and its people stranded in between the past and future, with the problems of both and the benefits of neither.

The reason these strategies fail is that most change in human systems is complex, unpredictable, and dynamical. Static change leadership and static planning are not very helpful in the everyday world of open, high-dimension, and nonlinear change processes such as the ones that emerge in complex adaptive human systems.

In this chapter, you will read the stories of individuals who used Adaptive Action to lead change whether from inside an organization, as an external consultant, or as an individual navigating personal transitions and creative life choices. As different as these stories sound, they all share the wisdom of Adaptive Action as a leadership strategy.

Systemic Change: Sustainable School Reform

The Story of Wendy Gudalewicz

Organizational change is never easy, and leading change can be a confusing and frustrating process. Politically charged changes, especially in public institutions, often get stuck even before they begin. In the next story, a committed and creative school administrator successfully leads a change process that could have gotten stuck in a dozen ways. Adaptive Action cycles in many places by many groups over an entire project process allowed her local school district to navigate a complex challenge and reach a sustainable and equitable outcome.

Wendy Gudalewicz is a lifelong educator who became an HSD Institute Associate by participating in the education certification cohort held in the winter of 2010. She had been hired as chief academic officer of the New Haven Unified School District (NHUSD) in a suburb of San Francisco about a year before coming to us and had been a principal, district-level administrator, and consultant for several years prior to that. She came to the class as part of her ongoing search for ways to deal effectively with the complexity of creating environments where students and staff engage in rich, productive learning experiences. She knew that traditional models of change and leadership fell short of what she needed and was open to learning a new approach.

What?   When Wendy stepped into her position in the NHUSD, she began to learn the district by examining policies and procedures around the various programs for serving students. One large challenge she found was the process for identifying and selecting students to enter the program for gifted and talented students (GATE). She knew from experience that this was a highly controversial and delicate question to bring up, generally built on tradition and local experience.

What she found was a process that was highly subjective. The process generated little or no data about its effectiveness. Her first question focused on *What?* of the Adaptive Action cycle: What benefit did the subjectivity provide, and what was the impact of that degree of subjectivity? She and the director of the program, Joe, began to sort through the data first just to see what they could find out about who was being identified through the existing process. They began to disaggregate the data in as many ways as they could think of to identify the ramifications of the selection process. For instance, the largest consequence they identified was that in some instructional settings students who were not selected in this highly subjective process were automatically barred from other opportunities as they progressed through school. This and other challenges, although they were similar to what goes on in school districts across the country, did not seem equitable to her. So she and Joe engaged others as they began to explore what actually happened in the assessment process for selection.

They found that a student was assessed for the GATE program only if a parent pushed for the assessment or if recommended by a teacher. They found that a teacher recommendation was, by policy, based on a child's performance on one test and overall grade point measures. In further exploration, they found that data showed bias in economic status, ethnicity, and gender. A Chinese student was ten times more likely to be identified as gifted than a Latino student. Only 4 percent of all Latino and African American males were selected or recommended for the program. Affluent schools identified more students than schools that served children from lower socioeconomic homes. And at two of the affluent schools, they found significant gender imbalances, with a strong preference for boys over girls at one school and a strong preference for girls over boys at the other.

The inequities were glaring; Wendy and Joe knew they had to do something about it. They just didn't know what to do. So they decided to engage others in their Adaptive Action to create awareness about the data. They engaged others to help understand the data and to move into action to address the inequities.

So What?   When Joe shared the data with principals, they identified the same concerns and ramifications Wendy and he had already seen. The principals knew they had to change the process. They also knew they would not be able to do it without the support and engagement of the parents, staff, and community members who felt they had a stake in the viability and services of the program.

So the next step was to take the information to the school communities to get their input about what needed to be done. Together, Wendy and Joe decided he should present the information first, so that if people wanted to protest or complain, they would come to Wendy. She would be able to respond to their concerns, reinforcing Joe's message and showing there was unity of purpose about this issue. They scheduled several meetings where he presented the data clearly and unambiguously, responding to questions, explaining the problems, and asking for input about next steps and what should be done.

Because the system was so inequitable, and because any change would be extremely disruptive across the system, Wendy and Joe decided on a one-year moratorium on identification of new GATE students. No one would enter the program until a more equitable selection process was implemented.

They put together a task force, with representatives from across the district—staff, parents, and community members from each school. They set a monthly meeting schedule to carry out their charge to make recommendations about how to establish a more equitable system. The task force was given the option of recommending two processes. The only requirements were that both programs had to (1) transcend ethnicity, socioeconomic, and gender bias and (2) be fluid to allow for differences among students across the district. Central office made a commitment to implement one of the recommendations, as long as both of them fit the criteria.

The discussions of the task force went deep into the *So what?* of the question. Their initial exploration focused on finding a shared definition of giftedness and creating a set of assumptions about the program. Meeting minutes were posted online, and halfway through the process task force members went into the community to share their ideas and gather feedback and input into the process.

After meeting for several months, the task force sent forward two recommendations meeting the associated criteria. The task force members presented their report to the school board, explaining their information, describing their process of decision making, and expressing their belief in and support for the final decisions.

Members of the task force believed either process would ensure equity and decrease subjectivity, and they were committed to supporting whichever plan the district decided to implement. Ultimately the district chose the one that was more popular with the task force and began to map out the implementation plan.

Now What?   As the new process was shared across the system, Wendy expected to be inundated by conflict and disagreement about the change in procedure. What she found, however, was that the task force members dealt with the challenges. As a group, they were highly committed to the success of their recommendations and stood together to respond to questions and the impact of a change of this magnitude.

She and Joe did experience some challenges internally from principals as the program was first implemented. At a meeting with principals about their concerns, Wendy and Joe returned to conversations after the principals complained about the original policy, walking them through the task force's process and reminding them of their support and agreement at every step. Ultimately a major concern came out of the conversations. The new plan called for more documentation and constructs around the process, and principals did not have time or resources to put those procedures in place. Wendy and Joe took on that responsibility and made a commitment to support the principals in this new work by whatever means. They agreed to small shifts: providing support to the schools receiving the most requests, phasing in the process so not all grades were engaged at once, monitoring data to be sure the outcomes aligned with their intentions, and exploring any barriers that prevented that alignment.

Wendy's Conclusions

Through the interview, Wendy recognized that even though she was describing one large Adaptive Action process she had designed, they also went through several smaller iterations of Adaptive Action along the way. The cycle began with the two focusing on the issue of selection, moved into looking at the data carefully, and resulted in a realization that they had to do something. It was the first small Adaptive Action iteration. Getting the principals, staff, and community members to see the issue, own its implications, and decide to take action was another cycle. The task force itself conducted their work through a cycle of *What?*, *So what?*, and *Now what?* as they came to their recommendations. Even in the implementation, as challenges arose and new barriers emerged, she and Joe and the principals were intentional in their continued use of Adaptive Action to see the patterns in the system, understand where they were generating desirable outcomes and where they were not, and make decisions about how to shift those patterns toward a more equitable and flexible selection process for students to be placed in the GATE program.

Wendy knew from the beginning that she would have to change the program selection process, but this particular path wasn't all preplanned or organized. From the beginning, using Adaptive Action, she was comfortable knowing the solution was emergent and that shared commitment, data, and multiple voices in the process would generate patterns she hoped to see.

Wendy says that this experience has helped her see why this type of process works, and it helps her know that the messiness and confusion in the middle are just part of the emergent process. It helped her be more intentional in planning for something she knew she couldn't control and could go out of control very quickly. Because they were working in short cycles of *What?*, *So what?*, and *Now what?*, they were able to defuse fear, frustrations, and challenges as they emerged throughout the process.

Dynamical Leadership: Engaging Change

The Story of Kristine Quade

Over time, organizations establish patterns of identity and policy that sometimes get them stuck. Circumstances change faster than the patterns of performance, and people and teams find themselves stuck in the middle. The story that follows outlines a situation with a much different outcome. With help, the players were able to shift containers, differences, and exchanges to generate new and more successful patterns for their products, their organizational structure, and their client relationships.

Kristine Quade has been an Associate of HSD Institute since the first cohort was certified in the winter of 2003. She chose the training because of a growing awareness that more traditional models of change and organizational theory were just not flexible or creative enough to meet the demands of the twenty-first century. Besides that, traditional models no longer matched her experience as a seasoned and respected organization development specialist. She has, over time, continued to explore HSD and its applications and has co-authored, with Royce, two books using HSD principles. The first was a primer for leaders about HSD,[1] and the second used HSD concepts as the core framework for leaders who want to build adaptive capacity.[2]

Kristine reports that she has always looked at patterns in systems but didn't know how to—or even that she could—label or influence them intentionally. She knew intuitively that a system could be moved by understanding its patterns, but she had no theory base to support or inform her intuitions. It wasn't until she began to study HSD that she was able to name and use her intuitions intentionally to bring about organizational and personal change. Her experience with complex systems and unwieldy dynamics now had a framework to continue to build her perspective and skill in providing leadership in change. This is the adaptive capacity she relied on as she worked with a client who was looking for new strategies in product development and marketing.

What?   Kristine entered a consulting relationship with a second-generation, family-owned manufacturing firm that found itself in a difficult position. As a third-party producer of other companies' products, their business consisted of taking clients' product ideas and designing creative ways to take the product to market. Through recent strategic planning, the company had decided to expand its revenue base by marketing one product it had developed and patented on its own but had never placed on the market.

During a strategic planning session, the members of the leadership team explored how their own patented product would compete with products they developed for their clients. Having made a commitment not to compete with their clients, the leaders felt they could not pursue the product and were reconsidering their original decision to enter this additional line of development activity. They were stuck. Kristine knew they needed a new perspective to explore options for action in response to their current challenges.

Kristine realized this system was reinforcing its own difficult position by focusing solely on the pros and cons of launching a proprietary product, rather than seeking other options for action. She worked with them to formulate their guiding question: "How can we honor our commitment to noncompetition and launch our own products without directly competing with our clients?" She engaged with them to look for an answer to that question.

To expand their current thinking, she encouraged management to engage the employees in creating other options for action. They called for volunteers and put in place a process for exploration that included no incentives or rewards. One team, calling itself the Innovators, formed to look for alternative packaging for the company's patented product. The team members were asked to explore the market and identify how to make their idea generate revenue for the company. This team explored several nontraditional markets, including the "green" industry, to identify a previously untapped market that could be penetrated with only a small investment.

A second Innovators team chose to examine the presence of the company in the external market and make recommendations for increasing or enhancing that presence. This team realized the company did not fully articulate the power of what it had to offer clients. Team members realized they were taking a high-stakes position in their report, essentially saying the current branding and marketing approach was not effective. After collecting data and images that represented a more accurate picture of the company's offerings, this team created a fast-paced, highly engaging video. They used powerful words and images to explain to potential customers how the company could and would meet their needs. On the day of their presentation to the top management group, team members were anxious about how their message would be heard. As the video ended and the screen went dark, the CEO stood and congratulated them publicly, saying this team was doing exactly what needed to be done. In the following days and weeks, that management team took significant steps to bring about an immediate change in the organization's strategy for branding and marketing.

Members of another team labeled themselves the Explorers and committed to surveying trends outside their own industry to identify new ways to serve their customers on the near horizon. Guided by their own question, "What should our customers be asking of their customers to understand external market potentials?" they looked at issues as diverse as outsourcing, social media, social causes, and potential population shifts. They gathered massive amounts of data and created a lively, information-rich sound-bite-type video, using fast music and flashing pictures to portray how the manufacturing and marketing world was changing. When they showed their video to the leadership team, several were moved to tears, amazed at the work of the Explorers and moved by their message.

So What?   After the team presentations, Kristine asked the leadership team to make meaning of all they had learned from this experiment in exploration and innovation. They recognized that they were most surprised and pleased with the out-of-the-box thinking the teams displayed, and they wanted to know how to support that level of involvement. Although these leaders were accustomed to reacting to and being creative in dealing with clients' new ideas, exploring innovative avenues for their own internally generated ideas was a new experience.

They learned that their employees could respond unexpectedly when asked. They also learned they had been locked inside their own traditional roles, at the same time that their employees had so effectively stepped outside of established roles and expectations.

The conversations during this strategic planning process helped them look at their own work differently and examine how they were operating as a leadership team. Kristine used this planning process to help everyone understand they were a part of a complex system subject to emergent patterns from inside and outside the organization. The message was that in large, high-dimensional, open systems, it is important for leaders to engage in ongoing conversation, learn from the past, explore today's impact, and consider tomorrow's possibilities. This Adaptive Action could help an organization leverage its own uncertainty.

Now What?   As they evaluated the process, the leadership team articulated how they had grown: "Given the patterns we found, what do we increase, reduce, eliminate, and/or create to extend those patterns into the future?" With this question in mind, the leadership team created an action plan.

They recognized and celebrated their company's ability to build value and relationship with the customer. They decided to raise awareness, expertise, and technology for building valued customer relationships. They began to identify measures to refine their processes and reduce overall costs to the organization by reducing time-to-market and clearing confusion in the process.

They chose to reduce distractions, deciding to eliminate a few undesirable accounts that didn't lead them forward in their focus.

They recognized a need to understand the market from a broader perspective and connect more effectively to their customers.

They began to increase their focus by picking one product at a time for exploring options for development and marketing.

Kristine helped them move beyond their current mind-set, by creating a "picture" of their strategy: a twenty-foot-long storyboard that articulated these bold actions to move into the future. They posted the storyboard for all to see, and teams were encouraged to reflect on its message as a shared vision—and to honor the teams' courageous actions.

Finally Kristine helped her client understand the role of a dynamical leader: to remain in tune with emerging and complex patterns and approach every new situation using Adaptive Action.

Kristine's Conclusion

After the work with this client, Kristine moved into a reflective mode to think about what she learned and how this experience might help to shape her work in the future. In her own *So what?* reflection, she articulated some basic foundations about her work.

She observed that clients usually present the easiest problem they want solved. She encourages them to seek alternative paths to discover what they don't know or to listen for unlikely sources of input and reflection. As Kristine enters new relationships with her clients, she interviews executives and key stakeholders. She asks the same questions of all and looks for patterns that indicate the how the team may be aligned or misaligned.

Her experience has been that the greatest opportunities present themselves when she begins to unravel the points of difference in their responses. This is where she begins to facilitate team growth and development through asking provocative questions about changing their approaches and looking at their worlds differently.

As Kristine works with a client, she uses Adaptive Action, moving them through the steps, helping them begin to see new possibilities. They may take unexpected turns, which can be delightful, but continuous cycles of adaptive responses help them understand what they need and where they want to be. Provocative questions help them find their next path.

For Kristine, an experienced and knowledgeable consultant, the most successful contracts are those that engage the clients in iterative cycles of inquiry, helping them identify a range of discovery and choices. She has learned that, through Adaptive Action, clients can clarify what they want, identify and engage in creative options for action, and articulate their own rationale for their actions. This level of adaptive capacity is her goal in working with leadership teams in any type of organization.

Simple Rules for Self: Adapting to a Changing Life

The Story of Mallary Tytel

Individuals can be stuck in the middle of uncertainty just as surely as their organizations and communities can. In this story, Adaptive Action opens unusual and satisfying paths for a gifted consultant.

Mallary Tytel is a longtime HSD Associate, having completed the certification as a member of the third cohort in 2004. Like Kristine, she has remained closely aligned with the institute, continuing to learn and apply HSD in her work. In 2010, she coauthored a book with Royce about using HSD principles to generate more productive and satisfying personal life patterns.[3] In it they talk about using Adaptive Action to bring about personal transformation, a process Mallary knew from firsthand experience. In the interview, she shared her personal story of transformation.

What?   Mallary has a broad range of skills. In her career, she has worked successfully as an evaluator, researcher, executive coach, and CEO. Her work experiences have taken her into the military, board rooms, nonprofits, and service organizations. In the late 1990s, she was recruited to take over and turn around an international nonprofit organization that was in severe trouble. She remained in the position, even after the organization made the shift toward success and viability. She and her staff were accomplishing good work and doing what needed to be done, when the attack on the Twin Towers occurred. The economy of their business sector shifted significantly, causing them to rethink their business model. A decision was made to divide and sell the company, and she was given the option of pursuing opportunities with the successor organizations.

It was a time of change, and Mallary decided to step back and review her options. In the first possible scenario, once the acquisitions were complete she had a chance to pursue a new direction in the business. In her second option, she knew she could take a similar position with another organization. As her third option, she could start her own business. She had, in fact, been considering the third option somewhat offhandedly for some time.

Fortunately for her, at that time she had the freedom and flexibility to look at what she wanted to do and the idea of working independently appealed to her more and more. Ultimately she decided to strike out on her own and start a consulting and coaching business. She was committed to supporting other CEOs and leaders as they developed organizations to support individuals' health—psychologically, professionally, and physically. Toward that end, she launched Healthy Workplaces, her own consulting and executive coaching business. It was around that time that she learned about Adaptive Action and used the cycle to reinforce her decision and support her planning as she moved ahead with her next steps.

Over the first months in her new business, Mallary developed a base of business and was doing well, generating relationships with clients across the country. Her success in this business, however, had unintended consequences. Her husband, retired from his career, wanted to travel. At the same time, she was traveling more and more, serving fewer and fewer clients locally, gaining more clients in distant cities and states. She traveled several days every month, often moving through client visits in a number of cities in one trip. That was the *What?* that described their life at that point.

So What?   As she and her husband looked at the amount of time she was on the road and in airports, they realized she could base her work anywhere; all she needed was to be close to an international airport. There was no reason for them to be tied to their country home in New England. This discovery led to their shared *So what?* relative to the needs and opportunities of their lifestyle.

Now What?   This next round of *Now what?* was launched when Mallary's husband, Stephen, proposed that they sell their home and all their possessions, and start a new life on the road in a motor home. After talking about other options and the ramifications of such a move, they did just that. They went through the accumulations of their lifetime, selling or donating most of it and putting what was left into a 100-square-foot storage space. Mallary and Stephen purchased a thirty-eight-foot motor home, moved into it with their two German shepherds, and set off on the road. They opened a continuous cycle of Adaptive Actions as they acclimated themselves to a new and quite different lifestyle.

Ongoing Adaptive Actions

Mallary continued working, maintaining her virtual office on the road in their RV, using her cell phone and Internet to stay connected to clients. She and Stephen planned their travels so that she had easy access to an airport when she needed to meet face-to-face with clients. She would fly out, leaving him and the dogs settled in a local campground until her return. When they were ready to move, they would start the engine and be on their way to the next stop in their journey.

This arrangement was one they enjoyed, traveling across the northern part of the country in the summer, moving to the south as the weather got colder, and settling in Arizona for the winter months. They were comfortable in this routine and were creating this new life that pleased and surprised them both.

Even with all the planning they had done for contingencies on the road, they found that new challenges and opportunities constantly invited them to step into new Adaptive Actions.

For example, it was time to rethink their plan when the economy fell apart in the fall of 2008. Their lifestyle allowed them to reevaluate their position and their choices for the future, so there were always alternatives to explore. They looked at the *What?* that considered the new economy and the skyrocketing price of gas. This forced them to admit the *So what?* that they were less willing to spend their summers on the move when it was so expensive and the future was even more unpredictable than it had been. Another part of this *So what?* discovery was that they were not finished with their explorations and wanted to find a way to continue their travels. In researching their options, they devised a *Now what?* that challenged them in many ways. In the summer of 2010, they made a decision to try out "workamping." They found public and private parks where they could take on seasonal jobs in exchange for the cost of living onsite through the summer months. This arrangement allowed them the adventure of living in nature without the added expenses of life on the road, but it also put them in work situations and experiences that were new to them.

Mallary and Stephen engaged in other rounds of Adaptive Action, as they realized how the road didn't support all the things they wanted and needed in life. Looking at the stages of their lives and the demands of the road, they recognized the challenge of having to be sure they were in a safe environment, with access to community supports in case one of them became ill or needed care. The remote nature of some of the places they wanted to visit made it more difficult to get to and from as she flew out to see clients.

Over time and through multiple cycles of Adaptive Action, Mallary has been much more proactive and selective about her work assignments, considering carefully the implications of travel, time away from home, and her expanding professional interests. Sometimes the shifts she makes in her work have to do with the job-related travel, sometimes they are about specific work requirements, and sometimes they are about her family and how she can balance all parts of her life. Every new question brings her to a new Adaptive Action and opens new options for this lifestyle adventure she and Stephen have taken on.

Mallary's Conclusion

Mallary recognized that her Adaptive Actions are sometimes intentional, and sometimes more intuitive. It's hard for her to separate the two, and quite often she finds herself pushing to get to the *Now what?* before she has really explored the meaning and perspectives of the *So what?* At those times, she has to slow herself down to deal with the continued search and the multiple options that emerge. For example, several times a year she receives calls from recruiters working on an assignment to find a senior-level executive. Sometimes she simply says she is not interested; sometimes she stops and thinks about the options and tradeoffs in giving up a life on the road and her own business for the stability and consistency of a "real" job in a house that stays put.

At other times, she gets so engaged with examining the options that she has to stop and make a decision. Very occasionally, when an intriguing position comes along, she will even go on a job interview, collect references, and become a finalist before she realizes what she truly wants. It is at those moments, however, when her bias for action pushes her toward the *Now what?*

Mallary recognizes that her career path has been a bit more unpredictable, unorthodox, and adventurous than most. She knows that her life path in last the five years has also been outside what might be considered normal expectations. She also owns that she cannot predict what might emerge in the coming months. What she does recognize is the value and elegance in the simplicity of the three questions of Adaptive Action.

Chapter Conclusion

In a tradition-bound institution like public education, in a family-owned business, and in personal decision making and life path planning, the old finite game, the command-and-control paradigm, locks people into patterns, even when the patterns no longer fit the purpose. Adaptive Action offers new ways to break out of obsolete patterns because it helps us see, understand, and influence the dynamics of the systems where we live and work. By engaging in iterative cycles that helped them explore and make meaning of their local environments, Adaptive Action helped Wendy, Kristine, and Mallary take action in the face of uncertainty and turbulence in the systems where they live and work.

WORKING AS A SOCIAL ACT

From our understanding of complex adaptive systems and how they influence people, we observe that individual understanding and emotional states also self-organize. Relationships self-organize between and among individuals. Teams go through many stages as they self-organize. Therapeutic environments self-organize as client and therapist come to know each other and build a productive relationship. Educational programs and the communities that inform them self-organize as information is shared, expanded, and passed on to others in the community. Leadership strategies for individuals and groups self-organize as talk becomes action and brings about change. In all these places and all these ways, Adaptive Action informs the processes and products of emergent change. The three simple Adaptive Action questions establish a rigorous and powerful framework for inquiry that reaches past uncertainty, engages with the real world, and leads to real action. This bottom-up process draws information and energy from the smaller parts of the system to inform the whole and the greater whole.

Our conception of self-organizing systems, however, involves an additional and very powerful set of relationships. Self-organizing processes influence patterns that are both within and beyond the agents of the system at the same time that those same patterns influence action and forces inside and even beyond the immediate system. Individuals, relationships, teams, programs, communities, and strategies all emerge from interactions of their parts. At the same time, they constrain the degree of freedom of the parts and set the conditions for the patterns that emerge within them.

These simultaneous top-down and bottom-up processes are essential to setting conditions for change in a complex adaptive system, but they are difficult to describe in popular language of change. Even before we found ways to describe it, we experienced influence from both directions in every walk of life.

The stories in this chapter focus on the intersections of organizing forces from below and above. They introduce many ways in which social and societal patterns shape individual and group behavior, but they also reinforce how behaviors of the parts shape the behavior of the whole.

Productive Groups: The Self-Organizing Team

The Story of Paul Reeves and Vickie Gray

As Larry and Denise shared in their story in Chapter 8, it can be helpful to think of adult learning as a self-organizing process for designers as well as for students. The power of the insight is even greater when instructional design takes into account self-organizing patterns of social interaction. As collaboration and teamwork weave themselves more deeply into ways of working in the twenty-first century, we experience an urgent need to develop the adaptive capacity of teams and communities as well as individual performers.

In the following story, Paul and Vickie share their own teaching experience of how complex adaptive social dynamics influence individual learning, group development, emergent instructional design, and group facilitation. Change in one sparks change in others, and Paul and Vickie see a more complex and coherent whole emerge before their eyes.

Paul Reeves and Vickie Gray are experts in using experiential learning to build high-performing teams. By immersing people in simulation activities, they build adaptive capacity for individuals and groups. They invite participants into a retreat setting to "design, implement, and deliver a course that teaches you everything you need to know to ship great products on time, every time." For the session, they provide a manual containing everything that other groups have learned over the past fifteen years as they accomplished the same goal. Throughout the session, Vickie and Paul observe. When they are asked, they help the team members use the learning of earlier teams at the same time that they help participants develop new useful tools.

In their interview, Vickie and Paul talked about what the founders of this approach, Jim and Michele McCarthy, and other instructor/facilitators have found. When team members engage in authentic work to develop a product, the powerful underlying dynamics of the team's interactions emerge. In action, those dynamics can be seen more clearly than interviews or group talk can reveal. The practice is to immerse the team in the collected rules and tools, support them in their own work, and then observe and coach as the team achieves its objective. Over the time they have been doing this work, Vickie and Paul have worked with many teams in many settings. They have been consistently successful in achieving their goals of building autonomy and high performance in teams.

Paul and Vickie had been doing this work together for many years when they came to the HSD Professional certification training in 2010. They attended the session with the intention of strengthening their practice by understanding the HSD perspective of underlying dynamics of team interactions. They wanted to use that perspective as a theory base to understand their work and enhance their approach in the future. As they plan for their team development sessions, Vickie and Paul now have a deeper understanding of the dynamics of the groups and of their roles as facilitators, instructors, and coaches.

First, they recognize that the prior learnings of other teams set initial conditions for the team members to be successful. Then, their role is to amplify the team members' strategies that work to move the group effectively toward its goal. They also know they have an opportunity to help the group restrict strategies that don't work or are less productive. Ultimately they recognize that they take action in response to the needs and experiences they observe and know to be emerging in the team, but they step in only when they are asked for help. They remain in a stance of inquiry, continuously observing and seeking to understand the needs, motivations, and understandings of the participants to inform how they respond to requests for help.

The story they shared was one of their first experiences after participating in the certification course, and they were very intentional in using the language, models, and methods they had learned from HSD. For them, their first Adaptive Action cycle came as they considered the conditions that make every session successful. They asked themselves the questions that guide the cycle.

What?   Paul and Vickie find the CDE model very instructive. If some members have been through the experience before and know what to expect, they form their own container, and these more experienced participants often do not wish to interfere as new participants discover things for themselves. Another container tends to form around groups of participants who work together regularly and believe they already have good teamwork practices. Paul and Vickie considered these dynamics as they reviewed information about the participants in preparation for upcoming session.

So What?   From experience, Paul and Vickie knew that participants who have
been through the training once tend to hold back because they want the newcomers to have the full experience. At the same time, the experienced participants bring whatever they learned the first time and try to carry this through
the subsequent experience. They also know that when people who have been
through the experience before come with people who haven't, there is a difference in the possibilities they imagine. New people are more constrained in
what they target as outcomes, while the experienced people know the outcomes
are going to be more awesome than the newcomers can imagine. Finally, as a
part of their *So what?* thinking, Vickie and Paul reminded themselves to be
prepared for constrained exchanges between the two groups of experienced
and inexperienced students.

Now What?   Over the years of development of this team-building process,
simple rules have emerged that are designed to support participants in dealing
with some of the pitfalls and challenges that are common to the teams. Accord-
ingly it is critical to share these simple rules as part of the pre-reading before
the session.

It is also standard practice to engage the experienced attendees as a separate container so they can be role models to inspire practice and comfort for
the new participants. Finally, Paul and Vickie planned to rely on their own
expertise and experience, bolstered by their knowledge of HSD principles, to
take informed Adaptive Action in the midst of the session if adaptation became necessary.

So the opening day arrived, and the group gathered to begin their shared
experience. As the hosts of the session, Vickie and Paul explained the tasks,
established the expectations at the highest level, and then put the participants
to work, explaining that they would step in only as they were asked to provide assistance and answer questions. As they observed and interacted across
the remainder of the session they were able to use Adaptive Action and other
models of HSD to see and influence patterns in the group.

What? in Action

Observations from the beginning of the exercise revealed that the team was
not using all the resources at its disposal. The team members were working in
various individual groups, ignoring the diversity and possible contributions
of the whole team. Just as Vickie and Paul had anticipated, two containers

emerged along the lines of experience and inexperience. These containers separated and worked in relative independence from one another. As a result, neither group of participants was getting the help it needed from the other. The newer participants were struggling with the initial stages of their work, and the experienced participants were not benefiting from the insights and creativity of the newer group.

So What? in Action

As Vickie and Paul reflected on what they were seeing, they recognized a common occurrence: this team was limiting its own greatness. As a group, individual members of the team were not as joyfully engaged as Vickie and Paul had observed in other groups; they were struggling far more than necessary. Additionally, the team as a whole was less agile and diverse. It was not as able to adapt because there were fewer ideas on the table, less connection to the work and to each other, and less engagement of all toward the commonly shared goal.

Vickie and Paul knew from experience, and from the HSD insight, that the connections across containers make "the magic" happen. When the group connects across significant differences and diversity, they become a great team. Vickie and Paul also recognized that emergent exchanges—or the absence of exchanges—are specific to the differences among and between the participants. In this case, the difference of experience was contributing to nonproductive patterns.

Though it contributed to negative patterns, in this situation the separation of the two containers also served a positive purpose. It enabled the experienced attendees to consider how to use what they had learned in their previous experience. They knew how painful, challenging, and exciting the learning journey could be, and they were open to trying measures to protect the new learners from feeling inferior.

In their first session, the experienced participants had already learned many tools to help them connect strongly with others. Those tools established powerful connections among all participants to nurture the collective creativity, interdependence, and decision making that moved the whole group to a higher level of functioning. They were missing opportunities to role model and contribute to the experiences of the new participants because they were not rigorously using the tools they had learned the first time around. Paul and Vickie observed and understood this pattern.

On the other hand, the inexperienced participants were assuming the people with experience were doing everything right. Those who had been through the session before seemed so busy and appeared to be so unapproachable, the newcomers tried not to get in their way. They withheld questions and suggestions to keep from bothering the others. Rather than interrupting the experienced group, the newcomers went only to Paul and Vickie to ask for help. Avoiding the trap of suboptimizing the learning process, Paul and Vickie asked that they request help from the experienced participants also.

In their work, Paul and Vickie were familiar with this emergence of patterns that appear to serve one purpose while actually causing trouble in the system. In their HSD learning, they came to understand that this phenomenon causes trouble because it optimizes the parts, rather than contributing to the success of the whole. They knew from experience that if they influenced the system toward different behaviors, those patterns were more likely to shift. Using the models and methods of HSD, they could identify ways to instigate radically different behaviors among the participants.

Now What? in Action

Vickie and Paul wanted the participants to generate more ideas, and they knew that new ideas would emerge only if the boundary between the containers was breached. They considered their options and decided to have the experienced participants be more welcoming of the new participants. They explained that this was a way of turning the old expectations inside out, making it clear that the experienced person's role was not just to teach but to welcome the new team members. Each of them was to engage with new people in their activities and to seek to assist them particularly through demonstrating how to use the tools.

This request interrupted the experienced group's desire to work alone. It helped them realize they were looking for a comfort zone, one solidly based on their earlier experience. They wanted to recreate that space and play there, assuming the other team would catch up with them eventually. Rather than waiting for their colleagues, they chose to move at their own speed, not realizing that the lack of exchange was an obstacle to the success of the whole team. It would be impossible for the new group to find its way through the process because they were on their own path, emerging out of different experiences of the same conditions.

Vickie and Paul set a challenge for the experienced attendees, who understood the rules. Their job was to get the new people to help them. When experienced participants become directive and try to teach new participants what they should do, the newcomers resist. To counteract this tendency, Paul and Vickie asked the experienced group to move toward and learn from the new group. They were to ask the new participant's questions about what they were doing, how they were using the tools, and what could be learned. The goal was to amplify the interactions between the two groups and damp the isolation across the boundary.

The result of this *Now what?* strategy caused some shifts in dynamics at first as the new people wondered what had happened. After a brief adaptation, the team took off and began to function at a higher level, moving clearly and directly toward the shared goals and desired outcomes.

Paul's and Vickie's Conclusion

In their role of setting the conditions for the teams to move toward successful learning, Paul and Vickie observe and offer options for action only when requested. Their suggestions may be more or less directive, depending on the needs of the group. As observers, they ask *What?* questions to identify patterns that are strong enough to influence the overall performance of the group. They reflect on the *So what?* and make meaning of the patterns they select. Options for action emerge from their analysis of the current conditions. Of all the possible patterns they observe, they choose those that promise greatest leverage for the *Now what?* step of Adaptive Acton. In that step, they identify options for action that are coherent with their own simple rules, details of the situation, and protocols for the established training process.

Paul and Vickie recognize that as trained observers they are more likely to see the whole system in ways that participants cannot. Because they see more, they can identify tools and be ready with suggestions that help the participants step back to see the whole. Then, as they see the whole, participants ask for help more insightfully and move themselves forward at an exponential rate.

The greatest clashes occur when participants engage across different expectations regarding *What?* they should work on. When these clashes happen, the participants are encouraged to come to Vickie and Paul for help. By focusing on the purpose of the group as the *So what?* of the Adaptive Action, Vickie and Paul help identify the differences that make a difference as they clarify their areas of focus. Participants are encouraged to ask each other for help; they are reminded to stand in inquiry as they strengthen their connections to each other and to the charge at hand. Vickie and Paul have found that their participants "fall" into the various behaviors accidentally as they try their own solutions. They also realize that if the participants step into inquiry and interdependence intentionally, they reap more benefits, and reap them sooner.

Paul and Vickie believe in their approach, and they see how the theory and practice of HSD through Adaptive Action has strengthened their understanding and ability to generate options for action for themselves as instructors and for their students as team members. They know their process always works. And now they realize it works because it is consistent with HSD principles. They use Adaptive Action to set initial conditions, let the team self-organize, and then encourage or discourage patterns in response to the team's emerging needs and challenges. The language of HSD and the discipline of the Adaptive Action help them work together more effectively and efficiently to see, understand, and influence what is going on.

Generative Engagements: Beyond Cultural Sensitivity

The Story of Mary Nations and Royce Holladay

HSD Associates choose to focus on some of the most sticky issues of our time. Chronic disease, collaborative work, emergent learning, school reform, and personal life changes—all of these are places where our culture is stuck, or will be stuck, in the middle of uncertainty. HSD Associates are committed to using Adaptive Action and other HSD models and methods to work through barriers to get individuals, teams, companies, and communities to move through and beyond their uncertainty. One of the most intractable issues of society today is bias. Racism, ageism, nationalism, and sexism generate all kinds of destructive social dynamics and distort healthy self-organizing patterns. In the next story, Royce Holladay and Mary Nations apply the CDE Model in the context of Adaptive Action to create a new theory and practice to inform diversity training.

Mary Nations is a consultant with an ongoing interest in the differences that make a difference when people are together. Steeped in formal and informal experiences in diversity and inclusion work, she has trained individuals and groups in institutions across multiple sectors. She was also instrumental in the strategic development of an internet radio show called Diversity

Matters, dedicated to exploring diversity and inclusion issues. Having less formal training in diversity issues, Royce nevertheless has been committed to working on diversity and equity in school districts and other organizations throughout her career.

In working with people from a variety of situations and perspectives, despite best efforts and practices both Mary and Royce perceived that the training they received and training they provided fell short of what was needed to fight workplace and institutional bias. Traditional approaches to these issues, though successful in some individual situations, still did not or could not furnish what people needed to bring about meaningful and lasting change in their lives and workplaces. They believed that earlier models established a strong foundation on which they could construct a broader approach to creating inclusive cultures.

What?   Mary knew many equity and inclusion approaches; Royce had a more limited repertoire. What they realized about the models they shared in their own work was that most of them did a good job of describing the patterns of "-isms" across the culture. Along with the descriptions of bigotry and prejudice, programs approached diversity by reinforcing the need to live and work together productively. These approaches attempted to help people respect each other and accept differences. Other programs focused on those differences, explaining cultural and social differences, increasing understanding between groups even when cultural backgrounds might be vastly different.

The programs Mary and Royce offered were well received by participants, and people generally engaged with the ideas enthusiastically. Mary received high marks for her knowledge and sensitivity in presentations; Royce got positive feedback about her work in this area as well. People professed new insights and learning as a result of their training. Both Royce and Mary were successful at what they did, but they both wondered if they were doing the right thing.

Mary and Royce still had the sense that what they offered was incomplete. Although people talked about how they were changed, they returned to workplaces and communities that were rife with bigotry, even at the institutional or cultural level. In those environments, many were unable to make translations of the descriptive language about cultural awareness into real applications. What participants learned seemed to increase their understanding of diversity and inform their personal awareness, but too often it fell short of helping them reach out to others to transcend differences that divided them.

When she attended the HSD certification program in the spring and summer of 2007, Mary saw a theory base that could build on the strengths of her mentors in the field of diversity and inclusion work. The HSD models and methods offered some new answers to the questions that challenged her work. She and Royce joined forces to see how HSD-inspired models and methods could transform diversity training into what it needed to be: a radically different approach that led to generative engagement and inclusive action across all differences.

Through their HSD training, Mary and Royce learned about seeing, understanding, and influencing patterns. They also learned to see racism and the other forms of prejudice as societal patterns, particular ways in which groups of people connect across similarities and differences. Through HSD, they found a theory base that helped to explain, rather than merely describe, the emergence of patterns of bigotry in social systems. Whether those patterns emerged from well-known issues such as race, age, sexual orientation, or religion, or whether they grew from subtler differences such as regional, political, or social differences, the dynamics of bigotry were always same. Mary and Royce found a way to talk about how bias emerged from conditions of the most basic interactions between individuals and among groups. The Eoyang CDE model gave Mary and Royce a theory base to understand the conditions that shaped emerging patterns. In addition, it contributed to even deeper understandings of many traditional approaches to diversity and inclusion.

Using the CDE, they saw that some formal approaches to diversity and equity focused on containers, pointing out that people who work and live together are in shared containers and need to work across differences that divide them. Some other types of diversity training described differences that were critical separators among people, defining multiple containers and explaining the major differences that made individual patterns unique. Each of these approaches talked about exchanges, how to interact with others in light of issues related to the containers or differences.

Most traditional diversity models pointed out that the exchanges needed to be transformed; they even described what needed to change. What they did not do, however, was explain how to reshape the cruel and exclusionary exchanges that characterize bias in the complex patterns of community. Earlier writers and developers of equity approaches did not know how to translate their descriptions of patterns into options for action, but Adaptive Action provided a path for Royce and Mary.

Armed with these insights, Mary and Royce engaged in an exploration of meaning making and learning. They wanted to see what would emerge if they considered bigotry from the foundational vantage point of HSD. Could they use HSD to inform new habits of exchange and as a result set conditions to transform the patterns of bias in social systems?

So What?   Using the CDE model, Mary and Royce talked about the conditions—containers, differences, and exchanges—that would generate patterns of greater understanding and respect for difference. They realized that what they really wanted was to help people engage to open up relationships to the possibility of growth, renewal, and mutual learning. To reflect this intention, they selected Generative Engagement as the name for the new form of relationship they hoped to encourage through their writing and teaching.

From their reading and knowledge of equity and inclusion literature, they explored how to identify conditions that might shape generative engagements. Toward that end, they began to create a midlevel abstraction of the CDE to name the specific container, differences, and exchanges they believed would be most helpful to inform action toward inclusion and generative engagement (Figure 10.1).

Mary and Royce realized that many traditional equity and diversity models described the need for people to build stronger understanding of others in spite of their differences. Phrases like "walk a mile in another's shoes" or "see the world through my eyes" are means of inviting people to stand together in a shared container. They reasoned that people standing together, identifying with each other's perspectives, would be more likely to engage with each other in generative ways. The container in their mid-level abstraction became "Identity."

The literature was clear that power imbalances lay at the heart of bias and bigotry. For their purposes, Royce and Mary defined *power* as the ability to influence or the willingness to be influenced. From past learning and experience, they saw bigotry and bias as the result of individuals who believe they are immune or isolated from the needs or concerns of others. When people see themselves as more important or more deserving than others, they use their power in the system to influence and shape the fabric of the social culture. Bigotry, defined from this frame, is the result of power imbalances that perpetuate this pattern. They chose "Power" as the difference that mattered in their midlevel abstraction.

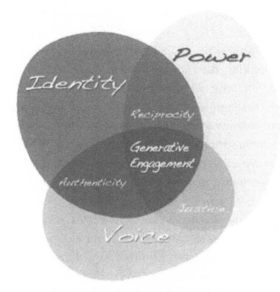

FIGURE 10.1. Generative Engagement.

Three conditions shape patterns associated with generative engagements. If we
make the choice to share identity, balance power, and grant and generate voice,
we are more likely to create patterns of reciprocity, authenticity, and justice.

Mary and Royce then turned to the third condition, exchange. Knowing
that exchanges are how energy, time, information, and other resources are
shared across the system, they considered the kinds of exchanges that would
support generative engagements. They chose to characterize those types of
exchanges across a system by describing them as "Voice." Granting or generating voice is about how people engage in exchanges that show honor and respect. People grant and generate voice in speaking and listening to each other,
in acting and observing each other, and in giving to each other and receiving
what is given.

After they identified the conditions of generative engagements as identity, power, and voice, Mary and Royce named a set of patterns that could
emerge from interactions that set those conditions. Over a series of conversations, they narrowed them to three basic patterns that would characterize the
openness, honesty, and fairness of situations that were free of bias or bigotry.
Considering the midlevel abstraction they developed, they asked how those
conditions might influence each other in real-life interactions. If people stand
together with shared identity and are willing to share power in that space,

Mary and Royce believed, those interactions would result in patterns that were characterized by reciprocity. Mary and Royce hypothesized that when people stood together in a shared identity, granting and generating voice together, the resulting patterns would be reflective of authenticity. Finally, when people grant and generate voice in ways that are open to influence, justice will likely be the dominant characteristic of the emergent patterns. Mary and Royce shared their ideas concerning the patterns with others, using feedback and input to refine their descriptions and insights about the patterns that constitute generative engagements: reciprocity, authenticity, and justice.

As they continued to get feedback and refine their picture of generative engagements, they realized conditions for moving toward or away from generative engagements are shaped at every point of choice in a relationship. In each moment, individuals choose, by the actions they take, to move toward generative engagements or away from them. They also recognized that these conditions can be set at multiple scales in a system. Individuals in friendships, families, teams, and organizations have the ability to set these conditions as they engage with each other. Organizations and communities can use the conditions of generative engagements to inform policies that govern individual interactions as well as how individuals are treated within those entities.

As their work began to settle into a coherent picture of a midlevel abstraction, they turned their attention to the next steps of deciding what to do with their model.

Now What?   Mary and Royce continue to learn and engage others in finding new meaning and understandings about generative engagement, even as they move forward to share in the greater environment. They return to Adaptive Action as they learn more and refine the model and as they think about how they want to share their model in the wider world, developing classes and workshops, engaging with others in various media venues, and in their consulting and coaching work. Additionally they find means to weave generative engagements into their work across a variety of fields and audiences to create broader interest in this work they believe in so strongly.

Mary's and Royce's Conclusion

Both Mary and Royce recognize the challenge of sharing a new approach in a field that is so solidly established in today's culture, and they are committed to showing the utmost respect and honor for those who have worked so hard for so many years to address issues of inequality and exclusion. They continue to expand their understanding of the power of generative engagements, and see them as the critical factor in building a culture of inclusion, understanding, and innovation.

They believe these ideas have implications for teaching and learning, and that generative engagements can be useful in helping individuals navigate the differences that divide them to avoid the eruption of violent conflict. And they know it will take time for people to come to understand, accept, and begin to incorporate the idea of generative engagements in moment-by-moment interactions to create powerful patterns that transcend bias and bigotry. Ultimately individually and as a team, Mary and Royce recognize that Adaptive Action will be the most effective method of finding their way and making a path for generative engagements to become the norm that informs relationships at all scales of interaction.

The Inside Game: Public Policy Advocacy Tomorrow

The Story of Ilir Zherka

One of the most powerful aspects of human systems dynamics in general, and of Adaptive Action in particular, is that the theory and practice are scalable. The preceding stories have demonstrated how Adaptive Action informs individual life changes, relationships, teamwork, institutional policy and procedure, and organizational strategy. The next story addresses an even larger scale: political discourse and public policy debate.

At the time he was interviewed for this book, Ilir Zherka was the executive director of DC Vote, a political advocacy group whose purpose was to gain full democracy and statehood for Americans who live in Washington, DC. As a career political operative, he has supported presidential campaigns, represented groups as a lobbyist, and led organizations that work for civil rights and political equity. When he came to HSD certification in 2010, he declared he had finally found a language and theory base that matched his own intuitions and practices.

As the leader of DC Vote, he established practices and expectations to help his staff adapt. In such a highly charged political environment and with such a high-profile mission, DC Vote must be adaptive to survive. As a result Ilir has come to see his leadership role as setting the conditions for adaptation and building adaptive capacity in his staff. After attending the certification program, he made sure his staff was introduced to HSD models and methods, particularly Adaptive Action. He hoped to create a level of shared language and practice of adaptation on a conscious, intentional level across all their work.

What?   The political stance of DC Vote leans to the left, falling along liberal lines of social engagement and responsibility. As an organization, they gain greatest support from liberal legislators, but sometimes that support is quieter and subtler than they would wish it to be. At times they feel a need to speak strongly in their requests for more public support.

Over the years, DC Vote has had great success organizing and holding "protests" to call attention to issues that are important to them. When they see a need for action (*What?*), they consider all the dissonant voices grabbing for attention (*So what?*), and use targeted protests as a means to stand out from the noise (*Now what?*). At one point a group gathered and stood in protest while some of them took tea to the home of a member of Congress supported by the Tea Party, a conservative political action group. That activity garnered good press and impressed and encouraged DC Vote's allies in Congress.

Soon after that successful foray, Ilir and his team went to the office of a more liberal legislator, traditionally an ally in the DC Vote cause (*What?*). In recent campaigns, however, he had not supported some key positions that would have benefited DC Vote. Despite public perception of his stance, he was not always friendly to DC Vote (*So what?*). The team planned to launch a silent protest at the door of this legislator's office. They set the time, invited supporters, and arrived at the office door with a large banner that read, "Don't tread on Washington!" (*Now what?*).

Unfortunately the tactic was a dismal failure, so the Adaptive Action process began again. Many people showed up to protest, but there was no representation from the press. Additionally there was no response from that particular legislator's office; he totally ignored their protest and public statement. Ilir and his team were frustrated and engaged in an Adaptive Action to evaluate their work and identify how they had failed (*What?*).

So What?   As they began the *So what?* step of this Adaptive Action, they reviewed their planning and activities. They had decided to pose the second event because the first had been so successful. Remembering the success, they were less attentive to details that would have created a greater scene. Through their analysis in this *So what?* step, Ilir and his staff realized they skipped the

So What? step of their initial planning. Their observation during *What?* and success of earlier action tricked them out of doing new and more meaningful analysis and planning. They realized that, given a more thorough process in support of *So what?* they might have realized the need for more than just silent presence. When they planned the first event, they created tension and exposed a conflict, but in the second one they did not. As a result, the second protest just didn't have the juicy impact of the first one. It simply didn't make as much difference to anyone because they were targeting an ally with a tactic of silent petitioning that did not reveal the underlying conflict created as the ally ignored the needs of DC in negotiations to gain his own political advantages.

As the team continued their debriefing activity, Ilir helped them realize that the second protest involved no real conflict. There was no "difference" to energize the self-organizing process. There was no "exchange" to ignite the conflict because no one had contacted the legislator's office to warn him of the protest. There was absolutely no response from the legislator. No response meant there was no conflict. No conflict meant there was no story. The team decided the event just was not "sexy" enough to capture the imagination of the press. There was no edge, no real drama to create a scene. It didn't set the conditions for a new and interesting pattern to emerge.

Now What?   As soon as Ilir's staff came to that conclusion, it was simple to identify what to do the next time they wanted to create a silent protest. They developed a plan of action for identifying the issues (D), contacting the target to generate some level of conflict or reaction (E), inviting people (C) who were passionate about the issue (D), and then, as drama was generated (D), they planned to contact the press (E) and amplify the pattern as it emerged.

The insights they gained in this Adaptive Action process led them to reconsider and enhance their plans for other events and actions designed to catch the attention of their constituents and the press.

Another Cycle

Ilir also shared a story about an event that was tied to another major piece of work. His team used Adaptive Action to frame and describe the issue they wanted to address in terms of their overall mission.

What About a Campaign for Sovereignty?   Recently, under Ilir's leadership the DC Vote movement was looking for a new voice, trying to bring in energy and gain some traction at the Capitol. Their former strategy had worked well for eight years, but they were realizing it was time to reexamine their approach because their current efforts were losing their impact.

The staff started by examining the long-term history of the democracy movement for the District of Columbia. Originally the movement started in 1801, when the city's government and sovereignty were dissolved. Over the years, a number of groups and movements had spoken out for fair representation and self-governance. The 1990s brought on the greatest challenge and lowest ebb of power for DC Vote and the movement it represented, when President Bill Clinton and the Congress set up a control board to govern the city.

It was also during the 1990s that efforts to resurrect the movement began. Realizing they needed to reframe their message, they chose a rallying cry that focused on "no taxation without representation." Not only did this approach shift away from the statehood challenges, its historical reference to the American Revolution had more power to stir the imaginations of potential supporters. This became the focus of the movement, as it exists now.

This *What?* existed when Ilir took the helm of DC Vote in 2002. The organization was struggling because, as Ilir realized after his HSD training, they had shifted the message but not the container. DC Vote staff members had continued to educate people and generate various solutions to choose from, but the challenge required a more complex solution. Ilir helped the staff realize that Congress was not going to take action without a concentrated campaign, so they needed to focus the Congress on specific legislation as the key container in this self-organizing process. The question for Ilir was how to start a national campaign and a legislative movement that was strategic and viable. To answer the question, he and his staff took inventory of their assets. They had their own passion and the support of some powerful national organizations and most of the Democratic Party. For Ilir and his staff, the next task had to be to make sense of what was possible, given this varied history, current situation, and list of assets.

So What About a Campaign for Sovereignty?   At the start of their *Now what?* step, Ilir and his staff and supporters asked themselves what the history and current situation meant in terms of a national campaign. For one thing, it meant they didn't have to educate the whole country; they could just look at the moderates in the middle and see who they could get from that list. This strategy shrank the target, changing the landscape of their campaign considerably. They also realized they didn't have to educate all Americans, or even the average Americans. This was a relief to Ilir and others, as their resources were limited. What they needed to do was to reach out to the top seven to ten senators to get their support and influence. This small number was all that would be needed to accumulate sixty senate votes to win the day.

They decided to reach out to certain groups in the states represented by those top senators. Ilir and staff contacted people they knew in various groups that might be sympathetic—civil and human rights groups, Common Cause, Unitarians, Jewish community action groups, certain fraternities and sororities, League of Women Voters—asking them to target specific senators and House representatives. Ilir referred to it as a campaign to engage both "the grass tops and the grass roots." Ilir also reached out to other organizations in the DC area whose missions were similar or at least coherent with the mission of DC Vote. With leaders from those other organizations, he formed a coalition to leverage the mutual support, power base, and energy of the whole.

Ilir and his staff knew they had defined a set of manageable containers and a viable approach to make their advocacy task more doable. The differences were captured in the slogan "No taxation without representation." The missing element was the exchange. They still lacked a legislative vehicle for instigating the change. Their struggle then was whether to maintain education as their primary means of exchange or shift it to advocacy. They had to get clear about an "ask" that was different from what DC Vote had asked for in the past. In addition, the coalition partners were questioning how they benefited from partnership with DC Vote. They also wondered what would be expected of them in the future. On top of that, the commitment to statehood had cost the support of some powerful Democrats.

For Ilir, this all meant DC Vote would need to give others something affirmative to embrace. So they moved away from statehood to look for another beginning point for a campaign. He embraced a suggestion made by a political friend.

The suggestion was to leverage demographic changes in the state of Utah to DC Vote's advantage. Representatives from Utah thought they were entitled to another congressional seat because of changes in their state's population. One problem was that adding one legislator would create an even number of representatives, but by law the number has to be odd. Utah would be more likely to win its case if they brought forth a plan to add two seats (one for Utah, one for DC) and retain an odd number in the House. The DC Vote strategy was to have two groups that felt aggrieved—Utah and DC Vote—join forces and accomplish the goals of both at the same time. The political calculus of the day meant that this proposal would be vote-neutral in the House overall, as it would probably add one liberal representative and one conservative representative to the overall political balance. Both DC Vote and Utah would get what they wanted while minimizing resistance all around.

Now What About a Campaign for Sovereignty?   Finally, Ilir and his staff felt they had a targeted campaign and vehicle to get the bipartisan support they needed. They mapped out a full-blown strategy to advocate for this change across two or three congressional sessions. These strategies reflected a major shift in their targets and campaigning, and they engaged in multiple small Adaptive Actions over time as they continued to learn from earlier activities and experiences. In 2009–10 DC Vote and its constituents were on the cusp of victory, with many sources of support and with a commitment by House and Senate to move early in the process and get the support they needed to ensure representation.

Then an unexpected difference arose to make a difference. One senator attached an amendment to the DC Vote bill that would eliminate DC's gun safety laws. As a result, liberals who would otherwise have supported the bill found themselves unable to support it. This move drew a total of twenty-two votes away from the DC Vote cause and destined it to failure. It was a poison pill, designed to force proponents of the bill to go against it. The senator had wanted to break DC Vote, and the leader of the Democrats wanted to increase the number of his colleagues who would vote for gun rights. The DC Vote movement did not really care that the outcome was more about the National Rifle Association. They were disappointed and hurt and angry.

Ilir and his staff knew they had to step into the next *What?* step of Adaptive Action to regroup and begin to redefine their next campaign. In making meaning of their experience, at the end of the campaign they realized they were not defeated by the people they had expected to be the greatest challenge. They had to recognize that their defeat came at the hands of the friends who deserted them on the basis of factors beyond their control. Ilir is convinced that without moving intentionally through the Adaptive Action cycles, they might not have realized this in such a powerful and empowering way.

The fact that friends could desert them so easily led DC Vote to understand that the movement's cost-to-benefit ratio was not high enough to get and hold the votes it needed. To secure bipartisan support out in the states, they would require more direct engagement and more protest activities. This change will shift the container by putting more pressure on the allies, making failure a greater threat to them and their interests.

Finally, Ilir and his team identified a more powerful platform and a more aggressive mechanism to involve Americans at higher levels of government. They recognized the opportunity to examine the underlying social and economic crisis in DC and expose it to the rest of the country. Revealing the city's struggle may help gain support across the country. Toward that end, the team created a new series of strategies, among them the standing protests described earlier. So, the next cycle of Adaptive Action begins.

Ilir's Conclusion

Over the years he directed DC Vote, Ilir and his staff were called on to respond and adapt to issues and challenges unfolding around them. Some changes have been triggered by their own actions and decisions. Some have been triggered by political and social forces that swirl around their work. Over time they have had to adjust language, clarify positions, and shift the focus of their actions to continue to move toward the goal that draws them forward.

When asked what it is that changed for them when they learned about Adaptive Action, Ilir responded that several long-held perspectives about their work had changed. He realized their long-term planning process would need to shift to allow shorter-term planning in iterative cycles of Adaptive Action. They have set broad parameters for two-year cycles, with aspirational goals that guide shorter-term increments. Ilir described how he and his staff have changed their thinking about planning. It has taken on greater significance for them. Before understanding the iterative and powerful impact of Adaptive Action, planning for the long run had held less meaning in their day-to-day decisions and activities.

The strong focus on learning in the *So what?* step has allowed them to be much more mindful about understanding the implications of their actions for their individual and group work, for DC Vote as an organization, and for them as a team of individuals. This planning and self-awareness at the organizational level has changed how Ilir and his team explain themselves and their work to each other, as well as how they present themselves to current and potential funders. Ilir and his staff believe they are able to shape an approach to their work that is much more vibrant and appropriate to the real world, with its chaos and unpredictability.

Understanding themselves as a complex adaptive system has helped them clarify their conversations with donors. During a recession, it is more difficult than ever to draw on the resources that are constrained by a struggling economy. Investors want to see the light at the end of the tunnel. This might have led to a shorter-term approach to planning and developing campaigns, but DC Vote no longer falls into that trap. Without a long-term legislative plan, they talk to funders about their capacity to adapt to the dynamics of the legislative landscape. Their examples and stories help the donors see the opportunity to own a winning campaign and be part of the bold, adaptive, and creative responses as change emerges from day to day and week to week.

Given their understandings now, Ilir and his staff have been able to describe and articulate their vision so their funders and coalition partners can accept and value it, given the current state of affairs in DC. Descriptions of how they adapt by creating or finding opportunities resonate with people.

Ilir is convinced that learning about HSD, and in particular about Adaptive Action, has saved their organization, and the movement. Using the models and methods of HSD, they have created a place to stand. He considers Adaptive Action as a necessary approach, given the rough-and-tumble, uncertain world of politics.

Since their devastating defeat in 2010, they are using Adaptive Action to regroup and see what they need to do now. This is particularly important, given the political changes and partisanship that now shadow the landscape of their work. Ilir and the staff used Adaptive Action to talk about their strengths and challenges as individuals and as a team. At the time of the interview, they continue to test adaptive strategies as they focus on the next twelve months out rather than two years.

Ilir and his staff use the Adaptive Action questions internally, even going so far as to have the Adaptive Action graphic printed on posters that hang in their offices. He has also used the model with his board of directors, and he introduced it in strategic planning with his coalition partners. He is currently engaged in writing a book about his experiences, using Adaptive Action to talk about how public political advocacy needs to change if it is to be a viable factor in shaping the future.[1] And so the next Adaptive Action cycle begins.

Chapter Conclusion

Work is a social act, whether at the individual, group, community, or global level. Humans make decisions and take actions that generate patterns of inter-action and behavior. Human systems are open to influence as individuals bring their own Decision Maps to interactions in a landscape that enables influences from the whole, part, and greater whole. They are high-dimension, as each in-dividual, group, or community brings its own rich diversity to play in the social and political relationships that move them forward. Finally, humans and their systems learn from today to shape tomorrow's Adaptive Actions. Whether their work is formal or informal, intuitive or intentional, they engage in the same questions: *What?*, *So what?*, and *Now what?*

PART III

NOW WHAT WILL YOU DO?

Adaptive Action is all about seeing patterns, understanding their dynamics, making sense, and taking action to shift toward greater productivity and coherence. We hope our passion for action has ignited your own, and that you are ready to make meaning of complexity in your own organization. This section provides a kind of guidebook to help you and your teams begin your own Adaptive Action cycles.

11

GAPS REVISITED

As the stories of our Associates show, Adaptive Action is a powerful way to explore new challenges as we build capacity; to identify options for moving forward in complex change; and to understand, name, and influence patterns of human interaction. These stories were told by individuals who have been Associates for several years, or only for a short time. They were told by people working alone and in teams and groups. The stories told of Adaptive Action as a guide for theory building, decision making, and action.

These nine stories represent only a slice of the multiple ways HSD is used by Associates at all scales, across business sectors and communities, and in support of a range of disciplines around the world. What we see in our own work and in the stories of our Associates is a growing capacity to play well in the infinite and uncertain game that is the social, economic, and political reality of the twenty-first century.

Adaptive Action Challenges in the Twenty-First Century

Our Associates talk with us about having been overwhelmed by uncertainty, and how HSD and Adaptive Action help them get unstuck as they contend with forces they cannot predict or control, in a landscape that shifts constantly. In the opening chapter, we posed a set of questions to describe the current condition of living and working in the twenty-first century. Let us return to them, now that you have seen Adaptive Action in practice, and explore just how Adaptive Action can help you think about these challenges anew, to make them less formidable—to help you get unstuck.

Economic foundations sit on quicksand of derived values and float on bubbles of speculation. Would it be possible to see, understand, and respond to economic turmoil in ways that reduced risk for ourselves and our organizations? Economic quicksand requires you to have enough data and information to form a comprehensive, if not complete, picture of today's patterns; to consider the data from many perspectives; to take action in the short run; and to reassess your next position quickly.

The *What?* step of Adaptive Action (as well as the short iterations of seeing, understanding, and acting) contributes to the possibility of agile response to unpredictable and risky economic situations. Of course, adaptive capacity is not enough. You also must have the ability to collect, analyze, and use data effectively, but without adaptive capacity you may not have an opportunity to use your other skills. Jerry Michalski leads a movement for what he calls Relationship Economy. Through his online salon, REXlab, Jerry and his colleagues imagine and implement a future economy that functions like a healthy complex adaptive system.[1]

Cultural and national loyalties shift too quickly or lock in too tightly for civil stability to be sustained. Might we see early signals of dissatisfaction so we could understand and influence the public discourse toward peaceful and productive dialogue? Cycles of Adaptive Action, coupled with the ability to see the conditions that shape patterns in self-organizing systems, contribute to deeper understanding of the underlying dynamics of the current social and political landscape. Because Adaptive Action invites you to see the patterns of interaction at deeper and more dynamical levels, you are able to explore beyond the symptoms of dissatisfaction or discontent, to see the underlying tensions and mechanisms that may be generating the public discourse. The Arab Spring did not emerge out of nothing in the spring and summer of 2011. Patterns of similarities, differences, and connections began shifting long before the public dissatisfaction disrupted. Some groups were able to see the shifting patterns and use them to forward their own agendas. The CDE Model and cycles of Adaptive Action can help individuals and groups discern and engage with patterns before they are obvious to others.

Technology moves from imagination to reality to obsolescence at breathtaking speed. Can we consumers, producers, suppliers, and service providers develop the capacity to keep up with the pace of technical change? Continuous and diverse cycles of *What?*, *So what?*, and *Now what?* help us to examine what's on the horizon from many perspectives. By considering multiple containers, diverse differences that make a difference, and connections that enliven change, we can respond quickly and adapt with agility when uncertainty distracts us, even in the short run. User groups and social networks provide both producers and consumers with details about the emergent patterns in the technology marketplace, but those messages are diffuse and change quickly. Adaptive Action and pattern-spotting tools help digest the data quickly and simply into actionable opportunities.

Massive, ubiquitous, and direct communications contribute to both intractable stability and incomprehensible disruption. Can we read the landscape and establish media and messages that support the patterns we choose to reinforce? Adaptive Action moves us through responsive cycles as we plan and take action in a manner that traditional planning does not allow. If we are constantly alert and collecting data about our clients' needs, our competitors' advantages, potential shifts in the landscape, and media opportunities, we can more carefully craft our messages to attune them to the audience. We can also shift those messages more quickly as we detect changes in the environment. The Obama campaign of 2008 relied on the adaptive capacity to craft, test, and revise their web and Twitter communications with lightning speed, ensuring that the message never got too far behind the electorate and their concerns.

Local climactic conditions change more quickly and more unpredictably than farmers, multinational corporations, or emergency services can manage to respond to. Can we collect data from around the world, consider it rationally and openly, and take collective action for the good of people and the planet? When we work in networks engaged in Adaptive Action, we can share the data we collect in our *What?* steps, make meaning together in the *So what?* steps, and learn together from the results of our actions in the *Now what?* steps. We increase the impact of understanding and action across multiple vistas. Farmers in the Andes work in some of the most climate-sensitive areas in the world. They move their fields up and down mountains, in continuous and traditional Adaptive Action, to accommodate changing conditions. What could they teach us about the speed and direction of change and options for sustainable response to climate variability?

These are some of the most intractable problems of our time. Adaptive Action alone will not solve them, but adaptive capacity can leverage our other capacities to increase options and decrease risk in open, high-dimension, nonlinear conditions of uncertainty. Adaptive Action can help us keep the infinite game in play.

Adaptive Action's Tips for Infinite Games

Each of these apparently intractable problems represents an infinite game. The rules of economic engagement continue to change as new and ever more creative ways of making, handling, and exploiting financial resources come into play. Boundary issues in today's world change too quickly, or they fail to shift as they need to, creating a volatile and unpredictable playing field where no one set of rules covers all questions. Ceaseless innovation in technology or any field makes a playbook obsolete as soon as it's written. You simply cannot create enough "perfect plays" to adjust to the multiple and unpredictable contingencies of innovation that moves at the speed of light. The game of understanding global climate challenges creates an unbounded playing field on a number of scales. In each of these situations that challenge us today, in each of the challenges described by the nine Associates' stories, in the many other stories we could not share here, Adaptive Action provides the flexibility and resilience needed to survive and thrive in an infinite game.

Across time in our own work and in the stories told by others, we have identified a set of tips and suggestions that contribute to increased success of Adaptive Action. The next three chapters share those suggestions, using examples from the Associates' stories. Chapter 12, "Lessons for *What?*" provides suggestions for how to see, value, and collect insights that are relevant and meaningful in the current challenge. Chapter 13, "Lessons for *So What?*" offers tips for making meaning from disparate pieces of data and using them to formulate a plan of action. Chapter 14, "Lessons for *Now What?*" features insights for effectively taking action to bring about complex change. Finally, Chapter 15, "Adaptive Innovation," reviews a number of business functions and how Adaptive Action can help them leverage uncertainty in today's organizational landscape.

12

LESSONS FOR *WHAT?*

The stories shared by our colleagues are powerful sources for learning about dynamics of the human systems where they live and work. We have found that, regardless of who tells us an HSD story, we continue to learn new insights about complex human systems. We see more clearly how individuals and groups adapt to the unique changes, challenges, and opportunities they encounter every day. The stories we shared here, in particular, offer a variety of insights about how these professionals use Adaptive Action to move their own practice forward. In their stories we see a number of lessons we have learned across time. What follows are lessons we've learned from the *What?* step of Adaptive Action.

- Start where you are.
- Dump your assumptions.
- Notice the patterns.
- Reveal the complexity in the tale.

Start Where You Are

In a self-organizing system, you must use the power of the present to reveal the patterns of the future. Starting where you are is not just the best way to practice the *What?* step of Adaptive Action in a complex system; it is the *only* way. You start where you are when you see and question the current conditions in your system, when you work with the networks of individuals and ideas connected to your current question, when you start with a thorough description of your situation and move toward deeper explanation. Wendy Gudalewicz's story of development of policy and procedure in her school district is a strong example of this lesson.

In mapping out a thorough process of exploration and development about reforming an inherently unfair practice in her district, Wendy took strategic actions that increased the chances of generating the patterns of inclusion and service to students. First, she helped others see and question the current conditions in the district. Without naming containers, differences, and exchanges, she made sure that people knew the dynamics of the system that currently existed. Wendy also ensured exchanges were rich and well informed by working with multiple networks connected with this issue in her district. Third, she made sure that stakeholders in the process had access to both descriptions of what existed as well as the explanation for what people saw and experienced.

When you start where you are, various features of the complex system become foregrounded. To accomplish this daunting task, you have to:

- See and question current conditions
- Work with networks
- Seek description and explanation

See and Question Current Conditions

What choices did Wendy have? No one can see everything, but she knew that this inquiry would be most efficient if they could focus on the conditions that generated the current process and their impact. During the *What?* step of their Adaptive Action, they collected this information and began to build a different future. She looked at current patterns around this issue and considered the conditions that had generated those patterns.

Wendy took the first step toward understanding those conditions by personally reviewing, and then taking a stand in support of, the board policy prohibiting bias (container). She engaged other district leaders and community members in conversations (exchanges) using the data about current processes, student representation in the gifted programs across schools, and student performance both inside the program and outside the program (differences that matter). Because she started where she was, Wendy and her colleagues were able to design a set of parameters around expectations that set the conditions for inclusion and fairness in the program.

Work with Networks

We generally think about a network as those individuals or groups with whom we have direct contact, but in a complex adaptive system, scale-free networks allow us to connect to and benefit from an even broader realm of research, insight, and creativity. In *Linked*, Albert-László Barabási[1] uses the internet, social networks, and interesting games of connection to help us understand how and at what point a network becomes scale-free, connecting widely diverse and distantly separated nodes to each other in a matter of a few links.

His description of the potential for powerful, distant connections across a broad and diverse network helps explain what we mean when we say that using your network is required if you are going to start where you are to move forward in Adaptive Action. When we try to understand new and unfamiliar phenomena in our landscapes, it is critical to seek a variety of sources to help make sense of what we see. Networks are made up of those closest to us who share the experience and are seeing the same data. They are also made up of friends of friends and distant neighbors who can share information and impressions about what we see. Our networks connect us as well to researchers and theorists who help us describe, name, explain, and understand our experiences.

In establishing the task force, Wendy recognized that the members had access to powerful networks with the capacity to design the best answer to the challenge. She relied on others in her professional network to inform and develop parameters according to the needs of the system. She also tapped into student and family networks to include their aspirations and knowledge about their children. Finally, she and others recognized the value of the network of research and practice related to gifted education programs across the country. For those reasons, Wendy made sure the task force was widely representative of students, parents, and educators. She helped the task force have at its disposal current districtwide data about students. She also confirmed that it had access to the most recent and compelling research about the topic.

Seek Description and Explanation

Because they knew that new information helps people step beyond their worldviews and previous assumptions, the leaders of the task force took time for members to make sense of the district's own data about the gifted programs. They explored patterns related to future options on the basis of a student's participation in certain classes in the middle and high school years. The task force looked at local and national trends and research that explored the issues at hand.

The information that came from data and research presented a clear description of the current state of gifted education in their district, but it didn't help provide any explanation about how they had gotten to that point or how to shift the program to allow more equitable participation across their district. That information, alone, could not inform action.

Wendy knew the task force required more than description to be able to design a process that would work in their district, so she furnished them with information about current activities and feedback from administrators and teachers as to why the current process emerged as it did. Wendy made it clear that resources—support, time, information, attention—would be shifted to ensure an effective, efficient selection process in support of full participation and representation in the gifted program across the district. She also worked with district leaders as the task force and individual administrators addressed deeper issues of stereotyping and expectations that came up with a fuller explanation of the local situation.

When all was said and done, Wendy was able to set the conditions to bring about significant change in the selection process and criteria for the middle school gifted program. She did it without major conflict or upheaval. She was able to do this because in the *What?* step of her Adaptive Action she mined the present for the raw materials to build the future. She started where she was.

When you deal with uncertainty in your organization, what is your current situation and how are you mining that information to understand and uncover the raw materials that will build a more sustainable future?

Dump Your Assumptions

Adaptive Action always begins and ends from a point of inquiry: open-ended questions that help us gather data and make meaning in the moment. It recognizes that previously held assumptions can get in the way of our ability to see and make sense of patterns of interaction that surround us.

Mallary Tytel has long recognized the need for questioning and eliminating assumptions that limit our vision. In fact, she has been faced with the reality of what it means to give up your assumptions in many areas of your life at the same time. After a full career as an evaluator, a consultant, a CEO, and professional coach, Mallary joined her husband to make a radical change in their lifestyle. As she explains in her story, this change required Mallary to dump a number of assumptions about what it is to live and work as a consultant from a stable home base, to live and grow old in a long-familiar location, and to hold onto a permanent structure that serves as a home base for grown children.

Her story helps us understand how assumptions influence the patterns in a CAS, how we must question our own assumptions, and how inquiry helps us move forward when we step away from the temptation to allow our assumptions to color our thinking.

To break the invisible boundaries of our own assumptions, we must:

- Consider others' assumptions
- Question your own assumptions
- Stand in inquiry

Consider Others' Assumptions

Assumptions prevent agents in the system from collecting data that might show them more of the whole picture. Without realizing it, we allow our assumptions to define and limit the questions we ask in our inquiry. As we live and work in a CAS, it's critical that we become conscious of and challenge commonly shared assumptions that help shape patterns of interaction and decision making for a group. Cultural norms, political stances, and social expectations are examples of individual and group assumptions manifesting as patterns that affect our uncertainty.

In Mallary's change of lifestyle, she had to shift her own assumptions about work and relationship, even as she responded to similar assumptions held by family, friends, colleagues, and clients across the country. She knew she would be influencing the patterns of interaction with these individuals and groups, and she wanted to escape the power of traditional assumptions about those relationships.

Question Your Own Assumptions

Every act of learning is a letting go. The most powerful and promising lessons, models, and methods ask the learner to challenge lifelong patterns of worldview, rules, and reality. Only then can the *What?* step of Adaptive Action reveal the most significant patterns emerging from complex environments and interactions.

After taking to the road, Mallary and Stephen responded individually to the many shifts of patterns they experienced. Over time, their Adaptive Action cycles led them to different conclusions and options for action, from moving south to buying a home, to joining "workamp."

At each point, as they made choices about where and how to live, they questioned the assumptions that influenced those decisions. They asked themselves what made sense. They reflected on why they preferred one particular response to any other. By constantly questioning their own assumptions, this adventurous couple sought and found the best fit between their needs and how they structured their life together.

Stand in Inquiry

Given the nature of complex systems (high-dimension, nonlinear, and open to multiple influences at multiple scales) there is no way to have one answer or established perspective that can serve well in every situation. Inquiry is not a process of gathering information to check against some arbitrarily established measure of what is "correct" in a system. Such measures come from assumptions about what is right and necessary in a CAS. Because there is no one combination of dimensionality, linearity, and openness that constitutes a "correct" system, systems (and solutions that work in systems) must continuously adjust to find "fitness" rather than "correctness."

Assumptions get in the way as we try to see the dimensions of our systems, understand patterns of interaction and decision making in our system, or know how we connect to each other across our systems. Mallary, along with her family, colleagues, and clients, remained in inquiry about their work together as they shifted assumptions from expectations of traditional working relationships to reestablish or sustain patterns that represented the best fit for their work together across evolving space and time.

> How might your own assumptions be limiting your ability to see and act through uncertainty in your organization?
>
> How are you and your team, limiting your vision, making yourselves blind to potential opportunities and barriers that can enhance your options for action?

Notice the Patterns

The conditions for self-organizing are embedded in the pattern of a moment. The similarities in the pattern bring stability as change begins to emerge. The differences in the pattern introduce the tension and asymmetry that spark change. The connections build pathways for transformation over time. If you want to understand the most essential aspects of the present and potential for the future, focus on the patterns.

Paul Reeves and Vickie Gray engage groups and teams in experiential learning events aimed at helping each participant function more effectively and productively individually and in the context of the whole group. As the facilitators of complex group process, the pair are in constant cycles of Adaptive Action as they observe what's going on with the participants, make sense of the patterns they're seeing, and take steps to intervene by helping the participants encourage interactions that are working or discourage interactions that are less productive.

We find that these practices support pattern spotting in all systemic situations:

- Start with freeze frame.
- Focus on the tension.
- Find the conditions for self-organizing.

Start with Freeze Frame

We experience self-organizing processes as uninterrupted flow, but we take action at single points and at specific times. Any *What?* step in Adaptive Action must choose a point in an evolutionary process and explore the patterns that exist then and there. Both relevant history and future potential are embedded in the pattern of the present moment.

The training sessions Paul and Vickie run are highly interactive. The action never stops as people engage in the assignments they're given. The self-organizing continues, even when it has little or nothing to do with the assignment itself. In this quickly moving and complex situation, the pair find ways to capture "snapshots" so they can talk about what's happening to inform their action.

This is the only way they can hope to describe what's going on in a particular frame of time so participants are better able to make sense of their own experience in *So what?* and plan their next action in *Now what?* Paul and Vickie can apply any number of models and methods to help understand what's going on, but only if they stop the action long enough to see individual patterns of behavior and interaction. Coherent explanations and effective action would not be possible if the descriptions were just constant, streaming, blow-by-blow commentary on the course of the day's interaction. On the contrary, in-the-moment interventions have to be quick and efficient, or the opportunity for intervention dissolves before the action is taken.

Focus on the Tension

Because Paul and Vickie stop action to create snapshots of how people are working together, they are better able to see the tension in the patterns. Tension emerges from the differences inherent in any lively and productive complex adaptive human system. In one possible scenario, if there were not enough difference in the system, nothing would trigger a change; patterns could not or would not emerge. If a system is at rest because the agents are all too similar, there will be no natural tension. The facilitators can amplify a difference in the system to bring some tension to life. When Paul and Vickie see low tension in a system, they can introduce difference or focus on an existing difference to increase the tension to a point of creativity or exploration.

The second option is that there may be too much difference in the system. When the team members are too far apart in their goals or aspirations or approaches, they essentially break into multiple groups and stop functioning as a whole. There is no tension because the groups no longer interact. This is what Paul and Vickie saw early in their story when the experienced participants and the newcomers were operating as though separate from each other. In that case, they brought the two groups back together to focus on the common work of the team by having the experienced participants act as hosts and mentors to accomplish their shared task.

By contrast, high tension in a system can also have an impact on a system's functionality. Unresolved or unrecognized differences that prevent or limit the interactions of a system will stop it from creating productive exchanges. It is a delicate balance that Paul and Vickie help their teams maintain. They coach participants to find the most productive tensions and then teach them to use Adaptive Action to maintain the tension as the system shifts in response to challenges it encounters.

Paul and Vickie can, by analyzing a pattern in a point of time, see the individual conditions that generate that pattern. Where the tension inside the pattern limits the system's fitness, they know this is a possible point of entry and intervention. They cannot predict the consequences of their actions, but their sensitivity to patterns and emerging tensions helps inform their choices.

Find the Conditions for Self-Organization

When Paul and Vickie see a level of tension that prevents functionality, they look at the conditions that give rise to those patterns. They ask themselves a variety of questions to see the conditions clearly. What containers hold exchanges across specific differences? What are the differences they see that have a significant impact on the functioning of the system, and what is the container that holds those differences? What exchanges connect the parts of the system such that those differences become important? What reward or feedback mechanisms has the team established that hold certain patterns in place? What prevents the team from adapting its patterns as the conditions shift? The tension in the system emerges from the interaction of the conditions. CDE analysis helps to name and describe those tensions in such a way as to point out explanations and options for action.

What are the patterns that make uncertainty intractable in your organization?

What are the tensions inherent in those patterns that hold them tightly in place?

What patterns would be more productive, and how can you establish the conditions that will help to generate them?

Reveal the Complexity in the Tale

At its fullest and most complete, a response to *What?* must include multiple kinds of data that reveal the many truths of complex systems. Quantitative data can reveal the objective and normative truths, while qualitative descriptions uncover both normative and subjective truths. The only way to come to the complex truth is to collect and analyze both.

Larry and Brenda each came to their writing partnership with deep and thorough understanding of the principles of TQM, Lean, and Six Sigma. They both worked with organizations to implement and refine programs using those principles. Between them, they were steeped in quantitative methods to track improvement over time. That knowledge had contributed to their successful careers.

In their experiences with TQM, Lean, and Six Sigma, neither believed that numbers told the whole story for their clients. For them, tales told by numbers represented only a portion of the full story about their clients' experiences in attempting to implement process improvement programs, and problems emerged when people tried to bring about change with only a portion of the story.

To complete their *What?* step, they (1) use both numbers and words to complete the picture, and (2) learn from stories.

Use Both Numbers and Words to Complete the Picture

A deep dive into Adaptive Action helped Brenda and Larry realize why their clients' struggles continued, even after declaring full implementation of Lean or Six Sigma programs. They realized that the stories told by numbers were true, but incomplete. The two of them talked to people, listening to the power of their words as individuals described experiences during and after the program implementation. Brenda and Larry realized that telling the whole story of process improvement programs required both numbers and words. So they worked together to author the book that says just that to the world. Their book tells their story about integrating numbers and words into a powerful *What?* step of Adaptive Action.

Learn from Stories

At the same time, Brenda and Larry shared stories that counted on both the numbers and the words to paint a picture of what they faced when they entered consulting relationships. Brenda worked with an engineering team created to help "fix" the numbers, which only got better as they learned to consider the words of their internal clients as well. Larry told of helping his clients go beyond blind faith in one specific program to understand the power of a fuller, more people-focused process.

In both stories, Brenda and Larry did their up-front work as consultants, engaging in the *What?* step of their own Adaptive Actions, as they told the story of the numbers and then as they revealed the story of the words from people involved in each organization. They knew that stories explore the open, high-dimension, and nonlinear relationships that emerge from real experiences in the real world. Stories were necessary to understand fully the dynamics they wanted to show their clients. They also knew that data alone are insufficient and that the best integration of insight happens in the real-life stories of the people who are living out the experience.

> What words will take you beyond just the numbers to reveal insights lurking in your organization's uncertainty?
>
> What stories do your own colleagues tell?
>
> What is your story that will help to create the most powerful *What?* and move you toward greater understanding and more powerful options for action?

Chapter Conclusion

What? is the step of Adaptive Action that asks us to inquire about the world around us. We have explored how some of our Associates engage in *What?* We have shared with you the lessons we saw again in the processes and questions that inspired their Adaptive Actions.

Questions are foundations for growth when we stand in inquiry. We rely on questions to gather the information we need to make good decisions. We rely on our questions to see the networks where we live and work, so that we can then understand and influence them. Questions help us identify and understand the conditions that give rise to the patterns in our lives. We come to understand both the words and the numbers by how we structure our inquiries and as we learn from the stories around us.

Asking the right question can help us abandon old assumptions that have ceased to be useful. They help us start right where we are without having to hear, yet again, about history that keeps us stuck. Finally, the right kinds of questions stop the action long enough for us to learn from the past, take action in the present, and prepare for the future. They help us find the points of leverage and tension in the system as we notice and examine the patterns we use to inform and shape our Adaptive Actions today and across time.

13

LESSONS FOR *SO WHAT?*

Engaging in the *So what?* step of the Adaptive Action cycle helps us make meaning of the data and information we collect during the *What?* In this step, we examine information to formulate possible options for action that move us toward adaptation and fitness in our environment. The descriptions and stories of the current situation are assessed in terms of the conditions they set for self-organizing. As the most relevant containers, differences, and exchanges are recognized and named, they begin to hint at options for effective action.

Associates who shared their stories with us for this book offer powerful reinforcements for the lessons we have learned for *So what?*

- Share the exploration.
- Visit the extreme edges.
- Find what fits.

Share the Exploration

As we pointed out in Chapter 3, the *What?* step of Adaptive Action depends on diverse points of view and a variety of insights because the purpose is to explore the widest possible range of reasonable interpretations. Raw material for this step comes from yourself and others; from near and far; from evidence of subjective, normative, and objective truths. Whether you are working in a static, dynamic, or dynamical change process, you are more likely to capture the fullness of the open, high-dimension, nonlinear reality that shapes your patterns if you include more, and different, perspectives in your analysis. "Share the exploration" is all about connecting with others who can help you see and gather information about the patterns that inform your Adaptive Action. It contains specific suggestions for how to include others effectively:

- Do it in dialogue and inquiry.
- Nurture generative relationships.
- Ask useful questions.
- Document, document, document.

Do It in Dialogue and Inquiry

As Janice Ryan developed an innovative and highly effective way to address the needs of Alzheimer's patients, she did not strike out on her own or just make it up as she went along. In her research and in practice, she relied on her own observations and hunches, even as she learned from and with colleagues. She also went to the literature to understand more about the physiology and neurology of the disease. She worked with other practitioners to understand current practice.

In building her theory and refining her practice, Janice stood in inquiry, engaging others in open-ended, but focused, dialogue. She relied on her HSD network to understand and name the complex dynamics she observed. She relied on her students to gather and help her interpret the data as they engaged in their own Adaptive Actions to design therapeutic spaces for patients.

In HSD we see dialogue as a way of engaging others in a group inquiry. In high-dimension, nonlinear, open systems, where inquiry is the stance that allows us to see and understand our environment, dialogue is the shared conversation that allows us to explore the environment with others. When we stand in inquiry with those around us, we benefit from their experiences, learn from their reading and theory building, and create a richer tapestry of understanding of the challenges we face. Many emerging facilitation and organization development practices support group inquiry and analysis. Art of Hosting,[1] Open Space,[2] Future Search,[3] and World Café[4] are some of the most popular methods to set conditions for shared inquiry. For more information about these and other dialogue methods, refer to *The Handbook of Large Group Methods: Creating Systemic Change in Organizations and Communities*[5] or *The Change Handbook: The Definitive Resource on Today's Best Methods for Engaging Whole Systems.*[6] However you go about it, this step of Adaptive Action will be much richer and more effective if you include more committed voices.

Nurture Generative Relationships

As we engage in dialogue to share ideas and learn together, it is important to use the STAR diagram to engage in generative dialogue. Paying attention to similarities and differences, engaging in authentic work, and sharing a common reason or goal for working together all contribute to effective inquiry in the *So what?* step of Adaptive Action. But most crucial is the requirement that we balance the second arm of the STAR: talking and listening.

When we engage in dialogue, it is an open conversation where we listen to each other as much as we speak. We seek to understand possible interpretations others bring to the data, and we listen to others' ideas for action options to move us toward adaptation. Taking a stance of inquiry does not just mean that we are open to what we see in the data, it also means that we are curious about others' perceptions and questions, listening to them as they share so that we may learn from them. We seek to know their questions and their answers, their barriers and their opportunities, their impressions and insights.

Ask Useful Questions

Standing in inquiry in the *So what?* step of Adaptive Action does not mean that we simply take in all the information and data that come to us. It means that we sort and categorize, select and discard data until we make meaning of the whole. We don't just ask questions for the sake of asking questions. We don't ask questions merely to reinforce the patterns we expect to see. We ask questions that help us make sense, and leverage the context, of today's environment and today's needs.

Earlier we suggested a series of "pattern spotting" questions. We use these questions in HSD to help us see patterns in the data. We need questions that help us generalize information to multiple areas of our lives, and other questions that reveal exceptions to those generalizations. We have to look for contradictions in the data, as well as surprises we didn't expect. Finally we define the questions that continue to puzzle us as we pose our next Adaptive Action cycle.

Janice asked many questions, in multiple forms, to help focus her exploration as she sought new insights to expand her understanding of Alzheimer's disease and possible treatment options for her patients. Useful questions are what helped her narrow her focus, even as she explored the edges of possibility around her challenge.

Document, Document, Document

"If it's not written down, it didn't happen." This phrase rings true across fields of endeavor and exploration. Documentation of what we see, understand, and consider true in a CAS is the only way to create the snapshot in time that captures today's experience. In systems that change drastically and quickly, documentation is the only way to be sure we remember and track patterns across time.

Documentation may be in written words, pictures, or snapshots that capture the instant. It may be a multimedia presentation that evokes meaning. It may be simple rules or the stories we tell each other. It is the documentation of today that we use to move into the possibilities and solutions for tomorrow.

In her work, Janice trains her students to observe and document stories gathered from observation and interaction with patients and their families. She asks them to create documentation in standard formats to convey meaning wherever people research or treat Alzheimer's disease. She uses videotapes of patients to prepare students to see, understand, and influence patterns of environment and behavior.

> How do you engage others to share exploration of uncertainty in your own organization?
>
> What questions do you ask, and of whom?
>
> Do you remain open to new interpretations and perspectives as you make meaning of what you see?
>
> How do you document the insights and understandings and actions that emerge for you?

Visit the Extreme Edges

Adaptive Action is an automatic habit with most people, but it is not always an effective habit. When you work with situations you think you understand, it is easy to skip the *So what?* step of the cycle and rely on your "ever and always" explanations. Complex adaptive systems, especially in times of dynamical change, demand more than that. Extraordinary times require extraordinary responses, and you will never find extraordinary in the middle of the pack. It exists only at the edges—beyond the tried and true.

"Visit the extreme edges" calls us to explore beyond the bounds of the familiar to find what is at the cutting edge of new thinking and questions that emerge around a challenge. As we visit those extreme edges, we stretch our thinking to free our minds and reach for creative and innovative meaning in the data and information we have. It covers a range of actions:

- Challenge general wisdom.
- Use multiple models.
- Look across scales.

Challenge General Wisdom

Denise Easton and Larry Solow built a partnership by challenging each other's assumptions about setting the conditions for learning and working in complexity. As their story explains, these two professionals spent many months pursuing elusive points of shared interest to identify similarities and differences that drove the quality of their individual work. They took the time to examine what they knew and how they applied that body of knowledge in their respective current practices. They were, as they explained, totally intentional about using Adaptive Action. Their discipline called for deep reflection about where they stood in the *So what?* step of their shared inquiry.

Larry and Denise began their work together by posing questions about their interest in adult learning and working in complex systems. What had they always been taught about adult learning? What had they learned by being instructors for adult learners? What had their experiences taught them about engaging adults productively and informatively? When they considered those questions against what they learned about HSD and complex change, Denise and Larry came to understand learning as a self-organizing process of a complex adaptive system. To embrace this new understanding, they had to step away from some long-held assumptions about the nature of learning and work. At this edge, they found innovative opportunities.

Use Multiple Models

Just as they do in the *What?* step of Adaptive Action, assumptions and "general wisdom" around our questions can blind us to seeing anew. Larry's and Denise's assumptions kept them tied to old paradigms that see learning as linear. They understood learning as static change, where the teacher provides information for learners to absorb (or not) in the process of teaching. Traditional teaching models kept them tied to a paradigm of learning as a predictable arc of developmental steps that can be traced for each learner. Neither of these assumptions describes the reality of learning as ongoing, dynamical adaptation and response. So Larry and Denise asked themselves about a model to represent the dynamical interaction among adults as they set conditions for patterns of understanding and action to change in complex systems beyond the classroom.

Denise and Larry looked more openly and realistically at the raw materials from their experiences and considered their observations through the HSD lens. They built a scaffold toward a new paradigm by developing multiple models to represent adult experience and learning. As this scaffold grew, they gained more confidence to step even farther away from the old assumptions and practices. New iterations of their work helped them refine their model of adult experience and learning. Every step opened their eyes and minds to seeing new meaning as they moved toward action in the *Now what?* step of their work.

Look Across Scales

Complex adaptive systems are connected across scales. An issue or question can take its meaning from action and experience at the individual level, from the shared experiences of a team, and from corporate- or organizational-level impacts. In human systems this phenomenon ensures coherence across all scales, from individual to community.

Knowing the nature of complex adaptive systems, Larry and Denise looked to see what they could discern about adult learning and interaction at different scales in a system. They looked at individual coaching and teaching, at how larger groups share and take in information, and how policy sets the conditions for learning in an organization. They also tested their own emerging models against those various levels.

"Look across scales" in the meaning making of the *So what?* step asks that we explore our questions at all levels across the system to see how they manifest on the various scales of interaction and decision making. We generate new options for action when we understand and look for opportunities in the whole, the part, and the greater whole.

> How are you getting at the extreme edges to make sense of the existing and emergent patterns in your organizational uncertainty?

> How are you exploring and incorporating new ideas and surprises into your perspectives?

> How does your emergent reality influence or how is it influenced by multiple scales of your system?

Find What Fits

In the same way that you look for tensions in *What?* you look for ways to re-solve those tensions in *So what?* Tensions are resolved when the parts of a sys-tem fit well together. In a complex adaptive system, two separate agents may be so different that they do not fit well together, or two patterns can clash in an obvious misfit. On the other hand, a shift in a system can establish conditions (container, difference, or exchange) that increase the fit, decrease the tension, and establish a more productive pattern. During the *So what?* step of Adaptive Action, you are looking for the strategies that will increase fit in the system as a whole.

Mary and Royce looked for a path to increase fitness between and among groups and individuals separated by difference. They recognized that patterns of bias and exclusion are based in system differences and that those patterns limit a system's ability to respond and adapt. As their story reflects, finding the best fit is not a simple process. Over the years, we have discovered many ways to find a fix that fits. We have some recommendations to help you seek what fits in the *So what?* of Adaptive Action:

- Go beyond description.
- Look past your first explanation.
- Attend to the whole, the part, and the greater whole.

Go Beyond Description

One of the limitations Mary and Royce saw in traditional approaches to di-versity training was the tendency of those models to describe differences that separate and interactions that were manifestations of bias around those differ-ences. These models created vivid descriptions to inform people about their own actions and helped them to see bias at multiple levels of interaction. They also gave suggestions about how to use those descriptions in varying situations to guide action. On the other hand, those models did not explain the condi-tions in a system that give rise to patterns of bias and exclusion. They could not inform the moment-by-moment decision making to influence the conditions that generate patterns of acceptance and inclusion. They focused on the differ-ence, rather than on the search for patterns of best fit.

The coauthors needed to explain the emergence of patterns and help people shape conditions to foster inclusive, equitable patterns in moment-by-moment interactions. Description of the bigoted patterns was not enough.

They used the CDE model to explain possible conditions that generate bias and exclusion; then they looked at possible conditions that might generate acceptance and inclusion. Both were useful explanations for understanding their own experiences and for influencing the experiences of others.

Look Past Your First Explanation

Their Generative Engagement model was designed to offer one explanation of the conditions that give rise to interactions that help people adapt toward fitness across their differences. The development of that model took time, as Mary and Royce looked at their experiences and knowledge through the lens of HSD in the *So what?* step of Adaptive Action. They searched for explanations of possible conditions of bias, explored ideas about possible conditions for inclusion, and searched for explanations of those conditions at different scales of interaction in a system. At each stage, their explanations continued to grow richer and more useful. In high-dimension, nonlinear, open systems, explanations are most effective when they are complex enough to answer a particular question fully, but simple enough to apply to other, related questions. Explanations that try to account for every possible contingency become too complicated to be useful, but simple explanations that reflect essential patterns apply equally to the general and to every particular. Mary and Royce continued to examine their model to find the simplest ways to see and explain what they saw.

Attend to the Whole, the Part, and the Greater Whole

Human systems are open to influences at multiple scales. Mary and Royce recognized that when individuals or teams attend training sessions about bias and exclusion, they represent a part of the system where they work. Change on one scale can affect local patterns, but it is difficult to sustain a single-level change in pattern. How can individuals behave without bias if their teams and families continue patterns of bias and prejudice? How can teams or families change their patterns if the communities and organizations of which they are a part don't change the policies and expectations that set the conditions for those patterns to emerge? Even knowing that individual and local action is the basis for systemwide change, understanding patterns across scales informs decision making to enhance both local and systemwide efforts.

As they moved from their *So what?* questions and began to explore *Now what?* challenges, Mary and Royce recognized the need to communicate these principles to address the needs of the whole, the part, and the greater whole in any system.

How are you describing the uncertainty in your organization? And what are the sources of your explanations about why that description is so?

What questions are you asking that help you understand the dynamics of human interaction that give rise to the patterns you see?

What is the impact of those patterns at various scales, and what can you learn about the dynamics by observing them at all those levels?

Chapter Conclusion

Meaning making in the *So what?* step of Adaptive Action helps us understand the context of the systems where we live and work. We examine the data collected in the *What?* step to help us explain the phenomenon of patterns and conditions we see. We bring together research and practice, theory and experience, and our stories and others' to make meaning of our worlds in the *So what?* step. We begin to formulate options for action to be taken in the *Now what?* step. The process may take days or months, or it may turn in the moment, and its gift to us is a greater understanding of our world and a way to base our next action on a reasoned and reasonable set of assumptions that emerge as we:

- Share the exploration
- Visit the extreme edges
- Find what fits

These lessons for action then guide us as we move into the *Now what?* step and engage with our questions as they help us leverage the uncertainty in our organizations.

14

LESSONS FOR *NOW WHAT?*

In Adaptive Action the *Now what?* step is a time of taking action, assessing impact, and moving on to the next question in your ongoing inquiry. It's both an ending and a beginning, as you carry out the action steps of one cycle and begin to collect data for the next cycle. The next cycle may, in fact, be the next logical extension of the current question, or it may shift the focus to another facet of the challenge. Whichever choice you make, the seeds of the next iteration come from the *Now what?* step of the current Adaptive Action.

Over time, we have identified three critical tips for moving into a successful *Now what?*

- Have a plan and hold it lightly.
- Just do it.
- Begin again.

Our Associates' stories reflect the rich and varied ways in which people carry out this last step of Adaptive Action, and each story brings its own personal touches to represent these lessons we have learned about taking the *Now what?* step.

Have a Plan and Hold It Lightly

On the other hand, you do have to be prepared. In a CAS, you can plan for the static and dynamic aspects of change, but there is no one way to plan for dynamical change or a complex situation that includes all three types of change.

Planning for the *Now what?* step of Adaptive Action depends on specifics of any given situation, including questions to be asked, the volatile nature of the environment, level of urgency, and any other factors that shape the possibilities for decision making and action. In the Associates' stories, each person created a plan to move forward. Each unique plan suited the purpose in a specific time and place. Each plan, however, represents a common set of expectations about planning in a complex system.

- Plan for your situation.
- Set a timeline.
- Develop measures for success.
- Clarify roles and expectations.

Plan for Your Situation

Janice Ryan's long-term search for treatment for Alzheimer's patients reflects multiple cycles of Adaptive Action. She engaged various containers, inquired about many differences, and built transforming exchanges across the system. Meaning making was sometimes simultaneous across more than one Adaptive Action. She brought together data and information from various cycles to enrich her understanding and practice.

Her cycles of inquiry addressed basic research about her own professional practice, data to inform her day-to-day choices inside that practice, and a broader tapestry of exploration to contribute to the field of study about treatment of Alzheimer's patients. Although her long-term goal was clear to her, she continuously recreated her plan as new information and insights came to light. She developed specific plans for her day-by-day research and for each individual cycle of learning, and she adjusted those plans as new information became available.

Just as Janice's planning met her needs in that unique time and place, Ilir Zherka used Adaptive Action more formally to engage his staff in planning processes. He and his staff examined the impact of their campaign to gain support from a political ally. Their conversation about what worked in one event contributed to a plan of action that was more reliable across multiple situations. The resulting plan will inform their campaigns in the future, even as it provides a guide for immediate action.

Two Associates' stories told of longer-term planning with less-defined outcomes. The planning that Mary and Royce did around the development and dissemination of their Generative Engagement model framed a path into the unknown. The similar Adaptive Action planning process of Larry and Denise shaped their inquiry about their model for learning inside a complex system. These two examples of planning into the unknown show how individuals and groups can engage in emergent processes of theory development, such as reading, reflection, and concept generation around specific ideas. In both cases, the work ultimately influences action in the *Now what?* step of Adaptive Action.

Kristine Quade's plan was effective for her client; Larry Solow and Brenda Fake worked on a plan that resulted in a new book; Paul and Vickie use a consistent approach to develop a different plan for every team of participants who go through their training; Wendy Gudalewicz engaged a whole community in her plan to address an issue; and Mallary Tytel's plan continues to shift as she and her husband adapt to emerging needs. Within the common structure of Adaptive Action, each plan takes unique steps to create multiple versions of a new and different future.

Set a Timeline

Any plan in its own way sets timelines for completion and expectations for success. At the least, a plan establishes indicators that point toward the next Adaptive Action. Timelines may not be full predictors of the future, but they can furnish reminders about when to collect data, when to reexamine the environment, or when to change the question and move to the next Adaptive Action. They help coordinate multiple actions of diverse players. There is no one right way to set a timeline in a complex system. Even after it is set, a timeline may need to shift in response to the unexpected. What is important is that each Adaptive Action cycle maintain focus and momentum in the inquiry, and specific schedules and milestones help maintain the necessary focus and energy.

Develop Measures for Success

Similarly, there is no one way to pose absolute measures of success in a planning process. Our Associates' stories reflected formal measures and informal observations, short-term indicators and longer-term outcomes, and descriptions of effectiveness and efficiency. All are acceptable means of assessing in the *Now what?* step. What is important is that measures be both true and useful for your own purposes. Measures should contribute to descriptions of current impact and explanations to inform future inquiry and action.

In complex systems, numbers are not always the most useful measures. Consider how stories and pattern descriptions can yield information about when and how transformation happens and success emerges. But whatever the method, measures are essential to effective Adaptive Action. They lay the groundwork for improving how one sees, understands, and influences patterns of uncertainty in organizations.

Clarify Roles and Expectations

Finally, in planning your action, be as clear as possible about expectations for who is doing what in the *Now what?* step. This is simple when the planning involves few people. Mallary and her husband can plan together. As their plan shifts, they can clarify their expectations in simple conversation and negotiation. By contrast, Janice's long-term, complex cycles of Adaptive Action require more explicit and evolving assignments of responsibility and expectations.

Just as in each of the other steps of Adaptive Action, decisions made in *Now what?* are unique to the specific needs and desired outcomes of the actual inquiry. The tips listed here as recommendations are all ways of individualizing and tracking the steps you take in inquiring into the uncertainty that challenges your organization today.

> How are you planning to move forward to address uncertainty in your organization?
>
> How are you accounting for the static and dynamic aspects of change in your situation?
>
> How will you communicate your plan and its expectations for completion, responsibility, and connection?

Just Do It

When you think of change as static or dynamic, you believe in the importance of careful planning before action. When you think you're planning for static change, there's just one chance to get it right, and there is only one right. So you increase the chances of making sure your outcomes are what you want if you map out a long-term, highly controlled plan for bringing about change. In the same way, planning for dynamic change means planning for a single, predictable path between where you are and where you want to be. You take the time to map out a complicated plan that tracks your milestones, predicts future conditions, and creates action steps to deal with what you predict.

But when you leverage dynamical change in a high-dimension, nonlinear, open system, all the pre-planning in the world will not and cannot prepare you for moving forward. In dynamical change, you explore patterns that set conditions, you consider how you might influence the change, and then you "just do it." A simple plan, active cycles of Adaptive Action, and attention to patterns in the part, the whole, and the greater whole help you co-evolve with your changing environment.

- Start with what's easy.
- Do one thing.
- Keep it simple.

Start with What's Easy

Kristine Quade, in her story of change in a family-owned business, began when she chose the easiest path for her work with the leadership team. She worked with them to analyze information they had already gathered, helping make sense of their current position and questions, and moving into action to continue to learn. She didn't try to map out a long and complicated process of data collection and analysis. She didn't try to push them to identify multiple goals, objectives, and action steps.

In high-dimension, highly interdependent, open systems, complicated and convoluted answers just serve to confuse the issues and the people who are trying to address them. Complicated approaches are designed with the idea that if only you can break a problem down into its smallest pieces, you can then solve each small problem and put the whole back together. This reductionist approach simply does not work in complex, dynamical systems.

The whole is greater than the sum of the parts in a CAS, so when you try to fix the parts, you are challenged by several factors. First, it's difficult to know where one "part" stops and another begins. In massively entangled systems, isolating the parts that matter may or may not be possible. Second, if you do figure out how to separate some of the parts, and try to fix them, you run into difficulty because of the interdependence of the parts. Parts that are nonfunctional in the whole may function fine in isolation. It may not be the parts themselves that are dysfunctional; it may be the relationships and connections among the parts. If that is the case, even if you can separate parts and fix them so that they work independently, you may or may not be able to put them back together into a functioning whole.

So when Kristine entered the organization and asked the leadership team to identify the one challenge they wanted to work on, she chose the simplest

approach to their challenge: let teams of individuals propose their own responses to the issue and see what this does for the whole.

Do One Thing

Kristine didn't sit with them for hours, considering options and weighing risks.
She didn't have them map out a long-range, multilayered plan based on artifi-
cially derived goals, objectives, and action steps. Instead, she helped the leadership team identify one question they wanted to explore, name teams to explore
it, and set the teams to work in Adaptive Actions of their own.

It is important to notice that many separate things were happening in parallel across the organization. This approach does not demand that you do A,
then B, then C, but that you focus on A, and as you do it in many places and
many ways you capture what is changing in B and C. You plan for your next
Adaptive Action cycle.

Keep It Simple

Moving directly into action, Kristine didn't worry about trying to predict the
future or creating a complicated "plan of attack." The assignment for each team
was simply to address the most pressing challenge from the leadership team:
identify new ideas for customer engagement and relationships. Starting with
the "low hanging fruit," she engaged the teams in pursuing their assignments,
encouraging them to keep it simple and be creative in sharing their ideas and
insights with the leadership team.

Kristine gave the teams their assignments, outlined the parameters, and
set them to work. She supported them as they needed it, helping adapt and
adjust as they moved forward. Ultimately each team was able to communicate
its learning creatively and compellingly to inform the leadership team's next
cycle of Adaptive Action.

Even in the follow-up reflection time with the leadership team, they didn't
go into complicated analysis of what worked and what didn't. They created a
storyboard that retold their story, celebrated their learnings, and represented
to the whole organization the shift in focus that had occurred as a result of the
work done by the teams.

Choosing simple tasks and taking one action at a time are possible when
you recognize that change occurs in ongoing cycles of Adaptive Action, and
when you recognize that change in any part of the system can trigger changes
throughout the system. You just don't have to take complicated action across

the whole. If you understand the dynamical nature of change in complex systems, you understand that elaborate plans and efforts to orchestrate the full change process consume resources without conferring much benefit. You are free to find creative and responsive ways to accommodate changes, opportunities, or challenges in each step as you move in alignment with your ever-changing environment.

How are you able to uncomplicate your organization's uncertainties?

Are you able to simplify the steps you take to address your patterns?

What have you found at the heart of your uncertainty that suggests one simple response?

How are you and others creating ongoing cycles of Adaptive Action that move you all forward together?

Begin Again

Even as you take action in the last *So what?* step, it is natural to gather data about the impact of those steps. What difference did your actions make? What is the situation now? What changes do you see in the issue? If these questions sound like the next *What?* step, you are right. The conclusion of the *Now what?* of any Adaptive Action moves you into data collection for either the next iteration of the same question or the pursuit of an entirely new inquiry. This recommended tip, "Begin again," brings you to closure on the current inquiry, even as it moves you to the next. Your journey will be enriched as you keep these hints in mind:

- See where you are now.
- Learn from failure.
- Move to the next *What?*

See Where You Are Now

Ilir Zherka is a political operative who knows his business well. His job is to understand the current landscape as he advocates for his particular issues and causes. For him, influencing change is about finding the system's current tension and shifting that tension toward support for his cause. Each experience informs the next adaptation and maintains adaptive potential as the social and political landscape changes. His story illustrates his use of the *Now what?* step to fuel the next Adaptive Action to carry his cause forward.

Learn from Failure

Ilir opened his story with a brief telling of a less-than-successful attempt to engage one of the nation's political leaders in a public show of solidarity and support. As he and his staff used the Adaptive Action questions to examine their recent disappointing experience, they recognized their failure to focus on the point of greatest tension that could compel action. Because of the approach they chose, they got little reaction and no forward movement from their target. Looking realistically at where their decisions had led them, Ilir and his staff could identify the gaps in their understanding to fuel the next round of Adaptive Action.

Ilir is certain they won't make the same mistake again because he knows that the natural next iteration at the end of the *Now what?* step is to move into a new question, beginning the cycle again. He and his staff looked at where they were, considered how they got there, and learned what they could from that experience.

Move to the Next *What?*

Ilir also shared a story of how he and his staff moved forward after a stunning political loss. Recovering from defeat, Ilir and his staff were already examining the current state, gathering data about their loss, looking ahead at other possible points of tension, and asking powerful questions to move forward in the next round of adaptation.

How are you looking at fitness in your uncertainty and defining the progress you are or are not making?

How do you track changes in your patterns to know where you are and how you are performing against your hopes and expectations?

What are you learning, even as you complete your action steps, that will help you move to the next Adaptive Action cycle?

Chapter Conclusion

It probably comes as no surprise that, again in the *Now what?* step, recommendations are dependent on the specifics of the current Adaptive Action. Designed to support continuous exploration and learning, these recommendations inform your choices and decisions as you move to action.

- Have a plan and hold it lightly.

- Just do it.

- Begin again.

Traditional beliefs about planning are simply too complicated to be useful in the high-dimension, complex systems where we live and work. Additionally, old practices focus on getting it right rather than on moving to action. That was sufficient when change was slower and the world was less diverse, but it is no longer the case. The changes we deal with now are dynamical in nature and require faster and more sensitive cycles of adaptation. These specific recommendations in the *Now what?* step help you take powerful action, learn more about the impact of your action, and fuel future inquiry as you leverage uncertainty in your own organization.

ADAPTIVE INNOVATION

This final chapter serves multiple purposes, but the main goal is to convince you that there is no final chapter in the development and use of Adaptive Action. We have moved into a world with no permanent boundaries. We know that every effect is potentially a cause, and every cause an effect. Acceptance of this paradigm shows us that every boundary can be a doorway, every difference an opportunity, and every ending a new beginning. When we live in this paradigm, we may be challenged by uncertainty, but we can find a way to move forward. All we have to do is open the door, capture the opportunity, and leverage it to find a new beginning.

In this book, we introduced you to the concept of human systems dynamics and complex adaptive systems, using real-life examples of how these systems differ from a traditional conception of systems. We offered Adaptive Action as the path for ensuring sustainability and fitness in highly diverse, open, nonlinear environments. We discussed each step of that iterative cycle, offering HSD-based models and methods to use as you ask *What?*, *So what?*, and *Now what?* We've shared nine stories of our Associates having used Adaptive Action in a variety of settings as they addressed their own issues—organizational and personal.

Since HSD is a young field, ripe with untapped insights and great potential for further learning and applications, we know that the last chapter in this book is not the final chapter on HSD or Adaptive Action. Across the years of learning about Adaptive Action in our own work and supporting clients as they build adaptive capacity, we have developed new ways to think about core business functions that contribute to systemwide capacity. These core functions have been the focus of writing on leadership and organizations for a number of years, some of them for decades or centuries. The difference for us is that Adaptive Action and the basic principles, models, and methods of HSD have generated new ways to think and talk about uncertainty, and new ways to leverage it for success in today's evolving landscape.

Traditional organizational functions were originally formulated to support static or dynamic change in finite games of growth and management. They emerged in response to challenges in simpler circumstances. Alternatives to those functions must emerge for organizations and communities to play successfully in the dynamical, uncertain, infinite games of the twenty-first century. We invite you to engage with us as we consider the implications of Adaptive Action in these traditionally accepted functions of leadership and management.

This final chapter offers brief glimpses into how these traditional functions can be transformed to build adaptive capacity at all scales of human systems. We offer them as a laboratory for future learning and as a launch pad for new frontiers and opportunities for building power and performance by leveraging uncertainty in your organizations. We have organized our thinking by grouping relevant activities according to their basic nature and role in adaptation and sustainability: Setting the Cornerstone, Doing the Work, and Reaching out to Others. These nontraditional categories do not combine to create a linear, step-by-step checklist; nor do they present a comprehensive analysis of critical business functions. They do represent functions that work together, each enriching the effectiveness of the others, each contributing to the healthy functioning of the whole, and each requiring ongoing attention and consideration in the work of the system. If you seek to leverage your own uncertainty and to create change when you close this book, we invite you to begin by working under these umbrellas, which we engage every day.

Setting the Cornerstone

Setting the Cornerstone includes activities that establish the foundation of the systemwide culture and direction. Activities in this arena help set conditions for systemwide patterns. As such, the descriptions we offer here help you think about where you are going and how decisions will be made as the journey unfolds. We explore:

- Adaptive ethics
- Adaptive vision
- Adaptive learning

Adaptive Ethics

The fundamental ethical consideration that influences patterns of productivity and interaction in today's organizations emerges from the three kinds of change: static, dynamic, and dynamical. Just as there are more and less effective actions one can take in responding to each kind of change, there are distinct ways to think about ethics in each type of change and take ethical action.

In static change, an object moves from one stable place to another stable place. Ethical actions in static change situations look like the simple distinction between good and evil. The line is clear; the path is straight. A person can choose one or the other, but a choice must be made. Some individual and institutional decisions fall into this category, among them tax accounting, legal requirements, and contractual agreements. You make choices that are or are not allowed by statute, regulation, or contract. Ethical actions are defined by the constraints that define the change.

Dynamic change is like the path of a thrown ball. The beginning situation is really clear, and the path and endpoint are perfectly predictable. Ethical decisions in dynamic change rely on logical argument and consideration of alternatives. Once a choice is made, the future will unfold as destined by the choice and the systemic factors that influenced the choice. In an organization, this kind of ethical consideration affects decisions about factors such as cash flow management, product development, and managing projects. What is ethical is what maintains the integrity of the path or the outcomes. Good decisions lead to good consequences—always.

Dynamical change, however, emerges from the accumulated tensions of patterns in the moment. Unlike static change, the beginning is ambiguous, and the end is unknown. Unlike dynamic change, the initial state and the systemic forces are unknowable and unpredictable. In such a situation, neither absolute good and evil nor rational planning will lead to ethical action.

Ethics in dynamical change depends on transparent and rapid Adaptive Action cycles to find the most harmonious fit with a complex environment. Ethics amid dynamical change is not so much a decision and how it is made. It is, rather, a stance of inquiry in which the questions are about coherence, fit, and what brings the greatest good to the greatest number.

Adaptive Action is how we look for fit with the system to build coherence, and coherence is necessary to long-term sustainability of the system. At the level of the group—team, organization, neighborhood, community—decisions of the whole are sanctioned as they contribute to coherence and sustainability. The dominant patterns, as described in a society's rules, roles, and expectations, come to be known as the group's ethics, and they emerge to ensure coherence in the whole and increase its chances of survival.

Of course, too much fit or coherence with an unlawful or unwise pattern could destroy an ethical foundation. Consider the coherence and high degree of fit that is required of street gangs. The strength and local sustainability of a street gang calls for coherence around belonging and maintenance of boundaries—physical boundaries (turf), psychological boundaries (membership and loyalty), and power boundaries (money and intimidation). Coherence in these areas sets patterns that characterize the lifestyle we have come to associate with gang behavior. Factors in the environment influence decisions in the moment, relative to the context of demands and needs of the gang, and ethical considerations focus on patterns that support sustainability and fitness within that context.

To a lesser degree, this type of commitment to the sustainability of the part over sustainability of the greater whole emerges anytime groups focus only on their own needs and local sustainability, rather than the health of the greater system. Relativism or "groupthink" and loss of an ethical center are always risks of adaptation, but they are not inherent.

We step beyond this danger when we recognize that we work in a complex reality. Fit is not just fit to one thing or one level of a pattern, but fit with patterns in many containers, including the whole, the part, and the greater whole. Any action should be judged in relation to personal beliefs and values, group expectations and relationships, institutional mores and policies, public regulations and laws, and spiritual or religious expectations for behavior. If an action adapts and resolves key tensions in all these levels at the same time, or if it intentionally balances the tensions among them, then it will serve as an ethical action. A short list of simple rules, applied in iterative processes of decision making, provides a powerful guide for ethical decisions.

Consider the challenges of your own organization:

What are the forces that threaten sustainability and fitness in the greater whole?

What individual and group decisions do you face day to day, or even on the larger, longer-scale horizon?

How can you use Adaptive Action in this context to ensure decisions that move your system toward greater fitness and sustainability?

Adaptive Vision

In a traditional paradigm, the imagined end is a kind of cause. A dynamic change process, moving in a smooth path from a known beginning to known end, can appear to be driven as much by the target as it is by the initial conditions. Very literally, one might say that the target is what caused the arrow to fly as it did. From this dynamic perspective, a vision of the future becomes a magnet that draws decisions and actions to it, expecting a sure and predictable path.

There is no such certainty in dynamical change. The conditions in the moment motivate changes that appear in the evolution of a pattern. It is the tension in the present that sets the conditions for the emergent future. So, why do you need a vision?

George Johnson invited Glenda to create a vision video. This idea, initially discovered by Malcolm Cohan,[1] invites you to create a series of statements about the world as it will be in your best future. The statements, called a poem, are put into a video format with pictures and music. The idea is that you watch the video every morning and evening to embed the images into your perception, feeling, thought, and action.

This process of creating the video vision shows that in a complex adaptive system the visioning process is actually an exercise in pattern formation and Adaptive Action, rather than an exercise in target creation. Writing the poem challenges you to see patterns today and imagine patterns in the future. Similarities, differences, and connections become clear. The significant ones find their way into the vision, and the less significant ones fade away. Searching for images and finding music develops resonance around key patterns as they are reflected in visual and auditory patterns. Watching the video and sharing it with others reinforces the pattern with each cycle. Over time, the pattern becomes a standard part of every *So what?* step of Adaptive Action. *So what* are the connections between the pattern in the vision and a current opportunity for action? *Now what* can be done make the similarities more compelling, the significant differences more distinct, and the connections stronger?

Rather than pulling toward some predestined point, the vision captures a coherent pattern than can inform choices in the moment. Not only does this view of vision open a kind of freedom in the conversation, it also invigorates observation, decision making, and choice taking over time.

How is your vision a set-in-stone image of some future state that remains unchanged over time, looming in the future?

In contrast, can you clarify a vision that describes patterns of power and performance and informs day-to-day Adaptive Action at the whole, the part, and the greater whole in your own system?

Adaptive Learning

There is no question that at the time of publication of this book, the system of education in the United States is broken. Patterns in educational institutions show low graduation rates, persistent disparities, poor reading and math performance, violence, high teacher turnover, failed national policy, private sector influence, political agendas, bullying, and a variety of other social ills. Decades of investment in education reform have changed some schools in some communities, but the system as a whole continues to deteriorate.

In any type of reform or whole-scale change in uncertain times, Adaptive Action becomes the center of a theory of change. Conscious cycles of *What?*, *So what?*, and *Now what?* inform decision making and action for individuals at every organizational level: teams, classrooms, buildings, communities of practice, the board of education, and systemwide policies, processes, and procedures.

This approach to transforming schools and school districts can be embraced because it resonates with what educators know about excellent, adaptive learning. Adaptive Action may not match all the current, complicated theories of pedagogy and schooling, but it does reflect every gifted professional's experience of teaching and learning.

Essentially, committed individuals in a given school or district use what they know about how children really learn to see and influence all the social, instructional, and institutional patterns they participate in. Using Adaptive Action to see, understand, and influence learning in these uncertain times gives hope for the future of an education system that builds adaptive capacity for children, adults, and their communities through Adaptive Action.

Although less dramatic, large-scale change and reform efforts are sweeping through all kinds of organizations, they seek to deal with changing times. Systemic change depends on the ability of the system to use yesterday's learning to inform today's action as it attempts to influence tomorrow's patterns.

What is learned from schools and school districts can be transferred to the larger world as leaders contemplate how best to ensure sustainable organizational learning. By building adaptive capacity across their systems, leaders prepare for effective, sustainable responses in uncertain times. Using Adaptive Action as the centerpiece of change across the system builds skills among individuals, establishes adaptive and responsive policies and procedures, and positions the organization to deal with the challenges and opportunities of the frontiers they face.

How can your organization use Adaptive Action to formulate your system-wide theory of change?

What actions can you begin to take today to build adaptive capacity that leverages the uncertainty you face?

Setting the cornerstone is a critical role of leaders in complex systems. They understand that the dynamical nature of the landscapes where they live and work call for more adaptive responses by individuals as well as by the organizations that support them. Once the foundations are set, however, the day-to-day operations and business inside the organization also call for adaptive capacity.

Doing the Work

Doing the Work includes the functions that speak to moving forward through the day-to-day system activities to adjust to the multiple, massively entangled forces of uncertainty in an unknowable dynamical world. In this arena, we will briefly consider:

- Adaptive planning
- Adaptive sustainability
- Adaptive leadership and management
- Adaptive change management
- Adaptive performance management and evaluation

Adaptive Planning

Though some of our complexity colleagues spurn the idea of planning altogether, the need for practical approaches in uncertainty drive us to explore this practice. We know that best performance requires planning, but we also know that a plan can distort or interfere with our commitment to emergence. Over the years, we have recognized Adaptive Action as our planning practice. Here are some of the particulars of the adaptive planning practice we use for ourselves and share with clients.

Plan to Replan   Plans must be developed from the beginning, reviewed periodically, and revised as needed. Plans are critical to coherence across time and space, but they must be held lightly and altered according to emergent conditions.

Plan for Many Horizons   Staff members plan their days. Teams plan by the week. Financial status and marketing activities are reviewed monthly. The board considers policy quarterly, and the staff meets annually to plan strategy. What is critical is that these horizons inform each other and contribute to coherent patterns of productivity and interaction across the whole. Because they plan for horizons that make sense to them, individuals and groups see, understand, and embrace their roles in contributing to the fitness and sustainability of the whole over time.

Plan for Surprise   Adaptive Action serves to make us opportunistic. This is not the same as being reactive. In the first, you have a picture of where you're going and the pattern you want to create, then when something comes along that could fill in a bit of the pattern, you follow it. When opportunities arise that don't fit, you know it and can made a different choice. In the second, there is no plan, no intentional pattern. A reactive group will follow any shiny object. An opportunistic group is prepared to leverage surprise.

Stack Adaptive Actions   At a given moment, an organization is participating in more Adaptive Action cycles than can be counted. Projects, communities, client relationships, instructional designs, writing feedback, emails, wrong numbers all represent an opportunity for Adaptive Action.

Adaptive planning is a powerful tool for aligning and engaging the whole system in moving toward increased fitness and sustainability.

> How does your planning process allow you to shift your plans as need arises, plan at all levels of the organization, take advantage of emergent opportunities, and make sense of the infinite responses you must make at any moment?

> How can you use Adaptive Action to increase your organization's capacity to deal with an uncertain future?

Adaptive Sustainability

Sustainability is another term that requires redefinition in the world of dynamical complexity. It is no longer about holding a system still and stable to protect the status quo. Even if we had sufficient resources and insight to hold on to what we had, we would quickly find ourselves made obsolete as the world moves on and leaves us behind. Nor is it about focusing only on the external realities in the greater physical world. That is a necessary condition for consideration, but it is not the only arena where fitness and adaptability are important.

Sustainability in a complex adaptive system is about maintaining patterns of productivity and identity. Circumstances may change. Players may come and go. Resources may dribble away. New ideas will emerge. Old opportunities will fade, and new ones will arise. The goal is to sustain the pattern that serves the purpose of continually discerning and moving toward fitness.

A pattern, of course, self-organizes in accord with conditions that contain, differentiate, and connect. To sustain a pattern means to hold a useful boundary and/or maintain differences that make a difference and/or retain connections that are meaningful and fulfilling. The challenge is to discover the useful boundaries, relevant differences, and meaningful connections, and then decide which of them can and should be intentionally reinforced and which can be allowed to shift in response to changing conditions. It is truly this simple; but it is not easy.

Over recent years, the concept of sustainability has come to represent the relationship humans have to the physical environment. Of course, if we are to maintain patterns of life we cherish, we must learn to do so without overtaxing the water, air, and other natural resources that support human life on the planet. At the same time, however, we have to think about the patterns of interaction and decision making that sustain life across families, communities, organizations, regions, and the globe. What we do in our organizations to adapt in the face of uncertainty is not sustainable if it does not, in fact, sustain at the level of the parts (individuals, teams, departments) and the greater whole (the environment, the economy, the society).

One of the central challenges of sustainability work is the tension between individual behavior and collective outcomes. It is hard to connect the tiny actions of a citizen with the global effects of climate change. Adaptive Action and the CDE Model are helpful here because both work at every scale and across diverse contexts. Imagine each agent in the system completing micro-Adaptive Action cycles working from the CDE of the patterns he or she can observe. In the meantime, policy makers, corporate players, researchers, and politicians complete their meso-Adaptive Action cycles looking at the conditions for self-organizing related to the patterns at their level of scale. Finally, we can hope that the macro-Adaptive Action cycles of international coalitions can see, understand, and influence emerging conditions on a global scale. All of these cycles, all over the world, at every level of decision making and on every time horizon might set the conditions for a massive shift in ecological patterns and a stabilization of climactic conditions worldwide.

This definition of sustainability lies at the heart of the cornerstones that enable organizations to step into uncertainty. The ethical decisions we make, the adaptive visions that inform our decisions, and how we ensure adaptive learning all set the initial conditions for sustainability and fitness in our systems.

How do you define sustainability in your system?

How do you shape patterns that increase the chances of sustainability at the levels of the whole, the part, and the greater whole?

Adaptive Leadership

A leader sets the conditions for patterns of innovation and productivity in an organization. Each organization's most successful pattern is unique, and its leader must be able to see and understand current patterns while influencing those of the future.

Leadership is about influencing containers as conditions for change. At any level, the person who establishes the boundaries has tremendous power over conditions for self-organizing. A parent defines curfews; a president sets policy for military and foreign relations; a CEO determines strategy. In every case, the person who defines the size and permeability of the container has a privileged role in the system.

Leadership is about shaping differences as a condition for change. The distinctions that make a difference define the patterns of culture and set the tensions that motivate action, so they help to dictate the patterns that emerge across the system. Parents teach values; the president sets priorities; a CEO determines metrics. The person who has standing to determine the differences that make a difference is the person who has power over the self-organizing processes of a system. For example, when leaders use simple rules to distinguish their organizational patterns from others, they step into leadership that shapes the self-organizing processes at all levels and in all parts of their community.

Leadership is about encouraging exchanges as a condition for change. No one is surprised that Twitter fueled the Arab Spring of 2010 and hobbled the formal leadership in nation after nation. Those leaders—tyrants or not—were accustomed to controlling who was able to talk to whom about what. They used exchanges to stifle change they didn't want and to encourage the changes they did. Whatever stance the leader takes around exchanges will become the pattern across the whole. That pattern then becomes one of the targets if and when rebellion emerges.

Effective leaders consider the diverse perspectives that are possible across the Landscape Diagram. From random acts and events to highly controlled and coordinated work, all are necessary in the context of ensuring fitness of the whole. If the conditions (CDE) are highly constrained, the system will be predictable, and traditional management is not only possible, it is necessary. At the same time, diverse conditions require corresponding leadership. The system may be totally random or surprising and patterned. In those cases, traditional management may be irrelevant or counterproductive. One of the most important leadership competencies in uncertainty is to discern the appropriate level of constraint. A leader must decide whether or not it is time to manage, according to the relative stability of the system and balanced against the need for adaptability in the greater whole.

This recognition of a leader's role engaging in Adaptive Action supports our belief that leadership can emerge at any level in an organization. You don't have to be the CEO or even a member of the executive team to see and influence the patterns that surround you. Those who work directly with customers can influence the stability and flexibility of the system in how they provide service. Sales people influence system stability and flexibility as they mediate between buyers and production and marketing. Human resources influence system stability and flexibility as they develop policies and procedures that balance employee needs against organizational demands.

How does your system encourage and support adaptive leadership?

What conversations will amplify the patterns of adaptive leadership?

How can you set the conditions for those conversations to occur?

Adaptive Change Management

Change management presents an interesting challenge in dynamical environments. If it is dynamical change, it isn't manageable. If it is manageable, it is not dynamical. The dynamical situation is open to external forces, influenced by unknowable factors, and subject to mutual causal relationships. The future is not simply unknown; it is unknowable, because conditions influencing the complex environment may shift in any direction at any moment and leave you stranded up a nonlinear creek without a low-dimension paddle.

Still, organizations and communities experience and must cope with change. They have to prepare for it, weather it, and find a new normal as a wave of change passes through and the future lands at the doorstep. By now it may be obvious to you, but we prefer to talk about change "adaptation" rather than change "management." In our experience, the three steps of Adaptive Action—*What?*, *So what?*, *Now what?*—allow individuals and groups to engage with changes inside and outside their domains, observe changes in patterns as they emerge, make sense of them, take action in a reasonable response, gauge the effectiveness of an action, and try again.

Sometimes self-organizing processes of change can be faster than you can imagine. A flash mob or a two-year-old's tantrum can attest to that. On the other hand, self-organizing can be excruciatingly slow, like the adoption of policies and practices that ensure civil rights in South Africa, the United States, and Israel. The only certainty is that you cannot predict the amount of time a self-organizing process will take. You can set the conditions you control to hurry it along, but other conditions may hold it at a standstill. It is not the length of time but the uncertainty of time that makes change in dynamical systems such a challenge.

Adaptive Action addresses this problem. If you don't know when change will come, the best you can do is check for change frequently, make sense of what you see, and be prepared to take action when the time is right. As an organization engages in Adaptive Actions around your work and the development of your organization, you continue to check for the emergent patterns you want, see and understand the patterns you have, and influence conditions to generate or amplify patterns that will move you toward sustainability and fit.

Consider the series of tragic events that brought about such pain and loss in Japan in 2011. They experienced first the earthquake, then the tsunami, then the nuclear disaster, then economic, social, and health challenges resulting from the dire circumstances. We have had some opportunities to talk with real people who lived through these traumatic events. Their stories are heart-wrenching, but the survivors we talked to all hold one thing in common. They paid attention to what was really happening, they separated what really mattered from differences that didn't make a difference, they took action, and they paid attention to the results and began again. Even as the world they knew literally shifted under their feet, they stayed standing or quickly picked themselves up when they fell, and they went on to do it again.

How many of us actually have to respond in such tragic and dramatic scenarios? The same principles of using Adaptive Action as the theory of change hold true in the day-to-day change processes of operating any organization. Leaders who engage in ongoing and frequent Adaptive Action see shifts in their data long before those trends might show up in annual or even quarterly reports. When leaders throughout the organization know about and engage in Adaptive Action, there is heightened sensitivity to changes, challenges, and opportunities as they emerge. Leaders, wherever they stand in the organization, pay attention to what is really happening, separate what matters from the mundane, take action, pay attention to the results, and start again. It's as easy—and as challenging—as that.

> How is your organization positioned to see, understand, and influence changing patterns in your market, industry, and workforce?

> How does it engage in the ongoing change necessary for adaptation and sustainability?

> How can you establish Adaptive Action as the norm across all levels and functions of your organization to see, understand, and influence patterns of interaction and decision making in the face of uncertainty and change?

> How can you expand your adaptive capacity to leverage uncertainty of change?

Adaptive Performance Management and Evaluation

Measurement and evaluation in complex systems present a puzzle. If there are no boundaries of time or space, and an infinite set of potentially important factors, you cannot know what to measure. When a system has nonlinear causality, there is no simple relationship between the action and the result, so you cannot connect a specific outcome with any specific intervention. Measurement, as we know it, is meaningless in a complex adaptive system when it is in a state of dynamical change. On the other hand, measurement still makes sense when systems are in static or dynamic change. When they are, traditional performance measurement and evaluation methods are perfectly effective. The challenge is to know when measurement is and is not meaningful and to find means to evaluate action in either case.

In times of uncertainty, the questions you ask, the data you use, and the information you have available determine the quality of your Adaptive Action. At all levels of your system, whether you are measuring performance of individuals or processes, Adaptive Action depends on your ability to know what questions to ask, how they can be asked to gather the most effective data, and how best to use the data to inform your decisions. In assessment and evaluation systems we design, we ensure that what can be measured is measured well, but we also do not delude ourselves into measuring things that are fundamentally unmeasurable. For those, we return to the CDE Model and Adaptive Action.

Adaptive Action is a core component of Michael Quinn Patton's approach to developmental evaluation, *Developmental Evaluation: Applying Complexity Concepts to Enhance Innovation and Use.*[2] He acknowledges that when people are learning and a system is changing, the best one can do is engage in iterations of data collection, meaning making, and revised action. Repeating this process over time generates knowledge about performance while simultaneously improving practice. Feeding two birds with one scone, as a friend of ours likes to say. The question still remains, what do you track and how do you track it? We have designed two kinds of adaptive evaluation methods.

One focuses on the patterns that emerge. The CDE Model has proven helpful to us in tracking and reporting on systemic change and unintended consequences from program interventions and training to improve performance. The method is simple. We record a CDE portrait of the conditions of self-organizing at multiple points in space or time. Then we convene discussions of participants to compare and contrast those portraits. We consider whether tension is increasing or decreasing, and whether the observed change is supporting or interfering with system performance.

Again, because the CDE is scale-free, our evaluations look at multiple system levels at the same time. One project we completed recently tracked change over time with individuals, diverse service projects, systems, and infrastructure change, as well as evolution of bureaucratic policies, procedures, and practices. There was also supposed to be a facet of the project that looked at patterns in joblessness over the same time period, but external forces of economic transformation swamped any pattern-generating influence our client might have claimed.

The second uses Adaptive Action explicitly. We drew on this method when we worked with the McKnight Foundation and on their international Collaborative Crop Research Program. The program included four levels of action: project-level activities, where the research was done; the regional level, where systemic patterns were investigated; the program level, where resources and information were coordinated; and the foundation, where strategy was determined and resource allocation decisions were made. Each level had its own evaluation questions, sources of data, and methods for data analysis. The purpose of the evaluation was to monitor performance as well as to support coherent learning and planning across the system.

Marah Moore, an HSD Associate, and Glenda designed an evaluation program called Integrated Monitoring and Evaluation (IMEP). Each group, at every level, used Adaptive Action to collect data to monitor performance, make shared meaning and plan for future action, coordinate action, and repeat the cycle of learning and planning and action. Adaptive Action on the part of each project fed into other projects, the region, the program, and the foundation. Region, program, and foundation drew information from all the other levels and fed information into them. All parts of the program used the process to see and influence patterns in agricultural, social, and institutional systems around the world.

What this project did was capture adaptations as they occurred and assess the effects of those actions on the overall direction and performance of the system at whatever level we were examining at a given time. This process of feeding learning and system intelligence into the greater whole added to the richness of data for informing decisions about resources and support at the foundation. Additionally, because similar processes and expectations were set across the whole, diverse parts of the system could learn from Adaptive Actions being taken on the other side of the planet.

> How does your system gather data and assess adaptive capacity of individuals, teams, departments, and across the whole?

> What are the current patterns of data collection and use that inform your decisions at any level of your organization?

Adaptive leaders understand their organizations as dynamical systems and are intentional about planning for and investing in decisions and actions that help build flexibility and responsiveness into the ongoing work at all levels. Adaptive Action is the core capacity in the ongoing operational strategies that move organizations toward their goals. Adaptive leaders also recognize that their organizations are more than just operational systems, processes, and procedures. They recognize the value in ensuring that their organizations assess, understand, and influence patterns to build responsive relationships internally and externally.

Reaching Out to Others

Reaching Out to Others captures how adaptive systems build new relationships, both internally and externally. Whether it's through internal teaming activities or supervision or through external partnerships and marketing, these innovative functions help people connect effectively as they engage in the daily infinite game of working together.

- Adaptive marketing
- Adaptive collaboration
- Adaptive consulting

Adaptive Marketing

All too often, marketing and sales are seen as one-way exchanges. The pitch goes out, and the value exchange ensues. In complex adaptive systems, however, systems are so diverse and challenges are so sticky, it is almost impossible to make a pitch that is specific enough for the client to see its relevance to their own current challenge. At the same time, clients want answers that are flexible enough to work across the diverse challenges they experience. In times of uncertainty, the best marketing helps people see patterns that build capacity to deal with the challenges they face.

The most powerful sales connections occur when a rich exchange of information helps test and improve a fit between a potential client and a potential solution. In a complex relationship, seller and buyer work together in dialogue to discover whether they can be or will be generative partners. In such relationships, sometimes players discover there is no fit, and they go their separate ways. Often, though, they find a fit and establish a mutual relationship that meets the needs of both over time.

The most critical approach in an adaptive marketing arsenal is the ability to remain in inquiry. Listening carefully to the client's perspective, seeking to understand what they see as the needs, and finding ways to address the patterns they find troublesome are the keys to successful marketing in uncertain times.

How does your organization invite clients to participate in a dialogue to develop interventions and solutions?

How do you engage with clients and potential clients to see and understand their challenges and create a solution that is custom-designed to meet their needs?

How can you change the patterns of client engagement such that these patterns of sharing and co-evolution emerge?

Adaptive Collaboration

Whether you call it teaming, public-private partnership, or community engagement, collaboration has become a way of life in the twenty-first century. Sustainability, resources conservation, systemic change, and global reach are all factors that push institutions of all kinds into collaborative relationships. As we have observed in many complex phenomena, however, the habits that supported the finite game of collaboration in the past are of little use in the emerging infinite game of the future. In our practice, we have noted a number of lessons for successful collaboration in dynamical change in open, high-dimension, nonlinear relationships.

Don't Talk About It Too Much   Our individual institutional and cultural languages tend to mark strong distinctions that may not serve us well in practice. By focusing on shared work, collaborative relationships may bypass some differences that don't really matter.

Don't Compromise Identity   No collaboration should ask either partner to sacrifice who they are or what they consider their core mission. Shared work should draw out the complementary natures of partners, rather than erasing one or the other. Conversely, not all relationships are collaborations. There will be situations when the identity of one organization is subsumed by another. Such relationships result from mergers or acquisitions. They too can serve a purpose in a complex environment, but they are different in kind from healthy collaborations.

Begin Small   We have seen lots of resources invested in establishing the groundwork for collaboration, and resources ultimately wasted once the relationship failed to function as designed. The conditions of a healthy collaboration will evolve over time, and they can never be predicted. It is a much cheaper and lower-risk path to begin with a small project and repeat Adaptive Action cycles together as trust, understanding, and shared vision grow. At some point, formal documentation of the relationship may be required, but at least it will describe a reality that exists, rather than one that is just imagined.

Begin with an Exit Strategy   Sustainable complex systems assume and accommodate change, even if they may not know particulars of when and how the change will occur. No collaboration is likely to be of value in perpetuity. When both parties acknowledge this and have plans for a graceful exit, then fear of the end will not distort their shared work. Agreements about division of property and joint assets are much more easily determined far from the reality of separation.

Adaptive collaboration depends on the understanding that the partners are coming together as a system, generating shared patterns of productivity, interaction, and decision making. As partners come together, as they work together, and ultimately as they go their separate ways, Adaptive Action is a way of seeing, understanding, and influencing the underlying dynamics of the relationship as they emerge.

> What types of partnership does your organization form through its collaborative endeavors?

> How can you build the capacity to ensure that your collaborative relationships—whether at the individual or the organizational level—are adaptive and productive for all who are involved?

Adaptive Consulting

The most radical assumption of HSD consulting is that all change is self-organizing. No system, no client, no team will change until the tensions within it set conditions for a new pattern to emerge. This principle manifests in a variety of consulting practices.

Work Where You Are   If a project manager contracts with us, we work with the project. If it is the CEO, we work with the whole organization. Our radical belief in self-organizing means change can happen anywhere, so we don't have to engage leadership before we can help set conditions that move a system along.

Bring Questions, Not Answers   We noted earlier that answers have short shelf lives in complex systems, but good questions last forever. As consultants and coaches, our job is to support clients in their Adaptive Action processes by reflecting what we see and asking provocative questions. The only valid and sustainable answers will come from clients and their systems.

Offer Theory, but Don't Force It   Sometimes we share the underlying theory with clients and sometimes we don't. Our models and methods work because they are based on rigorous and reliable explanations of complex dynamics, not because clients know the explanations or understand the dynamics. We use whatever language is alive in the client's environment to name patterns we observe, and we let clients use whatever language they choose to capture the patterns that are significant to them. Of course we don't hide the theory. If someone wants to know, we are more than willing to share.

Surface and Challenge Patterns   Whether we do it explicitly or implicitly, our primary job is to help clients see for themselves the conditions they have set for self-organizing and become conscious of shifting those conditions to encourage new patterns to form. We engage our clients in their of Adaptive Actions and build their capacity to continue adaptation into the future.

Pay Attention to Details   Sometimes the most important change work lies in the most mundane tasks. Note taking, meeting making, room arrangement, who knows what when—all these things can be small changes that generate enormous effects that may mean the difference between transformation and staying stuck.

Attend to the Whole, the Part, and the Greater Whole   We constantly stretch to see patterns at multiple scales. We work at the scale where the client invites us, but we look for patterns above and below that level that may influence the system at the level where we work.

We continue to expand and advance our understanding of service delivery and consulting practice as we adapt to emerging patterns in health care, education, prevention, peace, governing, finance, and agriculture. On the one hand, every organization and every project is unique. On the other hand, they all depend on the conditions for their own self-organizing change to emerge.

Whether you are a consultant or not, this section offers tips and suggestions for building a helping relationship anywhere.

How are you and your organization poised to reach out to others in consultative relationships?

What patterns exist in your helping relationships now?

How can you add energy to effective patterns while sapping energy from those that are less useful?

How can you begin to establish conditions that generate the types of patterns that feed Adaptive Action?

Conclusion: Your Own Adaptive Action

These well-known practices take on a different twist when posed as applications of Adaptive Action in the dynamical, infinite game that drives organizations and communities in the twenty-first century. Used adaptively, these basic functions engage the system at a level that allows us to see, understand, and influence the dynamic patterns of human interaction. We can describe what we see at the heart of these interactions, but more importantly we can take action to shift those interactions to find greater fit in the system.

We invite you to join us on this journey to find the next frontiers and blossoming opportunities that are possible in systems that are highly diverse, open to multiple influences, and able to learn from history. As your ticket to join our journey, we offer you models and methods based in human systems dynamics as a way of seeing, understanding, and influencing patterns in your system. We encourage you to choose the flexibility and simplicity of Adaptive Action as the key to leveraging your organizational uncertainty, and we look forward to engaging—dynamically, of course—with the products of your fine work.

REFERENCE MATTER

NOTES

CHAPTER 1

1. James P. Carse, *Finite and Infinite Games* (New York: Free Press, 1986).

2. James Gleick, *Chaos: Making a New Science* (New York: Viking, 1987).

3. Ilya Prigogine and Isabelle Stengers, *Order out of Chaos: Man's New Dialogue with Nature* (Toronto: Bantam Books, 1984).

4. Stuart A. Kauffman, *At Home in the Universe: The Search for Laws of Self-organization and Complexity* (New York: Oxford University Press, 1995).

5. John H. Holland, *Emergence: From Chaos to Order* (Reading, MA: Addison-Wesley, 1998).

6. P. Bak, *How Nature Works: The Science of Self-organized Criticality* (New York: Copernicus, 1996).

7. Murray Gell-Mann, *The Quark and the Jaguar: Adventures in the Simple and the Complex* (New York: W. H. Freeman, 1994).

8. Ian Stewart, *Does God Play Dice?: The New Mathematics of Chaos* (Cambridge, MA: Blackwell, 2002).

9. Jack Cohen and Ian Stewart, *The Collapse of Chaos: Discovering Simplicity in a Complex World* (New York: Viking, 1994).

10. Ralph D. Stacey, *Complex Responsive Processes in Organizations: Learning and Knowledge* (Abingdon, Oxon, UK: Routledge, 2001).

11. M. Poole, A. Van de Ven, K. Dooley, and M. Holmes, *Organizational Change and Innovation Processes: Theory and Methods for Research* (Oxford, UK: Oxford University Press, 2000).

12. Jeff Goldstein, *The Unshackled Organization: Facing the Challenge of Unpredictability Through Spontaneous Reorganization* (Portland, OR: Productivity Press, 1994).

13. Dave Snowden, *Cognitive Edge*, http://www.cognitive-edge.com/, accessed January 17, 2012.

14. Brenda Zimmerman, Curt Lindberg, and Paul Plsek, *Edgeware: Lessons for Complexity Science for Health Care Leaders* (Dallas: VHA, 1998).

15. Margaret Wheatley, *Leadership and the New Science: Discovering Order in a Chaotic World*, 3rd ed. (San Francisco: Berrett-Koehler, 2006).

16. Ludwig Von Bertalanffy, *General System Theory: Foundations, Development, Applications* (New York: G. Braziller, 1973).

17. Werner Ulrich, *Epistemological Foundations of a Critical Systems Approach for Social Planners: From Critical Rationalism and Critical Theory to Critical Heuristics* (Ann Arbor, MI: University Microfilm International, 1981).

18. Gerald Midgley, *Systems Thinking* (London: Sage, 2003).

19. Paulo Freire, *Pedagogy of Freedom: Ethics, Democracy, and Civic Courage* (Lanham, MD: Rowman & Littlefield, 1998).

20. Jürgen Habermas, *Logique des sciences sociales: Et autres essais* (Paris: Presses Universitaires De France, 1987).

21. Peter M. Senge, *The Fifth Discipline: The Art and Practice of the Learning Organization* (New York: Doubleday/Currency, 2006).

22. Bob Williams, http://users.actrix.co.nz/bobwill/, accessed October 4, 2012.

23. Glenda Eoyang, ed., *Voices from the Field: An Introduction to Human Systems Dynamics* (Circle Pines, MN: Human Systems Dynamics Press, 2003).

CHAPTER 2

1. Barry Johnson, *Polarity Management: Identifying and Managing Unsolvable Problems* (Amherst, MA: HRD Press, 1996).

2. Jay Wright Forrester, *Industrial Dynamics* (Waltham, MA: Pegasus Communications, 1999).

3. A. B. Katok and Boris Hasselblatt, *Introduction to the Modern Theory of Dynamical Systems* (Cambridge, UK: Cambridge University Press, 1995).

4. Malcolm Gladwell, *The Tipping Point: How Little Things Can Make a Big Difference* (Boston: Little, Brown, 2000).

CHAPTER 3

1. Bob Williams, http://users.actrix.co.nz/bobwill/, accessed September 29, 2012.

2. Jürgen Habermas, *Logique des sciences sociales: Et autres essais* (Paris: Presses Universitaires de France, 1987).

3. John P. Kotter, *Leading Change* (Boston: Harvard Business School Press, 1996).

4. Bruce Tuckman, "Developmental Sequence in Small Groups," *Psychological Bulletin* (1965), 63(6): 384–99.

CHAPTER 4

1. Peter M. Senge, *The Fifth Discipline: The Art and Practice of the Learning Organization* (New York: Doubleday/Currency, 2006).

2. Karl E. Weick, *The Social Psychology of Organizing* (Reading, MA: Addison-Wesley, 1969).

3. Dave Snowden, *Cognitive Edge*, http://www.cognitive-edge.com/, accessed January 17, 2012.

4. John P. Kotter, *Leading Change* (Boston: Harvard Business School Press, 1996).

5. Richard H. Axelrod, *Terms of Engagement: Changing the Way We Change Organizations* (San Francisco: Berrett-Koehler, 2000).

6. Ralph D. Stacey, *Complex Responsive Processes in Organizations: Learning and Knowledge* (London: Routledge, 2001).

7. Brenda Zimmerman, Curt Lindberg, and Paul Plsek, *Edgeware: Lessons for Complexity Science for Health Care Leaders* (Dallas: VHA, 1998).

8. Ibid.

CHAPTER 5

1. James Gleick, *Chaos: Making a New Science* (New York: Viking, 1987).

2. Glenda Eoyang, "Conditions for Self-Organizing Systems" (unpublished dissertation, Union Institute and University, 2001).

3. Glenda Eoyang, *Coping with Chaos: Seven Simple Tools* (Circle Pines, MN: Lagumo, 1997).

4. B. P. Belousov, "A Periodic Reaction and Its Mechanism," *Compilation of Abstracts on Radiation Medicine* (1959), 147: 145.

5. Glenda Eoyang, ed., *Voices from the Field: An Introduction to Human Systems Dynamics* (Circle Pines, MN: Human Systems Dynamics Press, 2003).

6. "Boids (Flocks, Herds, and Schools: A Distributed Behavioral Model)." Reynolds Engineering and Design, http://www.red3d.com/cwr/boids/, accessed January 17, 2012.

7. Brenda Zimmerman, Curt Lindberg, and Paul Plsek, *Edgeware: Lessons for Complexity Science for Health Care Leaders* (Dallas: VHA, 1998).

8. Royce Holladay and Mallary Tytel, *Simple Rules: Radical Inquiry into Self* (Apache Junction, AZ: Gold Canyon Press, 2011).

9. Kristine Quade, "Simple Rules Leaders Use to Guide Their Organizations in Times of Rapid Change" (unpublished dissertation, 2011).

10. D. F. Snowden and M. E. Moon, "A Leader's Framework for Decision Making," *Harvard Business Review* (2007), 85(11): 68–76.

CHAPTER 6

1. Peter M. Senge, *The Fifth Discipline: The Art and Practice of the Learning Organization* (New York: Doubleday/Currency, 2006).

CHAPTER 7

1. Joel Arthur Barker, *Future Edge: Discovering the New Paradigms of Success* (New York: Morrow, 1992).

2. Thomas S. Kuhn and Ian Hacking, *The Structure of Scientific Revolutions* (Chicago: University of Chicago Press, 2012).

CHAPTER 8

1. Lawrence Solow and Brenda Fake, *What Works for GE May Not Work for You: Using Human Systems Dynamics to Build a Culture of Process Improvement* (New York: Productivity Press, 2010).

CHAPTER 9

1. Royce Holladay and Kristine Quade, *Influencing Patterns for Change: A Human Systems Dynamics Primer for Leaders* (Los Angeles: Createspace, 2008).

2. Kristine Quade and Royce Holladay, *Dynamical Leadership: Building Adaptive Capacity for Uncertain Times* (Apache Junction, AZ: Gold Canyon Press, 2010).

3. Royce Holladay and Mallary Tytel, *Simple Rules: A Radical Inquiry into Self* (Apache Junction, AZ: Gold Canyon Press, 2011).

CHAPTER 10

1. Ilir Zherka, *Winning the Inside Game: The Handbook of Advocacy Strategies* (Apache Junction, AZ: Gold Canyon Press, 2012).

CHAPTER 11

1. Jerry Michalski, http://therexpedition.com/?page_id=69, accessed November 8, 2012.

CHAPTER 12

1. Albert-LászlóBarabási, *Linked: How Everything Is Connected to Everything Else and What It Means for Business, Science, and Everyday Life* (New York: Plume, 2003).

CHAPTER 13

1. "The Art of Hosting," http://www.artofhosting.org/home/.

2. Harrison Owen, *Open Space Technology: A User's Guide*, 3rd ed. (San Francisco: Berrett-Koehler, 1997).

3. Marvin Weisbord, *Discovering Common Ground: How Future Search Conferences Bring People Together to Achieve Breakthrough Innovation, Empowerment, Shared Vision, and Collaborative Action* (San Francisco: Berrett-Koehler, 1992).

4. Juanita Brown and D. Isaacs, *The World Café Book: Shaping Our Futures Through Conversations That Matter* (San Francisco: Berrett-Koehler, 2005).

5. Barbara Bunker and B. Alban, *The Handbook of Large Group Methods: Creating Systemic Change in Organizations and Communities* (San Francisco: Jossey-Bass, 2006).

6. Peggy Holman, T. Devane, and S. Cady, *The Change Handbook: The Definitive Resource on Today's Best Methods for Engaging Whole Systems* (San Francisco: Berrett-Koehler, 2007).

CHAPTER 15

1. Malcolm Cohan, http://www.malcolmcohan.com/.

2. Michael Patton, *Developmental Evaluation: Applying Complexity Concepts to Enhance Innovation and Use* (New York: Guilford Press, 2010).

INDEX

CPSIA information can be obtained
at www.ICGtesting.com
Printed in the USA
LVHW111716150519
617947LV00009B/116/P

9 780804 781961